Feminist Erasures

Feminist Erasures

Challenging Backlash Culture

Edited by

Kumarini Silva
University of North Carolina at Chapel Hill, USA

and

Kaitlynn Mendes
University of Leicester, UK

First published 2015 by
PALGRAVE MACMILLAN

Palgrave Macmillan in the UK is an imprint of Macmillan Publishers Limited, registered in England, company number 785998, of Houndmills, Basingstoke, Hampshire RG21 6XS.

Palgrave Macmillan in the US is a division of St Martin's Press LLC, 175 Fifth Avenue, New York, NY 10010.

Palgrave Macmillan is the global academic imprint of the above companies and has companies and representatives throughout the world.

Palgrave® and Macmillan® are registered trademarks in the United States, the United Kingdom, Europe and other countries.

ISBN 978–1–137–45491–1

This book is printed on paper suitable for recycling and made from fully managed and sustained forest sources. Logging, pulping and manufacturing processes are expected to conform to the environmental regulations of the country of origin.

A catalogue record for this book is available from the British Library.

A catalog record for this book is available from the Library of Congress.

Typeset by MPS Limited, Chennai, India.

*This book is dedicated to women, across the globe,
whose feminist activisms inspire us*

Contents

Acknowledgments

Our collaborations began as co-editors of Commentary and Criticism for *Feminist Media Studies*. We sincerely thank Lisa McLaughlin and Cindy Carter for giving us that opportunity, and for introducing us to each other. They are exemplary scholars, mentors, and friends, who have long influenced our feminist interventions.

This project was interrupted by several, wonderful, life events for both authors, and it took considerably longer than the one year that we had envisioned it would take us from the CFP to the end product! We are incredibly grateful to all the contributors who stuck with us through the extended process. Without them there would be no anthology. Alexandra, Andrea, Celiany, Elise, Eric, Jennifer, Katherine, Lauren, Mel, Micky, Monika, Natalie, Rosemary, Sara, and Susan, we are deeply grateful for your commitment to the project and for your patience. Thank you.

We are also indebted to the editorial staff at Palgrave-UK who have worked with us so closely on this book. We are especially grateful to Felicity Plester for her enthusiastic support of the project. Our thanks also to the anonymous reviewers, who provided important feedback for individual chapters, as well as the entire collection.

We start the introduction to the anthology by explaining that we are both many things to many people, especially our families. Their support of us, and this work, has been amazing.

KS thanks David Monje, Ruby Monje Silva, and her family in Sri Lanka for their loving support. They make all things possible.

KM thanks her family, Ben Wells, Brayden Wells, and Adam Wells, for their patience and support.

Kumarini Silva
Kaitlynn Mendes

Notes on Contributors

Sara T. Bernstein received her PhD in Cultural Studies with a designated emphasis in feminist theory and research from the University of California, Davis. She has published several articles that explore intersectional gender and representation issues using fashion, media and cultural studies, including 'Fashion Out of Place: Experiencing Fashion in a Small American Town' (co-authored with Dr Susan B. Kaiser), which recently appeared in *Critical Studies in Fashion and Beauty*. She currently teaches film studies at Portland State University.

Susan Berridge is a Teaching Fellow in Communications, Media and Culture and Member of the Centre for Feminist and Gender Studies at Stirling University. Previously, she has taught film and television studies at Glasgow University and Royal Holloway, University of London. Her research is centrally concerned with the relationship between genre, narrative structures, and representations of gender, sexuality and sexual violence in popular film and television. Berridge has published on these themes in journals such as *Feminist Media Studies*, *New Review of Film and Television Studies* and *The Journal of British Cinema and Television*.

Elise M. Chatelain is currently a visiting assistant professor at the University of New Orleans. She received her PhD in Cultural Studies from the University of California, Davis, with a designated emphasis in feminist theory and research. Much of Chatelain's academic work focuses on the representation of labor in popular media. Other research and teaching interests include domesticity and the family, health and disease, and youth culture as entry points for exploring the relationship between geography, subjectivity, and the production and circulation of meaning in popular culture.

Natalie Havlin is an Assistant Professor of English at LaGuardia Community College at the City University of New York where she teaches Latina/o Literary Studies and Urban Studies. Her scholarship concerns the politics of coalition and alliance in Women of Color Feminism and urban Latina/o cultural production. She is currently working on a book manuscript titled 'Migrant Affinities: The Gendered and Sexual Politics of Interracial Alliance in Modern Latina/o Print and

Visual Culture.' With over ten years of experience in community and labor organizing, she also writes about the intersections of transformative justice and social justice unionism. Havlin is a past recipient of the Woodrow Wilson Doctoral Fellowship in Women's Studies and the Smalley Fellowship in Gender and Women's Studies.

Rosemary Hepworth is a Research Associate on the WHIM project with the Computational Creativity Group at Goldsmiths, University of London. She was awarded her PhD in 2012 from the University of Cambridge (Faculty of English). Her thesis assesses the avatar, borrowed from digital social environments, as an intermedia figure of self-portraiture in narratives by women writers and artists across media platforms.

Katherine Hindle completed her MRes in Gender Studies at Northumbria University in 2012, which she undertook after working for ten years as a solicitor. She is now a doctoral candidate at Goldsmiths College, University of London. Her research focuses on the relationship between public policy, popular culture, and female complaint.

Mél Hogan is an environmental media scholar and designer and Assistant Professor of Communication Studies, Illinois Institute of Technology. She recently completed a postdoc in Digital Curation at CU Boulder. melhogan.com.

Micky Lee is Associate Professor of Media Studies at Suffolk University, Boston. She has published journal articles on feminist political economy, telecommunications, new information and communication technologies, and media, information, and finance.

Eric Lohman is a Media Studies PhD candidate and lecturer in the Faculty of Information and Media Studies at the University of Western Ontario. His research focuses on the social reproduction of labor power and domestic labor in the mass media. He also studies wedding culture and wedding reality television. Lohman is currently finishing a dissertation project that focuses on telework, gender, and capitalist crisis. He lives in London, Ontario, with his partner and four children.

Jennifer McClearen is a PhD student in Communication at the University of Washington. Her research investigates the ways dominant ideologies in mediated texts depict the physical agency of bodies that are gendered, racialized, and/or queered as Other, and how audiences interpret these representations using dominant and/or resistive discourses. She is a member of the Communication and Difference Research Group in the Department of Communication, a fellow in the Simpson Center for the Humanities' Certificate in Public Scholarship, and a candidate for the Certificate in Cinema and Media Studies in the Department of Comparative Literature.

Lauren McNicol is a feminist cultural studies scholar and occasional blogger whose work focuses on sexual violence prevention, the popularization of feminist thought, and the politics of anti-racist feminist organizing. She made Queen's University, Canada, her home base for nearly a decade, earning her BA in Psychology, BA in Physical and Health Education, and MA in Sociocultural Studies from the School of Kinesiology and Health Studies. She has worked as a campus organizer, writing tutor, nanny, equity counselor, HIV research intern, and women's shelter board member. She currently works as a research coordinator at Women's College Research Institute in Toronto, Ontario.

Kaitlynn Mendes is a Lecturer in Media and Communications at the University of Leicester. Her research is primarily concerned with representations of feminism, feminist activism and their goals in mainstream news, feminist media, and social media. Mendes is author of *Feminism in the News* (2011) and *SlutWalk: Feminism, Activism and Media* (forthcoming) and has published in journals such as *Feminist Media Studies*; *Media, Culture and Society*; *The International Journal of Cultural Studies*; and *Social Movement Studies*.

Alexandra Moffett-Bateau is Assistant Professor of Political Science at John Jay College-CUNY. In 2012 she was a recipient of the prestigious Carter G. Woodson Pre-Doctoral Fellowship. Her research focuses on race and politics, urban politics and political behavior, with broad specialties in American politics and political theory.

Monika Raesch is Assistant Professor of Communication and Journalism at Suffolk University, Boston. She has published numerous articles on film analysis. She is the author of *The Kiarostami Brand: Creation of a Film Auteur* (2009).

Celiany Rivera-Velázquez is the Director of the NYU LGBTQ Student Center. She is a Latina educator, queer scholar, feminist filmmaker, bilingual social justice activist, diversity trainer, civic engagement expert, and globally minded Student Affairs practitioner. Originally from Puerto Rico, she has explored a broad range of LGBT/queer aesthetics and politics across the Spanish-speaking Caribbean and the United States. Throughout her career Rivera-Velázquez has combined written and visual knowledge production by publishing and screening her films in national and international symposia.

Kumarini Silva is Assistant Professor of Communication Studies at The University of North Carolina, Chapel Hill. Silva's research is at the various intersections of feminism, identity and Identification, postcolonial studies, and popular culture. Her most recent work has appeared in *Social Identities, South Asian Popular Culture,* and *Cultural Studies.* Silva is also the author of several book chapters on race, global media, and film.

Andrea Zeffiro is a contemporary media historian and Adjunct Professor in the Department of Communication, Popular Culture and Film, Brock University, Canada. andreazeffiro.com.

List of Abbreviations

AG	butch or aggressive (gender presentation)
AIDS	acquired immunodeficiency syndrome
BBC	British Broadcasting Corporation
CBC	Canadian Broadcasting Corporation
CBS	Columbia Broadcasting System
CEDAW	Convention on the Elimination of All Forms of Discrimination against Women
CEO	chief executive officer
CHA	Chicago Housing Authority
CIA	Central Intelligence Agency
CTV	Canadian Television Network
CV	curriculum vitae
DVD	digital versatile disc
HIV	human immunodeficiency virus
ICSI	intracytoplasmic sperm injection
IVF	in-vitro fertilization
LAC	Local Advisory Council
LGBTQ	Lesbian, Gay, Bisexual, Transsexual, and Queer
LWC	The London Women's Clinic
MPAA	Motion Picture Association of America
NGO	non-governmental organization
NRT	new reproductive technologies
NYC	New York City
NYCOT	New York Council of Trollops
PCR	People for Community Recovery
TA	teaching assistant
TV	television

TVO	Television Ontario
UK	United Kingdom
US	United States
WAM!	Women, Action, and the Media!
WIC	Women Infant Child

1

Introduction:
(In)visible and (Ir)relevant:
Setting a Context

Kumarini Silva and Kaitlynn Mendes

Who we are and why we care

We are feminist scholars and educators who live on opposite ends of the 'pond.' We are also, when not writing and teaching, mothers, partners, daughters, sisters, and friends to a myriad of people in our lives. Our own experiences as women who work, in a conventional sense, and then *work* as gendered beings provide a foundation for our approach to this book. We fully recognize the burdens our gender places on us; at the same time we acknowledge the many opportunities that feminism has given us. The historical struggles of the feminist movement have given us the tools, the means, the legislature, and the social context to thrive in the ways that are important to us in our personal and professional lives. In keeping with this, the diversity of this book reflects the many spaces that women occupy and perform gender, and the ways in which these performances translate to cultural norms and conventions about being female.

Over the last half-decade we've collaborated on various projects, and spent a great deal of time talking about feminism and feminist cultural politics with each other, as well as with broader audiences through our own individual research and projects. While our discussions have always been about the relationship between feminism, culture, and politics, the genesis for this particular project comes with the intersection of several political and popular events happening over the last few years in the US and UK where we live and work. While the following events might seem disparate, they have created the cultural context from which these essays emerge: from the discourses surrounding the vice-presidential candidacy of Sarah Palin in the US in 2008; to political discussions of rape as either 'legitimate' (in the US)[1] or 'bad sexual etiquette' (in the UK),[2] to controversies surrounding gay marriage in the US, to the rise of 'mommy porn,' in both literary and mediated contexts, these seemingly disparate conditions fuel a particular and often times contradictory narrative about women in contemporary culture. In addition, we have chosen to focus on North America and Western Europe, because we believe that it is important to interrogate the spaces we occupy in order to understand how our own lives are shaped by patriarchy and feminist interventions. Looking at the 'Other' as experiencing marginality, while ignoring your own, creates a false sense of accomplishment, while stifling progress and change. If we pay attention to our own context, we will recognize that in our everyday lives, misogynistic imagery and discourses about women are used over and over again as exemplars of women's control over their own bodies, their sexuality, and their lives. And the systemic (in that, this contradictory message is present in all aspects of society from mediated images to political discourse) distribution of these contradictory images results in a form of apathy about feminism and women's rights as either irrelevant or 'too much work.' Essentially, 'what to believe?' and 'whom to believe?' inevitably results in 'so what?' and 'who cares?'

What is at stake: *So what?* and *Who cares?*

If the broader context of feminism and its discontents are grounded in the fact that most young women (and men) believe that feminism is a choice, that can be discarded or appropriated as necessary, it begs the question, what is at stake? What do we have to lose through the abandonment of feminism and its genealogical history and contemporary manifestations? For us, what is at stake is the erasure of feminism as a completed project before its work is done. That the current circulation of postfeminist discourses, in both popular and political culture, creates a sense of 'after' that we, among other feminist scholars (see Douglas 2010; Negra 2009; Tasker & Negra 2007), feel is inaccurate. The apathetic approach to understanding the importance of feminism and its genealogical history makes us immune to the systemic backlash against women that has become part of everyday culture. Here, let us take a moment to explain what we mean by an apathetic approach to feminism: for us, it's a condition where the progress made by feminists and women's rights movements, on a global level, are presented as a *fait accompli* and any ongoing activism or commitment to feminism is seen as outmoded and unnecessary. It is the simple belief that 'women have arrived' in spite of significant evidence to the contrary. This contrary evidence can be seen in the continued use of sexualized imagery and violence against women to sell products, in the legislative practices that are routinely enacted which negatively affect women's health benefits, the continued double-burden that is placed on women who work both within and outside the home, the continued debates around welfare mothers and the general judgment placed on single mothers, just to name a few. In spite of these realities, women are continuously and relentlessly encouraged to believe that there is nothing more to be done. That women's liberation has arrived and triumphed. But, as the chapters in this anthology suggest, such a declaration is not only inaccurate, it can also have significant drawbacks for continued activism and engagement with issues of gender, class, race, and sexuality that are much needed in contemporary culture.

As Michel Foucault reminds us, none of these entities/discourses about social structure, power, and agency exists independently. Foucault writes that 'We must make allowances for the complex and unstable process whereby a discourse can be both an instrument and an effect of power, but also a hindrance, a stumbling point of resistance and a starting point for an opposing strategy. Discourse transmits and produces power; it reinforces it, but also undermines and exposes it, renders it fragile and makes it possible to thwart' (1998, pp. 100–1). In keeping with this, we approach various cultural and political events, materialities, and texts as a collection of discourses that reinforce each other to both stabilize and destabilize power structures within North American and European contexts.

We are especially cognizant that these discourses and power structures disproportionately affect women, and create a culture of implicit (and explicit) misogyny and disempowerment that becomes naturalized, systemic, and institutionalized. For example, neoconservative politics that limit women's rights and a mediated culture that commodifies and distributes images of misogyny as empowerment are interconnected in that they rewrite the new politics of feminism. This particular politic tells us that feminism is, in fact, irrelevant. As Angela McRobbie writes, 'this new kind of sophisticated anti-feminism has become a reoccurring feature across the landscape of both popular and political culture. It upholds the principles of gender equality, while denigrating the figure of the feminist' (2009, p. 179). This anti-feminist feminism is echoed in our classrooms, where we often hear from students that while they believe in 'equality,' feminism is a 'choice,' and that the word feminist carries too much 'baggage.' The contradictions between equality and choice, and the inherent privilege in enjoying the systemic and structural benefits that the feminist movement has brought about while discarding the politics of feminism, are lost in the midst of the cacophony that is con-temporary mediated culture. And political discourse joins the popular in appropriating the language of feminist liberation and empowerment in the construction of an essentializing feminism that re-marginalizes and domesticates women. That is, in fact, the definition of backlash culture: a negative reaction to the *possibility* of progress and/or change.

Backlash and the culture of 'choice'

On 16 January 2014 US talk show host Elizabeth Hasselbeck asked Nick Adams, author of *The American Boomerang* (2013) – a book that looks at the relationship between the decline of American exceptionalism and the (supposed) decline of masculinity – whether such a decline was 'in direct relation to feminism on the rise?,' continuing with 'Is it a result just sort of society seeing men that are not as masculine and men that are as masculine being kind of demonized?' Adams responded by telling her that she 'hit the nail on the head.' In the course of that interview Adams and Hasselbeck concluded that the rise of feminism, and the apparently (completely unfounded) co-relational decline of masculin-ity, resulted in a threat to national security. While this conversation was decried by many in various venues, the very existence of Adams's book and Hasselbeck's questions indicates the kind of misguided notions of feminism that circulate in contemporary culture. But such notions are not without precedent. In the 1970s, British columnist Christopher Ward noted satirically that:

> I hadn't realized just how much bad news we men have suffered until I came across this Liberated Woman's Appointment Calendar and Survival Handbook, which is rapidly becoming the pocket book of every bra-burning American lady. Every day this diary records the anniversary of some past female victory, which we men have been suffering for ever since. I mention here some of the more promi-nent landmarks in the history of Women's Liberation so that, while women celebrate them, we men can treat them as days of mourning of our formerly great sex. (Ward 1970, p. 7)

And in the early part of the new millennium, the British writer Deborah Orr noted that, 'Feminism is blamed, completely erroneously, for everything – spiralling property prices (working couples), unemployment (women stealing men's jobs), teenage delinquency (feminists driving men to abandon their sons), reality television (the "feminization" of the culture) and increasing sexual violence (now that women don't defer to them, men have suffered a violent "identity crisis")' (2003, p. 15). More recently, speaking to this ongoing condition of blame on and backlash against feminism, McRobbie (2009) writes:

> Elements of feminism have been taken into account, and have absolutely been incorporated into political and institutional life. Drawing on a vocabulary that includes words like 'empowerment' and 'choice,' these elements are then converted into a much more individualistic discourse, and they are deployed in this new guise, particularly in media and popular culture, but also by agents of the state, as a kind of substitute for feminism. (p. 1)

McRobbie goes on to call this *'faux* feminism.' And within faux feminism, 'choice' is the linchpin that promotes a false sense of empowerment for women in contemporary culture. This is perhaps most easily identifiable in advertising marketed to young female consumers, who are encouraged to make 'empowering choices' through consumption. Take, for example, the 'Rule the Air' advertising campaign by the largest mobile network operator in the US, Verizon.[3] Debuting in 2010, the company released a series of ads targeting the much coveted youth demographic. In an advertisement titled (rather ironically) 'prejudice,' a series of young women, from different ethnic backgrounds, relay the following message to the audience:

> Air has no prejudice, it does not carry the opinions of a man faster than those of a woman, it does not filter out an idea, because I'm 16 and not 30, Air is unaware if I'm black or white, and wouldn't care if it knew. So it stands to reason, my ideas will be powerful, if they are wise, infectious, if they are worthy, and if my thoughts have flawless delivery, I can lead the army that will follow. Rule the air. Verizon.

Here, a series of random thoughts, none of which factually, or even theoretically, make a coherent argument, are strung together to encourage a feeling of accomplishment and success by buying Verizon products. We are not expected to question the notion that ideas generally (at least, in theory) *do* need to be 'wise' to be powerful or infectious, or that the worth of ideas is measured by their capacity to gain power in and within a patriarchal society, where women are routinely and systematically marginalized. Such critiques are irrelevant as the advertisement winds down by reiterating the notion of perfection for these young women, because only 'flawless delivery' will allow leadership – and, of course, it ends with consumption as power: 'Rule the air. Verizon.' Essentially, as Susan Douglas (2010) writes: 'What the media have been giving us, then, are little more than fantasies of power. They assure girls and women, repeatedly, that women's liberation is a *fait accompli* and that we are stronger, more successful, more sexually in control, more fearless and more held in awe than we actually are' (p. 5).

It is this form of empty empowerment located within consumerist choice that is mirrored in recent political discourse. In both North America and Western Europe, feminism, women's rights, and politics have become recent news fodder.[4] For example, the 2008 US election was a watershed moment, not just in terms of racial politics, but also gender politics, with Hillary Clinton as a possible presidential candidate, and Sarah Palin as a vice-presidential candidate. The latter, then governor of Alaska, was an unknown political entity, selected to become the vice president to presidential candidate John McCain. During the campaign, Palin managed to parlay her Alaskan roots and religious beliefs into a new form of 'choice feminism,' rooted in conservative, pro-life values, that made her extremely popular among religiously conservative, anti-choice advocates. Her supporters read her commitment to a large family, including a special needs child, as a symbol of a 'new kind of feminism,' one which was grounded in anti-abortion, right-wing conservatism and 'family values.'[5] Palin documented this new feminism in her memoir titled: *America by Heart* (2010), where she states that 'The *new* feminism is telling women they are capable and strong. And if keeping a child isn't possible, adoption is a beautiful choice. It's about empowering women to make *real choices*, not forcing them to accept false ones' (p. 153). She goes on to explain that 'left-wing feminists are out of touch with the real America,' and that 'Judging by the emergence of the mama grizzlies, it's becoming more acceptable to call yourself a pro-career, pro-family, pro-motherhood, and pro-life feminist' (p. 137). While we do not critique Palin's commitment to her family and acknowledge that a special needs child presents unique challenges to childrearing, her glib and uncritical celebration of women's double-burden, economic and political marginality, and the right to no-choice, showcases what Susan Douglas calls 'pit bull feminism.'

According to Douglas, with pit bull feminism, 'you have the appearance of feminism – alleged superwoman, top executive, and mother of five – with a repudiation of everything feminism has fought for' (2010, p. 271). Indeed, Palin's kind of political pit bull feminism and its companion in popular culture, faux feminism, essentially positions feminism as a generational, economic, social or political difference, where discussions around misogyny, double-burden, and rights seem outdated and unnecessary. Here, a more nuanced discussion is whittled down to 'choice' without an accompanying discussion about the inherent privileges of having and making choices. This false sense of choice-as-empowerment is also closely tied to and exasperated by the ways in which we have married choice to democracy, especially within the capitalist democracies of North America and Western Europe. Because democracy, within hyper-consumerist societies, is tied largely to consumer freedom, that choice of consumption stands in for democratic rights and privileges. This notion of choice is seen as unique to Western democracies and is used as a way to separate the political, social, and consumer cultures of the West from the non-West. For example, there is a common assumption that the West (made up largely of the US and other Western European nations) is more progressive and politically democratic than 'non-Western' spaces. This, in spite of the fact that the US is the only industrialized nation to vote against the ratification of the United Nations Convention on the Elimination of All Forms of Discrimination against Women (CEDAW). Because of a combination of historical and contemporary trends – including colonialism, balkanization, and globalization – too long to document here, there is a common notion that the West defined women's rights and therefore practice them the best. Such a mentality leads to the assumption that gender 'issues' are problems in 'other places' and not true of progressive, first world nations. As the various issues raised in this anthology highlight, this is inaccurate, and has far-reaching repercussions. Mainly, that the focus on the 'plight' of women in 'other' spaces ignores challenges and problems in our own backyards.

But this belief that women in Western/first world nations have superior rights is not new, and has been long reinforced by both popular culture and political office. As Lynn Spigel (2004) has noted, media create a seamless history of women's progress through (false) representation – from the 1950s stay-at-home moms, through single girl Mary Tyler Moore in the 1970s, and *Sex and the City* 1990s, etc. – that documents a (fictionalized) narrative of progress. Certainly, women have come a long way, especially in the last half-century, but to see progress in relative terms, like the media invite us to do, is to be content with a false sense of accomplishment.

This kind of false accomplishment pervades even contemporary politics. In 1991, Susan Faludi facetiously critiqued the backlash culture of the late twentieth century, writing that according to President Ronald Reagan,

'Women have "so much," ... that the White House no longer needs to appoint them to higher office. Even American Express ads are saluting a woman's freedom to charge it. At last, women have received their full citizenship papers' (p. 1). When Faludi quoted Reagan in the 1990s, it was hard to imagine that a similar faux pas could be made over two decades later. But, when candidate Mitt Romney was asked, during the second debate between candidates in the 2012 US presidential elections, 'In what new ways do you intend to rectify the inequalities in the workplace, specifically regarding females making only 72 percent of what their male counterparts earn?,' Romney replied: 'we took a concerted effort to go out and find women who had backgrounds that could be qualified to become members of our cabinet. I went to a number of women's groups and said: "Can you help us find folks," and they brought us whole binders full of women' (Stern 2012). While 'binders full of women' went on to make its rounds on the late night comedy show circuit and also became one of the most popular Halloween costumes of 2012, its political legacy is that it articulates the general sentiments of political and consumer advocates who see women as an 'add on' to an already well-functioning and organized patriarchal system of power.

But this kind of 'add on' and revisionist history of equality is not unique to the US. In the UK, pit bull feminism has recently allowed for the posthumous commemoration of Margaret Thatcher as a feminist and a symbol of women's empowerment. When Baroness Thatcher passed away in 2013, tributes poured in from around the world, hailing the significant contribution she made to make women in public office a norm. While much scholarly work acknowledges Thatcher's considerable disdain for progressive politics, including women's rights, during her tenure as the 'Iron Lady,' what is of interest here is the popular celebration of her as 'sort of' feminist, for the simple reason that she was a woman in power. Yet her avid disavowal of feminism and its politics are overlooked as Thatcher has become immortalized as a romantic exemplar of women's progress. As Thatcher becomes a celebrated feminist icon in postfeminist culture, history and context are replaced by symbolic representation: she was a woman in power, so she was a feminist. Such dislocated celebrations of empowerment run contiguous to everyday transgressions against women. For example, in 2012, amidst the various scandals, including accusations of rape, that surrounded WikiLeaks founder Julian Assange, UK Member of Parliament George Galloway declared that the only thing Assange was guilty of in regards to the rape accusations was 'bad sexual etiquette.' According to Galloway, this was because 'not everybody needs to be asked prior to each insertion,' since the woman bringing the charges had already had consensual intercourse with Assange. We bring up this incident here, not to debate Assange's guilt, but to highlight the ways in which violence against women – specifically when rape is involved – is discussed in public office. By renaming the act of rape (whether connected to Assange or not) as 'bad etiquette' Galloway essentially neutralized the inherent violence of forced sexual intercourse, and normalized that violence as part of sexual relations. In turn, it is the dismissal of violence, through language like 'legitimate' and 'etiquette,' without any critical discussion, which allows for sexual violence to be commodified and resold to the public. Consider this example: Before online retailing giant Amazon suspended it due to public protest, Solid Gold Bomb – a US-based clothing company – capitalized on the resurgent popularity of the 'Keep Calm' slogan by selling a number of t-shirts, mainly to UK consumers, that said 'Keep Calm and Rape a Lot,' 'Keep Calm and Knife Her,' and 'Keep Calm and Hit Her.' While the company quickly issued a public apology, blaming a computer glitch for auto-generating the sentence combinations, the reality is that the t-shirts were created, marketed, and sold, even in small numbers, as an acceptable form of 'nudge-nudge, wink-wink' humor.

Now what?

In the previous sections we've outlined the broader cultural context which acts as a backdrop for this collection of essays. These essays individually provide in-depth examples of the various conditions, both popular and political, that feed feminist apathy, as we have outlined above, in contemporary North American and Western European culture, as well as organized and activist responses to this apathy. Collectively, through a range of cultural and political contexts, including the news media, popular fiction and television, the internet, higher education, employment, motherhood, and feminist activism, this book highlights – implicitly, by focusing on the problems, or explicitly by providing examples of feminist activism – the conditions that create feminist inertia, as well as possible and necessary responses. For us, these essays are especially timely considering a number of 'classic' feminist texts such as *The Feminine Mystique* (Friedan [1963] 2010), *The Female Eunuch* (Greer [1970] 2006), and *The Second Sex* (Beauvoir [1949] 2009) are being republished, possibly indicating a growing interest in the history and theory of feminism. Foregrounded by the republication of these classics, this collection of essays demonstrates how feminist critiques have at times been made invisible within contemporary discourses, and the challenges associated with convincing the public that feminism is not in fact dead, irrelevant, or redundant. The book also raises questions about the need to integrate more diverse perspectives into feminist theory and teaching, particularly developments introduced by transnational and other postmodern feminist theory. In keeping with this, the book is divided into four parts:

In Part 1: 'Teaching Feminism' the essays focus on the experiences of education and feminism through the perspective of feminist and women's studies academics. As we've mentioned earlier in the Introduction, our own experiences in the classroom – where students believe equality is important, but feel no need to engage with feminism's politics or history – resonate here, when the authors engage with pedagogical issues that emerge in classrooms. Sara T. Bernstein and Elise M. Chatelain in 'CEOs and Office Hos: Notes from the Trenches of Our Women's Studies Classrooms' engage with pedagogical challenges when dealing with issues connected to students' lived experiences, and their impact on feminist praxis. Andrea Zeffiro and Mél Hogan continue this discussion of feminist praxis by interrogating location, research, and research methods by making connections to feminist and women's labor in academic contexts in their chapter titled 'Suture and Scars: Evidencing the Struggles of Academic Feminism.' Alexandra Moffett-Bateau concludes this section with her essay titled 'Feminist Erasures: The Development of a Black Feminist Methodological Theory,' which argues that black feminist theory needs to take a more prominent role in the social sciences. These three essays provide an important context for both pedagogues and students to understand how the relationships and discussions in classrooms affect our own sense of empowerment and activism.

Following these contextualizing essays, Part II, titled 'Feminism in Popular Culture,' explores how feminism *(dis)appears* in mediated and consumer culture. For us, a discussion of popular culture is central to understanding where feminism is (not) located in contemporary culture. In our own teaching, we focus on mediated texts, and routinely respond to student questions regarding popular representations. Essentially, our pedagogy cannot be separated from the consumer and mediated culture that we, and our students, exist in. In keeping with this, and approaching popular culture from a variety of methodological and theoretical perspectives, the following five essays provide a variety of issues facing women in contemporary culture, and were selected because they collectively represent the importance of recognizing and acknowledging intersectionality when discussing 'rights' and 'choice.' Because the essays range from backlash culture, to sexual violence, to gay and lesbian rights, identity, and economics, they provide a broad and necessary context for understanding the significant influence that popular and mediated culture have on how we understand and negotiate contemporary feminism and feminist activism. In keeping with this, in her chapter titled 'Illegible Rage: Performing Femininity in *Manhattan Call Girl*,' Katherine Hindle positions the book series *Manhattan Call Girl* within backlash culture, arguing that the series provides a false sense of empowerment through sexual agency. The counterpoint of this (false) sexual agency is interrogated by Susan Berridge in her chapter titled 'Empowered Vulnerability?: A Feminist Response to the Ubiquity of Sexual Violence in the Pilots of Female-Fronted Teen Drama Series.' Berridge argues that sexual violence is used in television programming to suggest female sexual vulnerability is an avoidable context. She turns to several popular television dramas in the US and UK to interrogate how sexual violence functions narratively and ideologically. In the following chapter, titled 'Against Conformity: Families, Respectability and the Representation of Gender-Nonconforming Youth of Color in *Gun Hill Road* and *Pariah*,' Natalie Havlin and Celiany Rivera-Velázquez look at embodiment and sexuality to understand how gender queering interpolates with race and racialized identities in two films. Micky Lee and Monika Raesch in 'Women, Gender, and the Financial Markets in Hollywood Films,' examine the representation of women, Wall Street, and economic success, juxtaposing it against the economic incentives of Hollywood. Their political economic and ideological analysis finds a connection between the stereotyped representation of women's economic success in film, and Hollywood as primarily an economic enterprise. In 'Gladiator in a Suit? *Scandal*'s Olivia Pope and the Post-Identity Regulation of Physical Agency,' Jennifer McClearen looks at feminism and post-race culture in the hugely successful television series *Scandal*. Her critical analysis of both the show, and the discourses surrounding post-race politics in the US, provides insight into the ways that race and gender are intertwined and understood.

Because representations of femininity in both everyday culture and mediated culture are closely intertwined with women's reproductive abilities as the core feminine identity, Part III: 'Becoming Mother' focuses on several intersecting contemporary discourses around motherhood and feminism. The popularity of films like *What to Expect When You Are Expecting* (2012) – a tie-in to a popular pregnancy book in both the US and UK, as well as controversial discussions around Marissa Mayer, as both a parent and CEO, after she gave birth to a son shortly after taking over as head of internet giant Yahoo in 2012 – implicitly and explicitly highlights the challenges facing women as they (do not) perform what are seen as the essential biological functions of femininity. In 'Got Milk?: Motherhood, Breastfeeding, and (Re)domesticating Feminism' Kumarini Silva questions this notion of the 'essential feminine' within motherhood, the controversy surrounding attachment parenting and breastfeeding of toddlers, connecting it to the contradictions between the sexualization of the breast itself, and mothers as asexual individuals. In 'Running Mother Ragged: Women and Labor in the Age of Telework,' Eric Lohman assesses how telecommuting is discussed as *the* response to women's double-burden and its place within discourses of work–life balance. In the concluding chapter for the section, Rosemary Hepworth, in 'Infertility Blogging, Body, and the Avatar,' explores ways feminism is constructed in relation to the self through an analysis of body and infertility, and the presentation of both within narratives of infertility treatments on the blogosphere. Our interest in bringing these essays together was based on the diverse ways in which motherhood becomes (re)inscribed within contemporary culture.

We conclude this anthology with two case studies that look at the same event from different perspectives. Our intent here is to have the reader focus on a contemporary moment in feminist praxis, recognizing the diversity of its impact. Therefore, in Part IV: 'Feminism/Activism,' two essays, both focusing on the SlutWalk movement – a transnational protest against sexual violence – explores the varied ways feminist activism has been reanimated and understood in contemporary culture. In 'SlutWalk, Feminism, and News' Kaitlynn Mendes argues that the media unmoor the Walks from their feminist context thereby effectively removing feminism from media representations of feminist activism. Lauren McNicol continues the discussion of SlutWalks in 'A Critical Reading of SlutWalk in the News: Reproducing Postfeminism and Whiteness' by questioning the color politics of its activism and the media's focus on SlutWalk as a spectacle, rather than on violence prevention.

By focusing on diverse texts and moments, our intent is to convey the prevalence of anti-feminist thought, and a sense of urgency for the continued commitment and organization of feminism as a political and cultural tool for women's empowerment. In putting together this work, we also acknowledge that we have only covered a very small area of a very large problem. We are very cognizant of the fact that over the last several decades, both North America and Western Europe have dramatically diversified, especially as ethnic and racial spaces. The transnational circulation of commodities and peoples has ensured that the imagined homogeneity of these geographic regions is now defunct, and without merit. Through the years, feminist scholars have addressed these shifts, acknowledging that intersectionality of race, gender, and class (Crenshaw 1991) as an absolute necessity for rigorous and thoughtful feminist analysis. Certainly, since the second wave of feminism in the US and UK, influential feminist activist/scholars like Gloria Anzaldua (1981), Judith Butler (1999), Indrepal Grewal (2005), bell hooks (1981), Audre Lorde (1984), Chandra Mohanty (1991), Cherrie Moraga (2011), Gayatri Chakravorty Spivak (1988), Karen Ross (2010), and Liesbet van Zoonen (1994) have engaged the intersection of race, gender, sexuality, postcolonialism, and contemporary culture to write of and about feminism in the different parts of the globe. Our intent with this collection of essays is to add to, rather than provide a complete picture of, the voices that challenge the dismissal of feminism. This collection does not claim to address the entirety of the many manifestations and diversities of feminisms that are routinely policed and critiqued and managed by popular and political culture. Instead, it hopes to join others in the journey to make feminism relevant and visible.

Notes

1. On 10 April 2012, in response to a question on the views of conservatives on abortion in the case of rape, Todd Akin, a US Republican Congressman, and Senate candidate, from Missouri, responded that there was no possibility of pregnancy through 'legitimate rape.' According to Akin, 'It seems to be, first of all, from what I understand from doctors, it's really rare. If it's a legitimate rape, the female body has ways to try to shut the whole thing down' (cited in Moore 2012). In light of the ensuing outcry against this, his comments were denounced by the leadership of his own party, and he went on to lose the Senate race in 2012.
2. Comments made by UK Member of Parliament George Galloway regarding rape accusation against WikiLeaks founder Julian Assange.
3. Verizon is co-owned by Verizon Communications, US and Vodafone, UK.
4. The discussion of women and women's rights in news forums also gives credence to this belief that women are visible and have equal rights. But it is important to consider the *kinds of news stories* about women that gain prominence and visibility, when we make this claim.
5. 'Family values' is a catchphrase used by many US-based politicians to articulate their stand against same-sex marriage and gay rights.

References

Adams, N. (2013) *The American Boomerang* (US: CreateSpace Independent Publishing Platform).

Anzaldua, G. (1981) *This Bridge Called My Back: Writings by Radical Women of Color* (London: Persephone Press).

Butler, J. (1999) *Gender Trouble: Feminism and the Subversion of Identity* (New York: Routledge).

Crenshaw, K.W. (1991) 'Mapping the Margins: Intersectionality, Identity Politics, and Violence against Women of Color,' *Stanford Law Review*, 43(6), 1241–99.

Douglas, S. (2010) *Enlightened Sexism: The Seductive Message that Feminism's Work is Done* (New York: Times Books).

Faludi, S. (1991) *Backlash: The Undeclared War Against Feminism* (New York: Three Rivers Press).

Foucault, M. (1998) *The History of Sexuality: The Will to Knowledge* (London: Penguin).

Grewal, I. (2005) *Transnational America: Feminisms, Diasporas, Neoliberalisms* (Durham, NC: Duke University Press).

hooks, b. (1981) *Ain't I a Woman: Black Women and Feminism* (Boston: South End Press).

Lorde, A. (1984) *Sister Outsider: Essays and Speeches* (California: Crossing Press).

McRobbie, A. (2009) *The Aftermath of Feminism* (London: Sage).

McRobbie, A. (2011) 'Beyond Post-Feminism,' *Public Policy Research*, September–November, 179–84.

Mohanty, C.T. (1991) 'Under Western Eyes: Feminist Scholarship and Colonial Discourses,' in C.T. Mohanty, A. Russo, and L. Torres (eds) *Third World Women and the Politics of Feminism* (Bloomington: Indiana University Press), 51–80.

Moore, L. (2012) 'Rep. Todd Aiken: The Statement and the Reaction,' *The New York Times*, 20 August, www.nytimes.com/2012/08/21/us/politics/rep-todd-akin-legitimate-rape-statement-and-reaction.html?_r=0 (accessed 26 April 2014).

Moraga, C. (2011) *A Xicana Codex of Changing Consciousness: Writings 2000–2010* (Durham, NC: Duke University Press).

Negra, D. (2009) *What a Girl Wants? Fantasizing the Reclamation of Self in Postfeminism* (Abingdon: Routledge).

Orr, D. (2003) 'Who Would Want to Call Herself a Feminist?,' *Independent*, 4 July, 15.

Palin, S. (2010) *America by Heart: Reflections of Family, Faith, and Flag* (New York: HarperCollins).

Ross, K. (2010) *Gendered Media: Women, Men and Identity Politics* (Lanham, MD and Plymouth: Rowman & Littlefield).

Spigel, L. (2004) 'Theorising the Bachelorette "Waves" of Feminist Media Studies,' *Signs*, 30(1), 1209–21.

Spivak, G.C. (1988) 'Can the Subaltern Speak?,' in C. Nelson and L. Grossberg (eds) *Marxism and the Interpretation of Culture* (Urbana: University of Illinois Press), 271–313.

Stern, M. (2012) 'Mitt Romney's "Binders full of women" Comments Sets Internet Ablaze,' *The Daily Beast*, 17 October, www.thedailybeast.com/articles/

2012/10/17/mitt-romney-s-binders-full-of-women-comment-sets-internet-ablaze.html (accessed 15 April 2013).

Tasker, Y. and Negra, D. (eds) (2007) *Interrogating Post-Feminism* (Durham, NC: Duke University Press).

van Zoonen, L. (1994) *Feminist Media Studies* (London, Thousand Oaks, CA and New Delhi: Sage).

Ward, C. (1970) 'Christopher Ward,' *Daily Mirror*, 28 October, 7.

What to Expect When You Are Expecting (2012) (Film) (USA: Alcon Entertainment).

Part I
Teaching Feminism

2
CEOs and Office Hos: Notes from the Trenches of Our Women's Studies Classrooms

Sara T. Bernstein and Elise M. Chatelain

Introduction

An increasing trend on US college campuses is that of the CEOs and Office Hos party theme, whereby men show up 'all cleaned up and in a suit' and women dress in their most 'scandalous secretarial undergarments' ('CEOs and Office Hoes' 2011). As with any form of popular culture, students engage with this manifestation of unequal gender roles in a variety of ways – some with passive acceptance, some with ironic play, others with distaste and rejection. However, considering the range of issues young women continue to face on college campuses and beyond, including sexual violence, racism, class and sexuality anxieties, and body image concerns, it is unsettling that female students are attending parties that suggest, among other things, that they are not 'CEO material.'

It is our concern that the women's studies classroom seems less and less to be a space where we can, along with our students, deploy a critique of this phenomenon.[1] With the field's movement toward a transnational feminist perspective, discussing the concerns of 'first world women' can sometimes be viewed as passé. As teachers, we have struggled to balance keeping students engaged through addressing their particular obstacles with guiding them to think beyond their own perspectives. Unfortunately, at times we have found that one approach leads to the sidelining – or complete erasure – of another. Further, when reading through contemporary feminist pedagogical writing, we noticed that there is this constant tension between the desire to teach women and men to 'check their privilege' but also wanting to empower them. Very often, these tensions go unresolved and generate anxiety for both students and teachers, resulting in feelings of frustration, guilt, and/or apathy rather than a feminist consciousness.

19

The impetus to examine these issues was inspired by conversations, with each other and with our students, during which we struggled to articulate our commitment to feminism and feminist pedagogy and our frustrations with some of our actual experiences in the classroom. Part of the dilemma may be that (appropriately) women's studies is expected to encompass a much broader spectrum of issues than most disciplines – from global politics, media, economics, and structural power issues, to race, class, and sexuality – while simultaneously providing a 'safe space' (however out of fashion the term may be) for young people who may be coming to terms for the first time with issues relating to their own sexual, racial, economic, as well as gendered subjectivities. At the same time, the field is (still) plagued with the problem of continually being required to justify its existence.[2] Despite, or perhaps because of, these unique challenges we face as instructors, we feel strongly that women's studies must continue to pursue its unique potential to provide a meaningful, rigorous intellectual experience for our students that also adheres to the transformative goals of feminist pedagogy.

What follows is a reflective piece that is not intended to be a sweeping commentary on the state of women's studies curricula, but only our preliminary offerings to a conversation about the kinds of things that are – as well as what we think should be – happening in the classroom. Together we have acquired over a decade of experience teaching women's studies and women-centered coursework. Our roles have ranged from reader to teaching assistant to adjunct instructor. We've worked at large Research One and elite private institutions, contributed to the 'liberal studies' core at a well-known school for art and design, and taught online courses, all in the US. Through evaluation and analysis of our own successes and failures, reflections on conversations with colleagues and mentors, and an examination of some of the ways that feminist pedagogy has been framed in textbooks and scholarship, our purpose is to suggest some of the potential ways in which women's studies curricula can more explicitly connect the various struggles facing university women in the US (and other 'first world' locations) and the historical and global cultural processes in which these are entrenched.

Below we put forth several key (and often overlapping) challenges that we have faced while trying to teach gender-centered coursework or implement feminist pedagogical strategies in our classrooms, both directly in women's studies courses and in other disciplines that are (or, we think, should be) concerned with power relations and identity. Throughout, we attempt to point to some concrete ways we think we can address some of these concerns, particularly in terms of highlighting key assumptions and approaches in women's studies and feminist curricula. We conclude by asking what is at stake in these challenges – why they matter, and, more broadly, why and how gender studies matters on contemporary college campuses.

Our challenges in the classroom

Challenge one: students' preconceived beliefs: old assumptions need reframing

In their introductory textbook, *Women's Lives: Multicultural Perspectives*, Gwyn Kirk and Margo Okazawa-Ray (2007) offer students what has become a typical framing device for their initial foray into women, gender, and sexuality studies: a challenge to common assumptions about the field and about feminism itself. They unpack certain myths about feminism and women's studies and promise to offer a more complex, nuanced perspective than what is typically depicted in popular media. Alluding to the 1980s backlash against feminism, they refer to what is now an almost common-sense understanding of young women's relationship to feminism: the third wave or postfeminist identity that begins with 'I'm not a feminist, but ...' (pp. 6–9).[3]

While this phenomenon persists, we have found that increasingly our students are more apt to openly express their feminist identities or, at the least, not respond with a blank stare when asked about the definition of feminism itself. Importantly, though, this shift does not mean that our work is done. For instance, during a round of introductions on the first day of the term, Sara asked her class to recount key feminist figures; the most common responses were Hillary Clinton and Lady Gaga. These examples suggest that some basic assumptions and frameworks that have guided approaches to teaching feminist theory for the last 20 years or so need to be updated. On the one hand, they can be seen as very encouraging. Hillary Clinton and Lady Gaga were not listed because they are seen as 'hairy, man-hating, radicals.'[4] Rather, they are women that our students admire and find inspiring, suggesting that 'feminist' has, at least in our classrooms, become shorthand for prominent women (and yes, usually just women at this point in the term) who represent qualities to which they aspire. On the other hand, their larger reasons for labeling them 'feminists' are problematic. Hillary Clinton projects a classic 'second-wave' image of an already privileged, straight, white woman busting through glass-ceilings in her immaculate pant-suit. Meanwhile, Lady Gaga is an example of our students' favorite type: the vaguely defined 'strong, independent woman' who is, in effect, the author of her own exploitation, a Madonna figure 'updated' for the third wave whose radical gender performance isn't explicitly there to question larger structural inequalities.[5]

We provide these examples to illustrate certain shifts in our students' perceptions, although this is not to say that they don't enter the classroom with any of the 'old-fashioned' expectations described by authors such as Kirk and Okazawa-Rey (2007). Nor is it the case that the 'old work' is done. If anything, issues such as the media's objectification of women, women's sexual autonomy, and even the old 'glass-ceiling' or the barriers to women in high-ranking leadership positions are more urgent in the current decade than they have been in the previous 20 years. These problems not only persist, but have possibly become even more difficult to untangle than they were 20 or 30 years ago as our students, to some extent responding to mainstream culture, have become more comfortable with the language of feminism – but often as it has been enfolded into the persistent American progress narrative. That is, many of our students enter the class assuming that women's 'real' problems happened in some nebulous, corseted, olden time, and while obviously we still have some work to do, for the most part things are better now than they were then.[6] To come back to Lady Gaga and Hillary Clinton, the labeling of these two figures as feminists suggests that the language of feminism has been so thoroughly inculcated into popular culture that it becomes necessary, not to merely nurture a feminist identity or dispel negative stereotypes, but to trace and then denaturalize the many ways that the term has been deployed, and for what purposes.

Challenge two: curricular gaps

About three weeks into Sara's first experience as a teaching assistant for Introduction to Women's Studies, she was about to begin her usual review of the concepts covered that week. She was looking forward to discussing the unit on globalization and had prepared several exercises to help them unpack the reading material. As she did every week, Sara began by asking if anyone had any questions before they got started. After a pause, one student tentatively raised her hand and asked, 'Can you explain what second wave means?' A little bit surprised, Sara opened the question up to the group, asking if anyone wanted to have a go at responding. It turned out that nobody felt comfortable answering the question, so she asked if they wanted her to give an impromptu 'lesson' on the 'history of the feminist movement.' Heads eagerly nodded throughout the room. At the end of the quarter, many students named this off-the-cuff discussion as being among the most useful to them in their evaluations.

In our own classes, we have continued to find that it is necessary to offer a kind of disciplinary history, such as the above example regarding the history of feminism, which provided students with a clarifying framework for the fuzziness of the term and helped them to sort out the distinction between activist and academic projects. Students' responses in class and on course evaluations validate this approach, suggesting that there is not only a need, but a desire, to position knowledge historically and within the field of women's studies itself (as well as within other disciplines). At times, this history is minimally addressed in introductory textbooks or in the surrounding curriculum (for example, lectures for courses we have TAed). For instance, in the course described in Sara's above anecdote, the textbook did briefly cover this material. However, the professor had chosen not to assign that section. Her syllabus was trying to avoid chronology (and the implicit 'progress narrative' attached to designations such as 'first wave,' 'second wave,' etc.) and focus on 'issues' instead. This move is certainly understandable given the scope of what 'Intro' is expected to cover; it can be a struggle to provide an adequate history of the field while also drawing students' attention to contemporary debates.[7]

But at times, an 'issue-based' curricular structure runs the risk of not just sidelining the field's academic history, but also limiting students' ability to critically engage with key feminist issues themselves. In one example, when Elise presented a prospective Intro syllabus for review, her chair responded that it was too 'theory heavy' and that the central goal was to provide students with readings that provided them with a 'lens for analyzing contemporary gender issues.' On this syllabus were select readings from the second wave that offered specific examples from key theoretical paradigms the students would be reviewing in class, including short excerpts from Shulamith Firestone's *The Dialectic of Sex* (1970) and Susan Brownmiller's *Against our Will* (1975). While she knew it was a bit unorthodox to assign such pieces in an introductory course, her intention was to contextualize their review of feminist thought – a strategy that was informed by previous experiences in introductory courses. While at the chair's request she removed these particular readings in order to make room for a greater number of contemporary topical pieces, and while the course still contained a unit reviewing the different paradigms of second-wave academic thought, students seemed confused without the contextualizing readings. For instance, they reacted strongly to the radical feminist notion that all sex is rape, an idea that on its own sounds crazy, but in the context of the historical moment of the movement and the argumentative work of the author would have provided students with situated knowledge of the field, as well as some more general tools for understanding the relationship between gender and processes of power.

This observation brings us back to one of the central challenges we face in the classroom: being able to offer students an awareness of relevant contemporary issues in gender and sexuality while also providing them with the appropriate analytical tools for thinking through these issues. From our experiences, doing this 'double duty' effectively takes more than just having students read articles about how women are oppressed; they also need a framework that situates what they are learning as part of the process of knowledge production, in addition to theoretical tools that allow them to develop the capacity for abstract thought. Unfortunately, we and many of our colleagues continue to have difficulties generating this kind of all-encompassing curriculum. While we can't be expected to cover everything in an introductory course (or beyond), our ideal classes would offer a well-rounded curriculum that simultaneously situates the field, appeals to students' interests, and offers them adequate analytical frameworks for thinking about gender and power. The trick, of course, is finding the appropriate balance between these goals.

Challenge three: transnational feminism in a US women's studies classroom

In one introductory course for which we both TAed, the professor showed a short video to the students called *The F Word: A Video About Feminism* (1994) on the first day of the term. This informative piece provides students with a clear, nuanced understanding of feminism, but after the initial showing, there was very little mention of the video or the relationship between feminism and women's studies throughout the remainder of the term.

This disconnect had a lot to do with the professor's particular approach to the field, which is consistent with our own. Just as she did, we come to women's studies from a transnational perspective, informed by our position as cultural studies scholars invested in issues of representation, labor, and identity. Our courses reflect this point of view, although we have found that, very often, we end up excluding the perspectives of the women and men we teach. Importantly, too, the curriculum itself seems to suggest that these two perspectives are mutually exclusive. As an easy example, we can refer to the two textbooks that formed the basis of the introductory women and gender courses for which we TAed as graduate students. The first, *Women's Lives: Multicultural Perspectives* (Kirk & Okazawa-Rey 2007), highlights issues affecting US women/men, while the other, *An Introduction to Women's Studies: Gender in a Transnational World* (Grewal & Kaplan 2006), outlines processes of globalization, histories of colonialism, and issues like labor migration and global economic policies. Our point is not that one is better than the other, but that each one offers its own exclusions. For instance, *Women's Lives* doesn't touch upon some of the central theoretical concerns of postcolonialism and has little historical perspective on gender and sexuality. The other offers scant discussion of issues like health, the family, or other experiences that our students are likely to face over the course of their lives.

Ideally, our classrooms would bridge the gaps between these two frameworks, although we have not always managed to carry this out in practice. For instance, during her very first time teaching an introductory course, Elise designed a syllabus that delved into such topics as the global division of labor, the relationship between colonialism and the production of knowledge, and questions of representation and geography. But very quickly, she realized that she didn't leave much room for them to grapple with their own experiences of gender oppression and inequality. In fact, many students expressed frustration throughout the term that they weren't reading about things that affected them on a day-to-day level, such as body image concerns, reproductive rights, or domestic violence. While she reworked the second half of the syllabus to include a few readings that touched upon students' stated interests, such as date rape and gay marriage debates, a disconnect remained in this haphazardly reconstructed curriculum, and she struggled to help them draw lines between, for example, processes of imperialism and contemporary discourses of sexual violence.

One of the biggest challenges we face is helping students feel connected to material that isn't necessarily 'relevant' to their lives. In our experiences, they tend to respond more positively to a more US-centric framework offered by a text like *Women's Lives,* likely because they see themselves more prominently in this material. But this curriculum doesn't quite mesh with our own scholarly strengths, and it also doesn't introduce students to certain theoretical debates within women's studies. Further, we want them to be drawn to issues that *aren't* necessarily about them, as well as to issues that are near and dear to them. This 'bridging' is part of the process of helping our students to develop the capacity for empathy, and helping them to establish the tools to connect their own experiences of privilege and oppression to those of others. It is also a very large task that leaves one open to dismissing or downplaying the issues that they bring into the class with them.

Challenge four: academic rigor and the 'transformative' goals of women's studies

In *Teaching Introduction to Women's Studies: Expectations and Strategies* (Winkler & DiPalma 1999) the editors suggest that a thread connecting all of the essays is the need for the introductory course to 'be taught in ways that are both rigorously academic and responsibly caring' because, 'being introduced to the ways in which course material "matters" is often life-changing for students' (p. 8). Our bias, we freely admit, is toward the rigorously academic. But our belief is that this academic rigor is necessary for generating caring, but critical, thinkers in the classroom.

However, we know that our approach runs the risk of alienating students who, very often, struggle with what is surprisingly (to them) academically difficult material. In one notable class, Elise assigned a selection from Chris Weedon's *Feminist Practice and Poststructuralist Theory* (1987) as part of a unit on representation and subjectivity. This piece provides an example about discourses of rape in the courtroom. Students enthusiastically participated in the discussion – not to talk through processes of language and representation, but to express anger and frustration about their own experiences and understandings of sexual violence. As students became more and more engaged, she tried to balance the path they were forging in the discussion with continuing the lesson on the concepts of discourse, subjectivity, and power in relation to feminist thought. The students did good and necessary work on that day, although Elise reworked future classes in order to ensure that they were equipped with the appropriate analytical tools for thinking about language and power in the context of any gender-related concern.

We feel strongly that part of our job is to introduce our students to problems, power structures, histories, and critical lenses that they may not encounter otherwise. Ideally, these larger lenses can then be focused onto the world around them, not only as they relate to gender, but also other institutions and experiences that are embedded in processes of power. Very often, though, we do struggle with guiding students into this kind of abstract thinking, and as the above example illustrates, we and colleagues have found that there is often a tension between keeping students from becoming too invested in an issue they read about and helping them to extrapolate the larger point illustrated by this reading or concept.

For many students, their expectation of why and how the course material 'matters' – that is, has transformative, political potential – is quite different from our own understandings. In an upper division seminar on 'transnational issues in fashion, dress and gender,' Sara thought it would be logical to begin with looking at how the relationship between the nation state and individual subjects has been theorized and historicized. To that end, her first readings and lectures for the course were centered on Foucault's 'The Subject and Power' (1982) and Stuart Hall's 'The State in Question' from *The Idea of the Modern State* (1984). In retrospect, it's not surprising that this didn't go over well with students who were enticed by the 'fashion' part of the course title rather than the 'transnational.' While one student actually wrote in the evaluations that she especially liked the inclusion of readings that were 'not specifically about fashion,' those two essays in particular became part of a running joke throughout the term (whatever they were assigned, at least it wasn't Foucault!). But obviously, we are in the classroom to challenge their expectations, and as the discussions in the previous sections have also demonstrated, many of the challenges we're describing spring from the basic problem of managing student expectations. Or perhaps more accurately, *balancing* their expectations: between what brought them to the room in the first place and a teaching agenda that many students are not expecting.[8]

Challenge five: feminist pedagogies

A so-called 'student-driven' approach is one of the cornerstones of feminist pedagogy. In an ideal classroom, the advantages of this form of education are obvious. Unfortunately, we have only encountered that ideal classroom a handful of times: that magical place where students work together, actively engaging with the material, enthusiastically fashioning independent or collaborative projects or research questions, learning as much from each other as from us, and so on. But in all honesty, these experiences were as much the result of happy coincidence, a student group that cohered organically and 'connected' with our teaching style, as it is the result of our labors in planning the course. More often, we have had mixed success with a student-driven approach. To an extent, our less successful experiences are due to our particular teaching styles and personalities. As hard as we try, not all of us are equipped with the skills to delicately balance a circular discussion of students' frustrations about campus gender politics with a reading of Judith Butler's *Gender Trouble* (1990) – or even something more accessible, like Allen G. Johnson's 'Patriarchy, the System' (1997).

And the challenges come from both sides of the classroom. Students – most of whom have been encultured very differently in their pre-college education – often have a profound resistance to what we think are 'cutting edge' methods.[9] This topic comes up frequently in conversation among our colleagues, not only in women's studies, but also for peers who consider themselves feminist educators in fields like American studies, film studies, English, and others. As instructors, obviously, we put a lot of thought and energy into our course designs. And our goals are often lofty. We want our students not just to learn the material, but to gain a deep understanding of why it's important and how they are implicated within it. We also do this a lot. We want to try new things, experiment with creative ways of making our students part of the learning process and to ask their own questions of the material. So we develop a final project or in-class exercise that we think is giving them some autonomy in developing their research questions or methods, or a chance to think creatively and apply a different skill set to the problem. And sometimes, for some students, it works brilliantly. But as we have seen, very often students respond to this 'freedom' with resentment. What we see as guiding them toward becoming 'active agents,' they see as ambiguity and extra work. They have other courses to study for, college is expensive, and they may have jobs, clubs, sports, and/or complicated family or social lives. They want to know how to pass the class, not how to write an auto-ethnography that connects their part-time job at Starbucks to transnational labor/production/environmental inequity. And frankly, especially in the current culture where a college degree – and the massive debt that comes with it – is often construed as the new high school diploma, these concerns are valid.

Despite these obstacles, we remain invested in generating a student-centered classroom, although our experiences have shown that this environment still needs a lot of structure and direction, and simultaneously an appropriate amount of flexibility and student autonomy. It is a delicate balancing act, and one that needs transparency as well as a framework for teaching students to be comfortable with ambiguity and responsibility. We also know that, as educators, we need to be willing to experiment and run the risk of poor course evaluations, keeping in mind that mistakes provide an opportunity for learning and improvement.

Conclusion

Recently, Elise ran into one of her old students from an introduction to women's studies course. This woman, now in her early twenties and in graduate school, was one of the most enthusiastic members of the class, excitedly generating a growing feminist and anti-racist consciousness throughout the term. During an experience when the majority of students at this particular institution seemed totally disconnected from the course, this woman stood out. But a few years later, Elise watched with some horror in a social setting where the former student's boyfriend policed her drinking with great bravado, shaming his girlfriend in front of her friends for letting loose at a bar and even going to the extent of asking the bartender to not serve her another drink. While somewhat of an outsider, Elise couldn't make a fully accurate judgment about the situation, the patriarchal, controlling tone of the interaction made her cringe, especially knowing this woman's proposed commitment to feminist principles. She couldn't help but feel like she had failed the woman.

Our ultimate concern is that, despite our best intentions, the classes we teach are not adding up to something that is relevant to what our students actually deal with on campuses or preparing them for their roles within the larger power structure. As the previous anecdote and, indeed, the title of this chapter suggests, we have both found ourselves somewhat troubled by the ways in which broader gender politics are playing out in our students' lives. The campus culture itself even seems to affirm gender stereotypes that don't serve women once they graduate and enter into the workforce. For instance, Sara recorded some interesting observations when interviewing young women in their late teens and early twenties of varying class backgrounds. What she found was a stark contrast between the working-class women who attended community college, had children, and/or worked full-time jobs, and the middle-class women attending a four-year university. While the women who went straight from high school to a full-time job (and often childrearing) presented themselves with confidence and authority on the subject at hand, the college students were often timid, almost child-like, and performed as though what they had to say was silly or irrelevant. Certainly, these were just casual observations, but what struck us was how very familiar the latter gender performance was and how consistent with our own experiences of many women in our classrooms. We have a concern that the university environment seems to reward 'girlish' behavior, especially among the more middle-class performing students, affirming what Julie Bettie (2003) has observed to be a period of extended adolescence among middle-class women when compared to counterparts who must enter the workforce at a young age (p. 61).

Much has been made of the news that, in 2011 US female college graduates 'across all racial and ethnic groups' outnumbered males by as much as 25 percent (Gonzalez 2012). However, this increase in college degrees has not, for example, closed the pay gap,[10] ended discriminatory policies relating to health care, or translated to more women in leadership positions in general.

To a large extent, these kinds of gender issues aren't being addressed in our women's studies classrooms. They are sometimes thought of as the 'old' concerns, but they really haven't gone anywhere. Instead there are just more women, of more diverse backgrounds, on the quad. It's not that we believe that women's studies should have changed the world by now, but it's obviously urgently needed, and, frankly, could be doing more. And this is why we believe it necessary that women's studies continue to insist on its transformative goals.

At the bottom of it all, we are cultural studies scholars invested in women's studies and feminist pedagogy. For the most part, our classes are *not* filled with women's studies majors. And we don't teach exclusively in women's studies departments. While we passionately believe that the field should remain an established and autonomous entity, we are also engaged in its interdisciplinary perspective. To an extent, we have some concerns about the dangers of 'roping off' a field that is, by its very nature, interdisciplinary. When Sara taught a freshman writing course on the topic of fashion and gender, she was shocked by the profound resistance from some students who explicitly told her that they 'signed up for English, not women's studies.' Funnily enough, one of the most successful units in this course – a section on masculinity and popular culture – was actually the most women's studies-y part of the syllabus. This experience illustrates that students continue to have a misunderstanding of what women's studies actually means – that is, it's not just about reading essays by women or queer writers – and also that there needs to be some kind of recognition, across departments, about how different disciplines speak to one another, and how one might be useful for another. And in line with our cultural studies background, we believe that part of the goal of interdisciplinary work is, consistent with the ideas of foundational scholars like Stuart Hall (1990), to 'decenter or destabilize a series of interdisciplinary fields' (cited in Grossberg 2010, p. 108).

How, then, might women's studies, consistent with its interdisciplinary foundations, work in conjunction with other fields of study to both destabilize itself and other modes of knowledge? One thing we have noticed is that, very often, curricula across disciplines that are invested in teaching students about issues of power and politics emphasize the tactic of training students to be better consumers. For Sara, especially, who has taught many courses centered on fashion, she has found that the 'shop better' motto infiltrates both student discussions as well as many of the readings available for such classes. This is a problem that Elise also encountered when teaching environmental sociology, where she had to work hard to challenge students' assumptions that being a better consumer was the only way to 'do' environmental activism. When students learn about problems like the pay gap, worker exploitation, or gendered violence, they also learn that large-scale, structural shifts are necessary. But they want to know what they can do immediately, and consumer activism offers students immediate, concrete solutions – although not necessarily the most effective solutions. We try to make our students understand that what they are learning in our classes is not straightforward, and that, very often, what we offer them is a foundation for generating a more critical perspective of the world – not necessarily concrete, step-by-step guidelines for fixing global hierarchies once and for all. To some extent, this is an issue of micropolitics: empowering students to engage, on a day-to-day level, with the larger power issues that they face. Although we understand that this 'personal is political' motto is not the sole end goal, there is a way in which this mantra is a central tenet of academic feminism. Further, since these students really are our future, we believe it is necessary to instill a sense of patience.

And more subtly, the assumption within much of the curricula of a student body of consumers problematically aligns traditional notions of femininity and consumption, failing to consider the ways in which our students actually are, and will be, 'producers' in and of the world. While our classrooms are quite diverse, just about everyone – even those from outside the US – enters assuming some level of first world privilege.[11] This is especially the case at the R1 and private liberal arts institutions we have taught in, although the very entry into almost any space of higher education within the US offers some kind of contextual status. These students will bring their critical academic training into their future lives: as workers, parents, community members, etc. Very few of them will end up working directly on gender-related issues in a specifically activist or academic space, but we want them to think critically about gender (and race, and sexuality, and class, etc.) in whatever life path they choose. And some of them *will* go on to become CEOs – as well as politicians, activists, church and community leaders, military personnel, teachers, administrators, etc. And in these roles, they will have the power to change not just their individual habits, but make policy-level decisions that can, for instance, effect real changes in the global economic system, in women's rights as workers, etc. Even if they don't end up in some high-ranking political office or as the CEO of a Fortune 500 company, we want them to know that they still have to move through the world making decisions in various positions of power: from hiring a domestic worker to managing a women's clothing department at Target to having to deal with sexism in a relationship or in the workplace. In essence, we want our students to graduate knowing that they *do* produce things in the world – and if we can help it, we want to help these 'productions' happen in a feminist way.

Notes

1. While the debate about how to name the academic field of women's studies still remains, and we have in fact taught under a range of departmental monikers (including 'Women and Gender Studies' and 'Gender and Sexuality Studies'), for ease of discussion we largely stick with the foundational 'women's studies' throughout this chapter. At times, we refer to the more general 'feminist studies' or 'feminist curriculum' to allude to ways that the study of gender and sexuality are integrated into other fields, and how we have grappled with these challenges in our own classrooms. The debate itself is revealing, especially for how it speaks to the 'marketability' of the field and the need to attract majors. One colleague commended a program's decision to name its department 'Feminist, Gender, and Sexuality Studies,' with the department's chair's response being, 'maybe ... but we only have eleven majors.'

2. If not to administration, then to students. In 'The Ideologue, the Pervert, and the Nurturer, or Negotiating Student Perceptions in Teaching Introductory Women's Studies Courses,' Vivian May (1999) writes, 'women's studies is thought to be "easy" because it is about everyday life, "soft" because it is about women, and therefore a seeming "waste of time" if required and obnoxious if challenging or "hard." Yet underneath expectations of "an easy A" are often internalized notions that women's ideas, art forms, bodies, and histories are inherently less important than matters of direct importance to traditional disciplines' (p. 24). Michele Tracy Berger and Cheryl Radeloff (2011) provide an interesting and useful framework for managing these assumptions from the perspective of women's studies students in their book *Transforming Scholarship: Why Women's and Gender Studies Students are Changing Themselves and the World*.

3. Versions of this sentiment also come up throughout Winkler and DiPalma's *Teaching Introduction to Women's Studies: Expectations and Strategies* (1999). For example, laying out the key challenges instructors face as women's studies has been successfully institutionalized and student enrollment broadened, the editors list the 'concerted backlash (to feminism), both within the academy and in the larger political environment, that affects students'

knowledge of what feminism is, the history of the women's movement, and the ability of women and men to contribute to effective social change' (p. 5).

4. Contrast this response, for example, with the one Katherine Ann Rhodes (1999) describes in 'Border Zones: Identification, Resistance and Transgressive Teaching in Introductory Women's Studies Courses.' In this essay, written in the 1990s, Rhodes summarizes the most common responses from her students thusly: 'Taken together, their descriptions construct feminists as a large, undifferentiated, angry mass of women who are out of control ("raging"); hateful toward men ("male bashers") and yet masculine ("brutes"); and zealously and exclusively committed to feminist causes' (p. 66).

5. While we don't have much room to discuss the limitations of the post-1990s third-wave visions of feminism, the popularization of apolitical female empowerment through figures like Lady Gaga has its precedent in such performances as the Spice Girls' 'girl power!' campaign, a spin on liberal feminist principles that sold particularly well during this era and has continued to be highly marketable.

6. In fact, in another course students watched the film *Miss Representation* (2011) and during a classroom discussion, a (white, male) student angrily insisted that the concerns raised in the film were no longer relevant political issues – because, as he argued, 'the truth is the US has more women in high-ranking political positions than at any time in history.' Not only was this claim just plain untrue, but it also showed a complete misunderstanding (midway through the term) of the term 'political' in the context of gender politics.

7. See Winkler and DiPalma (1999) for further discussion of the way the introductory course especially is assumed to 'speak' for the broader field of women's studies (p. 5).

8. From another field, Antoinette Burton (2003) notes a similar challenge that arises within her British Studies courses, whereby students arrive to her classroom and experience confusion when she asks them to think about race and colonialism – when what brought them there is a Merchant-Ivory film. This tension – between recognizing what makes a discipline 'marketable' so that it attracts new students but maintaining the academic rigor and especially the broader analysis of power that defines fields like women's studies – is a constant challenge that we face as educators invested in feminist pedagogy and content.

9. This resistance seems to have intensified in recent years as we are seeing the first cohorts of the 'no child left behind' generation begin to enter college.

10. Not only is it still the case that, in the US, female workers are paid an average of 77 percent of what their male counterparts earn (www.pay-equity.org/info-time.html), several 2011 studies have shown that the starting salaries of recent female college graduates average 17 percent less than that of males (Fairbanks 2011).

11. Our classrooms are typically racially and ethnically diverse, occupied by queer and straight folk, and filled with a mix of male and female students (although, very often, the majority are women, and transgender students enter now and again). Largely, there is not much variation in socioeconomic status, although one of us has taught at a couple of commuter institutions with more class diversity.

References

Berger, M.T. and Radeloff, C. (2011) *Transforming Scholarship: Why Women's and Gender Studies Students are Changing Themselves and the World* (New York: Routledge).

Bettie, J. (2003) *Women without Class: Girls, Race, and Identity* (Berkeley: University of California Press).

Brownmiller, S. (1975) *Against our Will: Men, Women, and Rape* (New York: Simon and Schuster).

Burton, A. (2003) 'When Was Britain? Nostalgia for the Nation at the End of the "American Century",' *The Journal of Modern History*, 75(2), 359–74.

Butler, J. (1990) *Gender Trouble: Feminism and the Subversion of Identity* (New York: Routledge).

'CEOs and Office Hoes,' *The Campus Companion*, 11 May, www.thecampuscompanion.com/party-lab/2011/05/11/ceos-and-office-hoes/ (accessed 3 April 2013).

Fairbanks, A. (2011) '"They Don't Negotiate": Why Young Women College Graduates are Still Paid Less Than Men,' *The Huffington Post Online*, 13 June, www.huffingtonpost.com/2011/06/13/negotiate-young-women-college-graduates-first-job_n_875650.html (accessed 3 April 2013).

Firestone, S. (1970) *The Dialectic of Sex* (New York: William Morrow).

Foucault, M. (1982) 'The Subject and Power,' *Critical Inquiry*, 8(4), 777–95.

Gallagher, E. and Jarmel, M. (1994) (Film) *Feminism: The F Word* (US: Women Make Movies).

Gonzalez, J. (2012) 'Young Women are More Likely than Men to Aspire to College, and to Graduate,' *The Chronicle of Higher Education Online*, 28 August, http://chronicle.com/article/Young-Women-Are-More-Likely/133980/ (accessed 3 April 2013).

Grewal, I. and Kaplan, C. (2006) *An Introduction to Women's Studies: Gender in a Transnational World*, 2nd edn (New York: McGraw Hill).

Grossberg, L. (2010) *Cultural Studies in the Future Tense* (Durham, NC: Duke University Press).

Hall, S. (1984) 'The State in Question,' in G. Maclennan, D. Held and S. Hall (eds) *The Idea of the Modern State* (London: Open University Press), 1–28.

Johnson, Allan G. (1997) 'Chapter 2: Patriarchy, the System: An It, Not a He, a Them, or an Us,' in *The Gender Knot: Unraveling Our Patriarchal Legacy* (Philadelphia: Temple University Press), 27–50.

Kirk, G. and Okazawa-Rey, M. (eds) (2007) *Women's Lives: Multicultural Perspectives*, 4th edn (New York: McGraw-Hill).

May, V. (1999) 'The Ideologue, the Pervert, and the Nurturer, or Negotiating Student Perceptions in Teaching Introductory Women's Studies Courses,' in B.S. Winkler and C. DiPalma (eds) *Teaching Introduction to Women's Studies: Expectations and Strategies* (Greenwood, CT: Praeger), 21–36.

Newsom, J.S. (2011) (Film) *Miss Representation* (US: Girls' Club Entertainment).

Rhodes, K.A. (1999) 'Border Zones: Identification, Resistance and Transgressive Teaching in Introductory Women's Studies Courses,' in B.S. Winkler and

C. DiPalma (eds) *Teaching Introduction to Women's Studies: Expectations and Strategies* (Greenwood, CT: Praeger), 61–72.

Weedon, Chris (1987) *Feminist Practice and Poststructuralist Theory* (Malden, MA: Blackwell).

Winkler, B.S. and DiPalma, C. (eds) (1999) *Teaching Introduction to Women's Studies: Expectations and Strategies* (Greenwood, CT: Praeger).

3

Suture and Scars: Evidencing the Struggles of Academic Feminism

Andrea Zeffiro and Mél Hogan

> Ideally, feminist labour/mentorship/activism are all aspects of the same thing, that is, living one's politics. Fostering real collectivity and questioning the hierarchies entrenched in academia. Respecting people as people, while stirring the pot.
>
> – Anonymous

Introduction

Our personal experiences as emerging scholars[1] shape the contours of this chapter. What began as a conversation many years ago over a cup of coffee has become a deeper reflection, channeling the various opinions and feelings of our graduate cohort,[2] and presented here as a first iteration that attempts to make sense of these shared experiences. The validity afforded to drawing from our 'personal experience' has itself long informed feminist modes of meaning-making: we have learned to value the personal as political, to find our voice, to enunciate, and also to acknowledge the limitations of our point of view. Because an important part of our training as feminist scholars has been to locate relations of power, this reflection has meant locating ourselves within a complex network of agents, to willfully complicate, rather than reduce the complexities of, the issues with which we are confronted. The feminist struggle is ongoing, and at once internal, structural, and institutional.

In this piece we reflect on our specific conjuncture as a means of opening up a broader discussion about feminism within academia, or academia *through* feminism. This reflection is likely to also raise important issues that we have unwittingly failed to address, downplayed, or altogether overlooked. We also recognize that much of what informs our feminism is the work of our predecessors: the artists, activists, and academics who continue to fight for the inclusion and legitimacy of our voices. For us, feminism is always rooted in the work of those who have made new modes of thinking possible, through its politics and applications. As such, a critical intervention such as we present here is also an acknowledgment of the struggles that came before our own.[3] These have enabled new venues, possibilities, openings, and modalities for thinking through feminism. In this way, the unified voice with which we speak in this chapter is comprised of many voices, and necessarily includes the contradictions, tensions, assumptions, and blind spots that are all integral to an ongoing conversation about feminism.

This personal introduction is necessary because, in our opinion, the academic trajectory is still too often understood as a logical (though competitive) progression: from student to faculty. In many ways the only thing that (really) counts on an academic CV is what is produced during the PhD, and for its own propagation: conferences, publications, and teaching experience.[4] Graduate students entering a PhD stream, with years of previous experience in arts administration, journalism, community organizing, corporate management, or with design and technology savviness (as few examples among many), are 'reset to zero' upon entering the academic field. 'Resetting' students in this manner is part of what breeds a transient army of laborers within the academy: student wages are much lower than those of freelancers doing the same work, for example, and university jobs are notoriously imbued with 'this will be good for your CV' logic or 'we did our time, do yours ...' rhetoric, particularly relating to research and acting as a teaching assistant. More often than not, this means that a clear work contract with defined tasks and hours is bypassed. This work environment, its conditions and hierarchy, are inherited, but become fertile grounds for a feminist revision and reconnection to life beyond the ivory towers.

The popular misconception of academia as separate from the 'real world' reinforces the idea that the university is always already a privileged space. However, the neoliberal insurgence on academic institutions has demanded that the university, as a space of intellectual curiosity and exploration, be replaced by the university as a service toward successful employment in the 'real world.' Yet what are we to make of the university as a service toward the employment *within* the university itself? Academic institutions are essentially set up to take advantage of transient student labor – graduate students in particular, within the humanities – which in turn, often falsely leads these individuals to believe they will find traditional (that is, tenure-track) employment within academia once they finish their doctoral degrees. The irony being that universities continue to accept a high level of enrollment, yet fail to offer resources to students that can prepare them for employment options outside of the university. Thesis and dissertation supervisors still often shun the very notion of 'their' students diverging from the academic track, thus rendering moot the possibility of even discussing other options. There is a way in which doctoral students remain affectively indebted to the institution they graduate from, as though there was an implicit understanding that the choices made after graduating are always somehow attached to, and a reflection on, the people and place that enabled graduation, as a rite of passage. For graduate students, this pattern can feel both paternalistic and infantilizing, and in direct contradiction to the professional status and independence it proclaims to have earned them (Fullick 2011; Zellner 2011).

The period after the PhD becomes a liminal space for many of us. However, we are neither disoriented nor, as it is too often assumed and implied, vying for a place in the ivory tower. It is certainly an option and ambition for many of us, but our feminist training has led us to question the implications of this assumed trajectory. That being said, having the academic accreditation that comes from successfully jumping through the flaming hoops of doctoral life is what places us in the ambivalent (if not seemingly hypocritical) position to question the burns (and ensuing scars) of graduate life. Having been through the process is also the very thing that places us in the position to speak to its issues most accurately. Post-PhD life offers a particular vantage point, but the ambiguities of what it produces are increasingly folded into how we perceive ourselves: you got your PhD, now what?

Our personal experiences are largely shaped by our privileged positions within, but also, in many ways, against, academia: we are always standing with one foot in and one foot out of the university's door, willingly or not. We hope this ambivalence can be productive. Rather than something to be resolved, ambivalence can serve as a thinking point about our collective assumptions about what it means to become, and continue to be, a feminist scholar.

As we write this, both of us are very happily working within universities, though neither of us feels beholden to the idea, nor considers it the only (or necessarily the best) use of our acquired creative thinking tools and critical production skills. We believe feminism can (and increasingly must) offer new modalities for thinking about the university as a less insular enterprise. Feminism – if academic feminism is to survive as more than a set of recycled ideals – must remain highly contested, debated, and open. But it also must consider its applications: what does it mean to produce a feminist scholar? How might feminism inform a postgraduate trajectory? Is a PhD *only* useful for the university? How do we equip feminist scholars with the skills to work within, alongside, and/or outside of a university context? Or, as is increasingly the case, as temporary workers or limited-term appointments within the university? It is in this vein that we prefer to poke at rather than censure the felt contradictions between feminism and academia, the very place we learned the immense potential of these politics. For this same reason, we look inward into ourselves and into academia to locate initiatives that demonstrate the potential of feminist scholarship through a *détournement* of the scholarly tradition, but that only serve to deepen our anchor.

Feminism – as a tactic, ideal, potential, politic, method, tool, and model – has the most potential for (re)opening the discussion about *why* we do academia in the first place. In deciphering the *why*, we can be brought important insights about the *how*: what might feminist methodologies offer, not only for academic research, but also for suturing contradictions between academia and feminism? How can academic feminism inform community activism, design, education, art, health, politics, etc? Our intention is to validate feminist scholarship and action beyond the university – not because of the lack of jobs in academia (though certainly with that in mind) – but because it is where feminism has brought us. If ignorance is bliss, knowledge is responsibility. So, rather than celebrating women in positions of academic power, we angle the discussion about the potentialities of feminism that put the contradictions of the trajectory at the forefront, as an undoing of this frame of reference that we deem a highly problematic ambition.

In our experience, to become a feminist scholar means to recognize and eventually embody a practice, mode of doing, and politic, even as it permeates and mutates. As an embodied practice, feminist scholarship is a modality independent of a particular object of study, despite a tradition of attention paid to power relations pertaining to gender equality. This modality carries over, and out of, academia. As such, feminism is a borrowed concept and a constantly reacquired position; one *is* not a feminist so much as one *does* feminism.

In redefining feminism as an active practice as well as a continuous and nomadic struggle (in the Braidotti sense), we approach the problems of feminism as also in flux (waves!), demanding constant revision to account for the myriad of issues addressed (if not redressed) in adopting any definition of 'feminism.' Braidotti (1994) refers to this moving state as 'as-if,' which she deems necessarily rooted in conscious agency and lived experience. It is within this purview that we propose a layered contribution to this anthology: we deconstruct the notion of 'feminist research methods' and explore its anchors for becoming a feminist scholar: Namely, the underlying structures that shape how research happens, in what spaces, and with what people. This is where our discontents and interventions lie.

Becoming (a feminist scholar)

The lessons of feminism are numerous. The waves of the feminist movement have increasingly complexified the interplay between various markers of identity, their representation, and the multiplicity of voices (Hart 2008; Hartsock 1998). From gender equality, to the body and pleasure, to freeing oneself of gender, the paradoxes and tensions within feminism are integral to its definition (Hey 2004). Feminism requires the category of women to exist, but insists on deconstructing its essence. As further argued by Ahmed (1998), power differentials *between* women are at the crux of the means and methods by which we conduct research, if feminism is to be framed as an enacted politic. As stated long ago in Audre Lorde's infamous conference talk 'The Master's Tools Will Never Dismantle the Master's House' where she states that 'Interdependency between women is the way to a freedom which allows the I to be, not in order to be used, but in order to be creative. This is a difference between the passive be and the active being' (2007, p. 111). This active being has revealed persistent threads which we take care in elaborating below. These come to shape not only research methods and methodologies, but also our everyday modes of navigating the world, as feminists. The more easily we can imagine feminisms as multiple embodied politics, the more we can strengthen the 'creative function of difference' itself (Lorde 2007, p. 111) to shape our *becoming* feminist scholars. By doing feminism – by actively and creatively engaging – we mark the importance of situatedness, enunciation, self-reflexivity, accountability, and collaboration. Together, these concepts shape the ways in which feminisms can best be understood, as intersecting and shifting ideals and practice, which in turn divulge, delimit, and determine their politics.

Situatedness

Through our academic and community-based feminist training, we have grasped that knowledge is socially constructed, partial, and situated (see: Clifford & Marcus 1986; Clifford 1988; Cook et al. 2005; Geertz 1973, 1983). Donna Haraway's (1991) feminist critique of the production of scientific knowledge is also a critique of academic knowledge production. The manner in which we devise, conduct, reflect on, and disseminate our research is intricately tied to the maintenance of hierarchical structures and production practices that affect the people, places, and things that become the 'objects' – willingly or unwillingly – of our research (see for example Engelstad & Gerrard 2005). Haraway reminds us that, 'feminist objectivity means quite simply *situated knowledges*' (1991, p. 188), which is 'a usable, but not an innocent, doctrine of objectivity' (p. 189). Knowledge that is generated through academic research is situated knowledge. It ought to be read (that is, situated) within the context of its production.

Feminist scholars are mindful of these considerations and work toward accentuating the manner in which sedimented structures of power are transported into the research process. For instance, academic feminists work directly with underrepresented groups and communities, and in partnerships and/or collectives that work against the traditional researcher/informant divisions. Yet we – a collective we, as in those of us invested, even partially, in the academy – are still swayed by the power of a 'god trick' (Haraway 1991, p. 191). For Haraway, this 'trick' concerns Western patriarchal visions of scientific knowledge, in which objectivity is equated with 'Truth' and 'Reason,' and knowledge is divorced from the social and cultural contexts in which it is produced. For us, the 'god trick' is extendable to the artifice of disseminating our research according to 'good' academic measures and conventions, and the accompanying pressures associated with favorable representations of our research context. The burden we feel is often a sense of responsibility to others, particularly within collaborative research projects and/ or settings. Inspired as we might be to translate our (research) experiences and feelings, we are confronted by measures of 'objectivity'; the pressure to make ourselves visible and present within the research, but without revealing *too much*. And when we formalize research or give our research form – be it a dissertation, report, journal article, or book chapter – we remain mindful that it will be read and interpreted by others. In other words, we imagine our audience. Who will read this? How are we positioning ourselves through this work? How will the work reflect on us? How are we to be positioned on account of this work? We often try to appease the audience and pacify potential conflicts. What are we permitted to reveal? What is too much? And who has the authority to decide?

Increasingly, graduate students are employed with collaborative research formations. These research networks are comprised of individuals with differing skills and institutional affiliations. Experiences within a single research formation vary, for instance, between faculty members or graduate students or industry specialists. The allocation of tasks and responsibilities contributes to the divergences, but so does the allocation of power. As graduate students, many of us were employed within similar research configurations. For many, the experiences were both positive and productive. In other instances, some of us were burdened by our lack in ability to alter our circumstances and those of other graduate students. Some of us stayed the course of a project for better or worse, while others sought other means of employment for both professional and personal reasons. In our introduction, we describe how this work started as a conversation between us (the authors) but extended into a wider-reaching dialogue with other graduate students, in which many of us shared our alienation from and within academic experiences and encounters. A considerable challenge, however, concerned our subjugation within what we designate here as an economy of disavowal. To be positioned within such a space is to feel disconnected from our experiences. How do we represent these kinds of experiences? How can we lay claim to both the favorable and difficult details of our experiences? To be positioned within an economy of disavowal is comparable to what Rebecca Solnit (2012) describes as 'an archipelago of arrogance' (par. 29). It is the means through which we are made to believe that we are unreliable witnesses to our own lives (and/or research), and it marks the process through which 'our right to speak, to have ideas, to be acknowledged to be in possession of facts and truths' (par. 29) is delegitimized and disavowed. How can research become a means of taking ownership of our emotions?

This work is a means through which we take ownership of our emotions. Many of us felt anger at the ways in which our experiences supplanted insecurities in relation to our own feminist politics, and the ways in which we became more vulnerable as a result. Our emotions became a launching point and we were 'moved' and are now 'moving' toward a vision of a different feminist future. '[E]motions work,' as Ahmed writes, 'as forms of mediation between knowledge/theory and practice/activism' (1998, p. 238). Our emotional responses, as individuals and as a cohort, signal hope for the future, toward an initiation of actions and reactions that improve others' (feminist) academic experiences.

Enunciation

Our capacity to enunciate our lived experiences into material forms – as speech acts, written accounts, or channeled through artistic practice – is to declare ownership not only over our emotions, but over our thoughts and experiences. Enunciative actions are also acts of critical agency through which we engage with the world around us, and respond accordingly. In this regard, to enunciate is to translate our singular introspections and transcode the personal to a larger political body. 'Translation,' as the late Canadian feminist scholar Barbara Godard writes, 'in its figurative meanings of transcoding and transformation, is a topos in feminist discourse used by women [writers] to evoke the difficulty of breaking out of silence in order to communicate new insights' (1989, p. 45). Through Godard we recognize the flip side of enunciation: silence. To be silenced is to be enacted on by outside forces. It is a form of oppression perhaps most easily recognizable through limitations placed on our enunciative agency: to speak, to respond, and to make ourselves heard. The negation of our enunciation occurs through direct silencing, but also when others step in and speak on our behalf. When we continuously 'speak for' or give voice to others, we are simultaneously silencing the already silent by denying them a right to speak, and we reposition ourselves at the locus of enunciative power and knowledge. Indeed, as feminist scholars, we have the responsibility to redistribute our privilege to misaligned individuals and groups. But what if these individuals or groups are purposefully unaligned? Who are we to impose alignment onto others? Nonalignment or misalignment is a definitive positionality. Therefore, if feminism is concerned with the power of representation, then as feminists, it is imperative that we not speak on behalf of (and therefore purport to know better) but rather enable, make room, and bring attention to underrepresented or undermined voices, so these groups and individuals can speak (or not) for themselves.

Increasingly, technology has become integral and plays a more central role in the construction of knowledge and a means by which to access and make available different realities. Researchers implicate user-generated content, social media, participatory platforms, and so on, as both source and pedagogical tool for their work. Media itself requires a level of awareness about how it shapes, limits, and informs the research outcome and how it informs the possibilities for storytelling (Chapman & Sawchuk 2012).

Thinking of research as adjoining political voices with technological practicalities has been important to the development of an increasingly self-reflexive approach that accounts for the documentation of research processes and academic deliverables, as not only integral to methodology but as elemental to rigorous scholarly output (Juhasz & Lerner 2006; Scalar 2013). To quote Julia Flanders and Trevor Muñoz (2012), 'raw and abstracted material created as part of research processes and which may be used again as the input to further research – carries with it the burden of capturing and preserving not only the data itself, but information about the methods by which it was produced' (p. 1). Determining the bounds of research is therefore inextricably linked to the possible knowledge produced about it, and the legitimacy (of voices, histories, testimonies) it enables. It is also, however, about what falls out and fails, and what these perceived failures reveal about a researcher's subject-position vis-à-vis their site of inquiry (Spivak 1992).

The generative elements of media engagement are therefore not exclusively about deliverables, but also – and more importantly perhaps – about process. A feminist engagement therefore includes careful documentation and description of the steps undertaken for research, serving to highlight the often iterative and invisible labor, experiments, tests, and prototyping. While Tara McPherson (2010) laments that, 'Many humanities scholars aren't really engaged with the technological: they're more likely to critique the social effects of technology than use it in their work' (p. 4), we believe these concerns can be redressed through self-reflexivity, in two interconnected ways. First, we counter the idea that media scholars must also be media makers (no more than films scholars are required to make films); and secondly – in tension with the first point – the necessary acknowledgment within research documentation that media is not neutral and must be accounted for methodologically. In this way we are proposing that media becomes a marker of identity (and class), and must be deconstructed with the same rigor as other intersecting factors that shape privilege, power, and voice (class, gender, ability, age, race, sexual orientation, and so on).

For many of us dealing with media technologies[5] in our research, as tools or sites of inquiry, we come to an understanding of self-reflexivity through the media at our disposal. We identify the role that the media – the Web, camera, audio recorder, etc. – plays in conducting oral histories interviews, focus groups, generating one's research archive, engaging in media archaeologies, as well as in various data-collection processes. These point to the myriad of ways in which media facilitates new modes of storytelling, showcases research findings, frames limitations, all as integral to the reflexive process.

Self-reflexivity

Self-reflexivity implies a critical personal examination of one's role as researcher, and the capacity to self-scrutinize research practices (England 1994; Gardner 2012). Feminists employing self-reflexivity offer critical interpretations of the difficulties associated with the research process, including academic networking, the role of researcher/subject, interpersonal dealings, and institutional and intellectual relationships (Nagar & Geiger 2007). As research cannot be removed from this greater context, and/or the tangled relations of power that facilitate research processes, self-reflexivity asks that we interrogate our individual identity as academics/researchers. As an awareness, if not practice, self-reflexivity intersects with the very modes by which we conduct our research, including how we edit and represent findings, and it informs the circuits and venues we choose to circulate our work. In this regard, self-reflexivity requires a 'radical consciousness' in which one purposefully interrogates 'the political dimensions of fieldwork and construction of knowledge' (Callaway 1992, p. 33 cited in Nagar & Geiger 2007, p. 269). Self-reflexivity must therefore extend beyond the acknowledgment and assessment of one's own presence in the research domain by asking: Is our role in the research process made visible? How are we entangled in processes of knowledge production and distribution? Why do we do what we do? How do we do what we do? (See also Acker 1994; Patai 1994; Rose 1997; Wolf 1997.)

In our own research endeavors, we have come to employ self-reflexive analysis in relation to the tools implicated in our creative and productive processes, but also in the formation of our identities as academics. As we have personally experienced in doctoral forums and conference contexts, feminism is still resisted within academia. To demand self-reflexivity is threatening because it asks of those who perceive themselves as neutral observers and as outside the purview of privilege altogether to consider – if only for a moment – their own body, position, and privilege (which often feels better negated). It remains entirely legitimate to remove yourself from your own writing in academia. Because the rejection of feminism, and women, is not reserved to the classroom, doing feminism – or, adopting a 'methodology of the oppressed' (Sandoval 1995) – becomes more than an academic tactic. It is a philosophy about human existence and networks. It is a mode by which to make sense of our lives, whereby the risk to disengage often feels greater than the cost of fighting. As Simone de Beauvoir put it, in 1948, 'It is in the knowledge of the genuine conditions of our life that we must draw our strength to live and our reason for acting' (p. 9). As feminist academics, we feel it our political responsibility to speak to and about (our own) privileged positions, whatever the markers of that privilege may be (as having/had access to an education and/or working within an institution that not everyone has access to). To study is a privilege. To study usually leads to opportunities that – simply put – make life better. To own this privilege is an act of unveiling, an acknowledgment, as transparency.

With transparency as a feminist ethic, we claim an openness and accept the vulnerability it transpires, as a mode of doing. However, the decision toward transparency also positions us in contradiction with that privilege. As we move 'up' from Masters to Doctorates to faculty – and increasingly contending for research positions over teaching ones – we are striving upward, and, in turn, buying into the (hierarchy within the) hierarchy that sustains it. It is also the hierarchy that largely facilitates our role and ability to write and reinvent widely circulated feminisms. It becomes impossible, in some sense, to distance ourselves from such ambition, while also portending its downfalls. This becomes concrete when we think about our own unease with privilege (with the identities, spaces, tools, and technologies), and even more so when we try to distance ourselves from those realities. Within our writings and academic interventions at large, the agency – the choice to participate or negate privilege – is where feminism lives out one of its biggest contradictions. Feminism is about noticing instances where power inserts itself – who we thank, assign credit to, put at the top of a list, nod toward, and acknowledge as a collaborator. Feminism means being aware of those rankings and resisting them. The risk it might be that feminism becomes a pool of guilt, producing an impossible liminality to wade in. But of course this is the easy way to avoid dealing with the ways in which we abide to rank and organize our work accordingly, because this might be the only way we have been told we can make sense of ourselves. This contradiction within feminism creates anxieties and grudges, expending large amounts of energy in attenuating those feelings at the expense of creative and productive ends.

Accountability

Having made the case for self-reflexivity as a means by which to enact feminist politics, we propose that accountability is a necessary byproduct. What does it mean to be accountable? How are we accountable to ourselves? To others? How do we ensure that accountability is threaded throughout our research agendas and practices? How do we make accountability visible? How are we accountable to the concept itself?

Accountability means acknowledging that research has consequences, in terms of both chosen methodologies and the means by which research findings are made available. Accountability, as Anita Allen explains, is 'a matter of actual and felt imperatives, including obligations, duties, and responsibilities' (2003, p. 17). Swayed by Allen, we posit here that accountability is complexified by the notion that 'self-regarding' actions are always already enmeshed within the larger social fabric, and therefore extend beyond the self.[6] Reframing accountability as pluralities, Allen points to its various facets: 'accountability functions, among other things, to enable and limit power, to enable and limit responsibility, and to foster intimacy and solidarity' (2003, p. 26). In this view, to be accountable is a continuation of self-reflexivity. It can be demanding, as it requires continuous check-ins with one's process; however, as we argue, this is a necessary and rewarding part of the process that should be valued in its own right. Assessing the 'what' and the 'how' of the enabling and limiting of responsibility suggested by Allen is where the possibility for feminist action and intervention lies.

As feminist scholars, we have social and emotional ties to a myriad of groups. Some of these bonds we actively forge ourselves through personal and professional relationships and collaborations, and shape research agendas. Other alliances are made on our behalf through institutional affiliations, roles, and titles. Each of these responsibilities becomes an opportunity to assess the ways in which they bring us closer to, or distance us from, the core responsibilities of research. How do our research agendas and practices frame us politically? How do they risk rendering us complicit in exploitative practices? Are we exploited at the expense of other research agendas and or/practices? How can we impose an ethical ecology on our research? Indeed, some of these questions are easier to answer but each belongs to an ongoing discussion that parallels our own trajectories within, alongside, and outside of academic feminisms. With this, we reiterate that becoming a feminist (scholar) is a continuous struggle that we owe ourselves. The core of accountability in this context is the recognition that pushing forward a feminist agenda means a dedication to its struggles, rather than a means by which to counter or appease notions of what counts as research, or as traditional research methods. This struggle is precisely what makes doing feminism so compelling, but it is also the reason why calling one-self a feminist or aligning oneself with feminism can often be exhaust-ing, sometimes unsexy, and often difficult to communicate effectively.

Collaboration

During our doctoral trajectories we participated in individual and collaborative research initiatives. In line with traditional scholarship, which honors independent research and authorship, we presided over individual research projects, most notably in the form of our doctoral dissertations. Yet, for many of us, it is increasingly difficult to view the prospect of research as a solitary enterprise. More often than not, the kind of research we are drawn too thrusts us into social contexts that are founded on a collaborative ethic.

Through feminism we have learned to identify different forms of col-laboration, from working with 'subjects,' participants/contributors, and collaborators. Feminist action research, for example, has tended toward positioning subjects as participants, and participants as collaborators (Clamen, Gillies & Salah 2013; Namaste et al. 2007). This has meant a politic of sharing both the project's decision-making roles and the related accreditation, often resulting in multiple authors.

This mode of thinking about contributors as collaborators often means a slower process; a way of working that can be counter to the usual academic pace. Instead of propagating one's own academic CV at the behest of publishing ideals and tenure dossiers that value sole authorship, collaboration is part of a comprehensive methodology that demands a renegotiation of the line between research and participa-tion. We call for a reassessment of the terms of collaboration because although it emerges from a multitude of experiences and perspectives, if we step outside of academia to perform research, we are bringing subjects into the institution's folds, where feminist ideals established by academia are applied (if not imposed).

As emerging feminist scholars and activists navigating the counters of the university and its limitations on our personal and political potentials, we have found respite in a burgeoning number of like-minded individuals for whom the university is neither friend nor foe. We count this, among other examples, as an important and worthy form of collaboration. As we have recounted throughout this essay, our concerns over the contradictions we identified within contemporary academic feminisms – those 'alien affects' that lead us toward identify-ing a disjuncture between how we felt and how we thought we should feel – enabled us to see beyond our singular encounters and formulate inquiries toward larger systemic issues. What does it mean to position ourselves as feminist academics? What do we expect from other feminist academics? How do we un/align ourselves with academic feminism? Ahmed (2010) has described the fractured experience of becoming a feminist as 'an alienation from happiness' (p. 5). Our alignment with an affective community ensues when we 'feel happiness in proximity to the right objects' and we become alienated when we 'do not experience happiness from the right things' (p. 5). But what if our alignment with an affective community transpires *because* of alienation? What if our need for an affective community is christened from a shared alienation? What if we reject not only feeling happiness in proximity to the right objects, but the objects altogether?

Indeed, feeling underappreciated (or alienated) as a graduate student is a common sentiment, but the universality of such 'soft degradation' (for lack of a better term) is by no means a reason to perpetuate forms of graduate student subordination. If the values and virtues associated with the university – as a tolerant and egalitarian space – are to be escorted into the future, and by us, then we need our feminist mentors and guides to begin that process immediately; first by recognizing what it is that they will come to expect from us, and second, by making those same demands on themselves at once.

Conclusion

This reflection piece was written by channeling the voices of our cohort; many of us at different stages in the academic trajectory, but all of us feeling a sense of urgency about the disconnect between the politics imparted through the theoretical interventions we engage with within the university setting, and the academic apparatus itself. Even though we learn to carefully think through the various modalities of feminism, and recognize its importance, our feminism is quieted within this same context. As such, we have attempted to use our own voices to outline and realign some of the essential contributions that have shaped feminist methods so as to imagine and insist on their wider applications and implications. We also look inward, to the ways in which we do feminism – and often fail to – within the confines of academia.

We recognize that the path toward this kind of intervention was paved by numerous feminist scholars whose journey started long before ours and who were in decidedly less favorable conditions than ours. This reflection piece is both a continuation of their work and an invitation to renew the context for feminist methodologies. In following Braidotti (1994), our reflection is also 'a discursive and political exercise in cross-generational female bonding' (p. 207); so without negating the progress of feminism, we've intentionally identified the scope of our intervention as 'here and now,' with the conundrums particular to having recently acquired a PhD. We started from a personal place in order to contextualize and acknowledge how different the *enjeux* are for everyone at this conjuncture. From the personal and speculative, we extrapolated various ideas – passed on from decades of feminism(s) – to propose five threads that highlight and push forward a new wave of feminist thinking. This new wave is about the continuity between academic modes of research and the practices of feminism as embodied, continuous, and carried with us beyond the context of the university.

As feminist researchers we recognize that any and all knowledge we produce is necessarily shaped by numerous competing factors. An interrogation of situatedness and self-reflexivity is a means through which we are able to lay the groundwork for a deeper discussion about the role of locating oneself in research as well as the potential impact our research might have for others, particularly groups or individuals seemingly disconnected from our research projects. If we continuously work within academia, then it is increasingly more difficult to envision the reach of our work beyond it. How do we make connections with and within broader communities? How can we make the process of research – its design, implementation, and dissemination – more applicable to others? Who are these 'other' individuals and/or groups? How can we broach divides? The simple answer to these questions would be an increase in accessibility to individuals and/or groups. But what do we even mean in terms of access? Access to our research reports? To obscure journal articles?

When we speak of access, we are insinuating the general inaccessibility to academic knowledge, from disciplinary journals, to rhetorical strategies and vocabulary, and indeed, accessibility of the documents themselves. And, many feminist academics and activists continue to work tirelessly at building venues for academics and non-academics alike that level the playing field, so to speak, in terms of how a public – not simply a specialized public – but a public with a set of shared politics are able to make contributions to the circulation of knowledge. The risk there, however, is the limit of academia – what it values and how it propagates those values – despite the best of intentions to break out of the model.

If we are to contribute to the feminist project within, alongside, and outside of the university, then it will demand enunciative action on our part, in that we invoke our critical agency as feminist researchers and activists (through collaborative actions), interact within the world and respond accordingly. Our enunciative function as academic feminists, however, is not only to use our voice but to provide an occasion for others to develop, refine, and practice their own enunciative agency. We discussed the importance of recognizing our own partial perspectives: that we do not know better than any individual or group, and therefore, cannot speak on its behalf. And we would like to extend this imperative to include graduate students. How can we encourage and nurture graduate students to develop a relationship with their enunciative agency that is simultaneously confident *and* compassionate? How would that translate in terms of mentorship? How can we cultivate future feminist mentors and guides that instill confidence and compassion in their students? As feminists, we are accountable to our colleagues (and sisters) who will continue *and* surpass our efforts and into the future.

Notes

1. Our chapter was written shortly after the completion of our PhDs and is reflective of a very specific moment in our personal and professional trajectories. The question of academic feminism is ongoing and ever shifting.
2. We asked our cohort to participate in an informal survey, which helped us think through the problems of feminism in academia.
3. Our critical intervention is an iterative process that parallels our own formations as feminist researchers and activists. Much like our own trajectories, which will mutate with new encounters and experiences, so too will our aims for our interventions. For us, this work lays the foundation for future projects, including collegial outreach and feminist academic and activist collaborative engagements, to name a few of many conceivable outcomes.
4. And in few places, exhibitions/performances/screenings, as creative interventions, still often remain difficult to assess within established academic standards.
5. To which we would also add communication and information technologies. See: Petty & Crow 2008; Sarikakis & Shade 2008; Shade & Crow 2004.
6. This is contrary to John Stuart Mill's (1974) deliberations on accountability in which individuals are accountable for actions on others as opposed to 'self-regarding' actions that affect the self.

References

Acker, S. (1994) *Gendered Education* (Buckingham: Open University Press).

Ahmed, S. (1998) *Differences that Matter: Feminist Theory and Postmodernism* (Cambridge University Press).

Ahmed, S. (2010) 'Feminist Killjoys (and Other Willful Subjects)', *The Scholar & Feminist Online*, 8(3), http://sfonline.barnard.edu/polyphonic/ahmed_01.htm (accessed 3 April 2013).

Allen, A. (2003) *Why Privacy Isn't Everything: Feminist Reflections on Personal Accountability* (Lanham, MD: Rowman & Littlefield).

Beauvoir, S. de (1948) *The Ethics of Ambiguity*, trans. Bernard Frechtman (Secaucus, NJ: Citadel).

Braidotti, R. (1994) *Nomadic Subjects: Embodiment and Sexual Difference in Contemporary Feminist Theory* (New York: Columbia University Press).

Callaway, H. (1992) 'Ethnography and Experience: Gender Implications in Fieldwork and Texts,' in E. Oakely and H. Callaway (eds) *Anthropology and Autobiography* (London and New York: Routledge), 29–48.

Chapman, O. and Sawchuk, K. (2012) 'Research-Creation: Intervention, Analysis and "Family Resemblances",' *Canadian Journal of Communication*, 37(1), 5–26.

Clamen, J., Gillies, K. and Salah, T. (2013) 'Working for Change: Sex Workers in the Union Struggle,' in E. Van der Meulen, E. Durisin and V. Love (eds) *Selling Sex: Experience, Advocacy and Research on Sex Work in Canada* (Vancouver: UBC Press), 113–29.

Clifford, J. (1988) *The Predicament of Culture: Twentieth-Century Ethnography, Literature, and Art* (Cambridge, MA: Harvard University Press).

Clifford, J. and Marcus, G.E. (eds) (1986) *Writing Culture: The Poetics and Politics of Ethnography* (Berkeley and Los Angeles: University of California Press).

Cook, I. et al. (2005) 'Positionality/Situated Knowledge,' in D. Sibley, P. Jackson, D. Atkinson, and N. Washbourne (eds) *Cultural Geography: A Critical Dictionary of Key Ideas* (London and New York: I.B. Tauris), 16–26.

Engelstad, E. and Gerrard, S. (eds) (2005) 'Challenging Situatedness,' in E. Engelstad and S. Gerrard (eds) *Challenging Situatedness: Gender, Culture and the Production of Knowledge* (University of Chicago Press), 1–26.

England, K.V.L. (1994) 'Getting Personal: Reflexivity, Positionality, and Feminist Research,' *The Professional Geographer*, 46(1), 80–9.

Flanders, J. and Muñoz, T. (2012) 'An Introduction to Humanities Data Curation,' *DH Curation Guides*, http://guide.dhcuration.org/intro/ (accessed 3 April 2013).

Fullick, M. (2011) '"My grief lies all within" – PhD Students, Depression and Attrition,' *University Affairs*, 14 December, www.universityaffairs.ca/speculative-diction/my-grief-lies-all-within-phd-students-depression-attrition/ (accessed 26 April 2014).

Gardner, P. (2012) 'Extended Session: Feminist Scholarship Division', www.icahdq.org/conf/2012/print_program.pdf (accessed 3 April 2013).

Geertz, C. (1973) *The Interpretation of Cultures: Selected Essays* (New York: Basic Books).

Geertz, C. (1983) *Local Knowledge: Further Essays in Interpretive Anthropology* (New York: Basic Books).

Godard, B. (1989) 'Theorizing *Feminist* Discourse/*Translation*,' *Tessera*, 6, 42–53.

Haraway, D. (1991) *Simians, Cyborgs and Women: The Reinvention of Nature* (New York: Routledge).

Hart, J. (2008) 'Mobilization Among Women Academics: The Interplay between Feminism and Professionalization,' *NWSA Journal*, 20(1), 184–208.

Hartsock, N. (1998) *The Feminist Standpoint Revisited and Other Essays* (Colorado: Westview Press).

Hey, V. (2004) 'Perverse Pleasures: Identity Work and the Paradoxes of Greedy Institutions,' *Journal of International Women's Studies*, 5(3), 33–43.

Juhasz, A. and Lerner, J. (eds) (2006) *F is for Phony: Fake Documentary and Truth's Undoing* (Minneapolis: University of Minnesota Press).

Lorde, A. (2007) 'The Master's Tools Will Never Dismantle the Master's House', in *Sister Outsider: Essays and Speeches* (Berkeley, CA: Crossing Press), 110–14.

McPherson, T. (2010) 'Animating the Archive: Old Codes and New Media,' 9 April, www4.uwm.edu/c21/pdfs/recaps/10spring/mcpherson_recap.pdf (accessed 3 April 2013).

Mill, J.S. (1974) *On Liberty*, ed. G. Himmelfarb (London: Penguin Books).

Nagar, R. and Geiger, S. (2007) 'Reflexivity and Positionality in Feminist Fieldwork Revisted,' in A. Tickell, E. Sheppard, J. Peck and T. Barnes (eds) *Politics and Practice in Economic Geography* (London: Sage), 267–78.

Namaste, V., Vukov, T., Saghie, N., Jean-Gilles, J., Lafrenière, M., Leclerc, N., Leroux, M., Monette, A. and Williamson, R. (2007) 'HIV and STD Prevention Needs of Bisexual Women: Results from Projet Polyvalence,' *Canadian Journal of Communication*, 32(3), 357–82.

Patai, D. (1994) 'When Method Becomes Power,' in A. Gitlin (ed.) *Power and Method* (New York: Routledge), 61–76.

Petty, S. and Crow, B. (2008) 'Introduction to Digital Feminisms,' *Atlantis*, 32(2), 2–5.

Rose, G. (1997) 'Situating Knowledges: Positionality, Reflexivities and Other Tactics,' *Progress in Human Geography*, 21(3), 305–20.

Sandoval, C. (1995) 'New Sciences: Cyborg Feminism and the Methodology of the Oppressed,' in C.H. Gray (ed.) *The Cyborg Handbook* (New York: Routledge), 407–22.

Sarikakis, K. and Shade, L. (eds) (2008) *Feminist Interventions in International Communication: Minding the Gap* (Lanham, MD: Rowman & Littlefield).

Scalar (2013) (Website), www.scalar.ca.

Shade, L. and Crow, B. (2004) 'Canadian Feminist Perspectives on Digital Technology,' *Topia*, 11, 161–76.

Solnit, R. (2012) 'Best of TomDispatch: Rebecca Solnit, The Archipelago of Arrogance,' *Tom Dispatch*, 19 August, www.tomdispatch.com/blog/175584/ (accessed 3 April 2013).

Spivak, G.C. (1992) 'Women in Difference: Mahasweta Devi's Douloti the Bountiful,' in A. Parker, M. Russo, D. Sommer and P. Yaeger (eds) *Nationalisms and Sexualities* (London: Routledge), 96–120.

Wolf, D.L. (1997) 'Situating Feminist Dilemmas in Fieldwork,' in D. Wolf (ed.) *Feminist Dilemmas in Fieldwork* (Boulder: Westview).

Zellner, A. (2011) 'Banishing Imposter Syndrome,' *Grad Hacker Industries*, 2 September, www.gradhacker.org/2011/09/02/banishing-impostor-syndrome/ (accessed 26 April 2014).

4
Feminist Erasures: The Development of a Black Feminist Methodological Theory

Alexandra Moffett-Bateau

Introduction

Within the social sciences, and particularly in political science,[1] feminist methods and theory are seen as valuable only within its own disciplinary boundaries, and limited to its own departments or program, often named women's studies, gender studies, and/or feminist studies. While the move within the academy to formalize the study of women, gender, and feminism is an important one,[2] these disciplinary boundaries unfortunately have the result of rendering the study and practice of feminist intellectual work invisible to the rest of the academy. Too often, feminist theory and methodological practice is only carried out by one or two female academics within individual departments, and these academics also happen to be connected with various iterations of women's studies departments, centers, or programs. As a result, feminist discourse is often absent from broader discourses within the larger academy, which is rife with methodological habits that fail to adequately measure and assess the lives, habits, and politics of marginalized populations at large. Contextualized within this broader condition, this chapter argues that feminism should have an important role in the methodological conventions of the social sciences, especially political science. More specifically, the chapter contends that black feminist theory should be more fully incorporated into the discipline of political science because it specifies how political scientists can better study populations on the margins of American society. In keeping with this, the black feminist methodological practice that is developed in this chapter illustrates the ways in which the use of first-person narratives, in surveys and interviews, is one of the most successful processes for a fuller and more nuanced study of all social and ethnic groups.

The context

Over the last century, tension has been increasing around the exclusion of women of color from mainstream feminism (Guy-Sheftall 1995). The absence of black women from mainstream feminist discourses in particular, has led to widespread debate within black communities at large about the degree to which feminism is relevant to the experience of black Americans in the United States (Guy-Sheftall 1995). As a result of this absence, feminism has indeed been rendered invisible and irrelevant in many mainstream black political and media spaces for decades. In spite of this, or perhaps because of this, black feminists, especially since the 1980s, have continuously sought to push back against anti-feminist arguments within communities of color. This 'double erasure' – an absence in the mainstream as well as in communities of color – of black feminist praxis makes its theoretical interventions even more relevant for thinking through the various approaches to studying populations that are rendered invisible within the larger American context.

Black feminist scholars' awareness of their unique marginalization within feminism, the broader US academy, as well as globally, makes their research a critical starting point for discovering methods in which to better understand larger marginalized communities. In keeping with this, the centrality of first-person narrative is a core component of the black feminist methodological theory developed here. Patricia Hill Collins (2000) argues that the individual narrative is black feminist practice. By providing women of color spaces to tell their stories, we are in fact engaging in a political act. Research methods like in-depth interviews and surveys, the latter of which allow for individual respondents to write in their own answers, provide space for individuals to tell their own stories, and thus potentially provide more accurate data. First-person narratives are particularly relevant for understudied, marginalized populations for whom data is difficult to gather (for example, low-income, highly transient communities) (Liebow 1993).

While high-residential mobility makes data collection of marginalized populations difficult, high-residential mobility alone is not the challenge. The reality is that low-income individuals, as well as people of color – who are often times the same community due to historical and systemic inequalities – fail to respond to researchers in large part because many research instruments, including the language used, are based on the cultural norms of privileged groups (Leighley & Vedlitz 1999). In other words, people outside of privileged communities are often unable to accurately respond to the questions posed to them simply due to a lack of intra-culture comprehension. As a number of scholars have noted (Leighley & Vedlitz 1999; Segura & Rodrigues 2006), the language within many academic studies – both qualitative and quantitative – is frequently inaccessible to marginalized populations (Leighley & Vedlitz 1999). The cultural capital used to construct these studies is usually most appropriate for middle-income-to-wealthy white Americans who are highly institutionally educated. As a result, frequently studied populations like low-to-middle-income black and Latino populations, and particularly youths within these communities, are unable to fully engage with the question sets posed to them in surveys and/or interview questions (Cohen 2010). The goal of the research documented and shared here, which utilizes feminist methodologies, is to remedy such limitations.

Access

In April 2012, I conducted a two-month pilot study in the Altgeld Gardens and Murray Homes Housing Development in Chicago's south side to assess if my project would be feasible. In order to gain access to the space, I began by contacting researchers and news reporters that had written previously about the Altgeld Gardens development. Initially it was recommended that I contact two women: Bernadette Williams, the Local Advisory Council President of Altgeld Gardens, and Cheryl Johnson, the President of the local community organization, People for Community Recovery (PCR). The PCR website provided Cheryl Johnson's email address, so I spent the entire month of April attempting to reach her. Meanwhile, I was able to get the office phone number for Bernadette Williams from the Chicago Central Advisory Council, and made contact with her relatively quickly.

When I first spoke with Bernadette Williams, she was exceptionally reluctant about communicating with me. She'd had many researchers interview her and study the Altgeld Gardens community in the past, and in her account, 'got nothing from it.' So her first question was, 'what makes you any different? Why should I talk to you?' I told her that my intention was to study the lives of black women in public housing in order to make a substantive difference in their lives. Unenthusiastically, she scheduled a meeting a couple of days later. When I arrived at her office, the genuine surprise on her face was palpable. Since I'd introduced myself as a doctoral candidate from the University of Chicago, she'd automatically assumed that I was white and much older.[3] Almost immediately she said that she 'didn't expect [me] to look like' me.

In fact, she was convinced that I looked just like one of her younger cousins and corroborated this with the other women in the office. The conversation that followed was familial in tone. She told me repeatedly that she was proud of me for getting a PhD from the University of Chicago (this was a theme repeated throughout my time at Altgeld). Open about her challenges and victories, Bernadette was also generous in sharing the dates and times of Altgeld Local Advisory Council (LAC) meetings, Chicago Housing Authority (CHA) Board meetings, and Tenant Services meetings. This initial meeting was critical because it served as my opening to a community with deep-rooted suspicions of 'researchers.' Because of her previous negative interactions with academics, Bernadette was clear that she expected me to keep in regular contact with her, as well as to show her my final dissertation. I agreed to these terms readily, because in the end it was her initial enthusiasm about my project, and her willingness to introduce me at meetings, as well as to individual residents, that allowed my project to take root.

Toward the end of April 2012, I was able to schedule an initial meeting with local activist Cheryl Johnson after continuing to email her throughout the spring.[4] As with Bernadette, my meeting with Cheryl was familial in tone. Cheryl was less surprised around my racial identity because she'd worked with quite a few black graduate students from around the city before. Like many other women I met in the development, she felt invested in my success, and did everything she could to help my study. She opened up about the challenges she faced as an activist in the Altgeld Gardens development. My meeting with Cheryl turned out to be another critical moment in the development of my project as she shared information about my project to a number of women who live in Altgeld and also informed me of meetings and protests hosted by PCR.

From these two initial meetings, I was able to reach out to a number of Altgeld residents to arrange interviews. As was the case with Bernadette, many interviewees were surprised to see me, a black woman, showing up at their door. Based on our screening conversations over the phone, almost all of them expected me to be a much older white woman. Many also expressed relief that I shared their racial identity and I heard many times that I looked just like their sister, cousin, or daughter. One other theme that appeared in many of my interviews was a sense of pride when respondents discovered I was working on my PhD, and woman after woman congratulated me for being in school and encouraged me to finish the degree and 'do something with my life.' Perhaps this was an expression of Michael Dawson's (1994) concept of linked fate. Many women seemed to closely identify with my perceived achievement and had an urgent desire to express a personal sense of pride.

The intersection of my race, age, and gender provided a certain level of access, trust, and comfort throughout my interviews. Looking like my respondents certainly opened up a space of trust that allowed them to express fears and anxieties, particularly concerning their treatment by the Chicago Housing Authority, as well as the violence that pervaded the housing development. While a shared racial and gendered identity provided a certain level of trust in many instances, it also created an assumption of a shared lived experience on the part of my respondents. There might have been moments within my interviews where I should have pushed or asked more questions, particularly in regards to aspects of my identity that I did not share with my respondents, knowing that they would likely complicate my relationship with them. But silencing such details and allowing myself to engage with respondents around assumptions of shared experience, also meant that there was usually a level of comfort in the room. Ultimately, despite these potential silences, I believe that the data I collected is rigorous, rich, deep, and theoretically meaningful. I was deliberate in the construction of the study and interview protocols, which ultimately facilitated a set of in-depth interviews with much to offer.

Method

As part of this year-long project, I interviewed 31 black women over the age of 18. The women had been living or lived in the development between two and 70 years. I was able to study a number of women with a diverse range of experiences. Within the study, I used traditional political science measures for efficacy and cynicism (which I will detail more below), and I followed up with simple questions, asking the respondents to interpret what they thought the previous questions meant. This approach allowed me to develop a black feminist methodological theory based on empirical evidence that outlines the challenges within current political science methods, and an alternate possibility that could potentially add more accurate and nuanced results.

Using a case study approach, I was able to interrogate not only the shifting political identities of black female tenants of the CHA, but I was also able to examine the way in which their lived experiences and environments contextualize, and in some ways shape, their understandings of themselves as members of the polity.

The in-depth interviews I collected with 31 female black residents of Altgeld Gardens allowed me to slowly get to know the women and the nuances of their lives within the housing project and surrounding neighborhoods. I asked questions about how these women understood politics as well as questions that examined whether or not they consider themselves to be citizens. Most significantly, the in-depth interviews examined how the women felt about the public housing space and the (non)presence of government actors in their lives.

While each in-depth interview was based loosely on the same interview guide, the questions were open-ended in nature so as to allow each individual woman's narrative to develop. It was not my goal to shape how the respondents told their stories. Instead, my aim was to get as close to an authentic self-description of their political selves as possible. All of the interviews were audio recorded and transcribed. I used what some researchers call a snowball or convenience sampling method. I interviewed the women who volunteered for the study who met the specifications of my sample and from there I continued to ask my respondents to recommend other women for the study. This sampling method enabled a better understanding of the community, political, and social networks of the women respondents.

Most interviews were held in the respondent's home, a location selected in order to minimize the inconvenience posed to them as well as facilitate their comfort and to build trust. Seeing their homes also allowed me the opportunity to further study their relationships to their place of residence, as well as to get a first-hand view of the aesthetics of their lived experience. A few interviewees were not comfortable inviting me into their homes, and alternative locations were thus selected. I deliberately chose not to interview respondents at the University of Chicago, or Chicago Housing Authority offices, where potential negative bureaucratic associations might exist.

Respondents were paid $20 in cash for their participation in the interviews. It was a priority to me that everyone was paid adequately for their time; as such, I was careful to always acknowledge my appreciation of their willingness to sacrifice time in their day for the benefit of the study. I chose to pay each respondent in cash because of the remoteness of the Altgeld Gardens from any major retail establishments. The closest shopping centers are at least 30 minutes away by bus, and many of the women do not shop online. In general I tried to schedule a maximum of four interviews per day, so that I never had more than $100 cash on my person when I visited the development. This was done to protect myself, as well as my respondents. Interviews on average were between

40 minutes to one hour long. However, the longest interview lasted three hours, and the shortest was 20 minutes. In general, the shorter interviews tended to be with women who were elderly, or battling various addictions or illnesses. As such, I kept the shorter interviews in my data set because they offered perspectives that were important to my study.

A secondary method used was participant observation, which I also conducted within the Altgeld Gardens and Murray Homes (this is the full name of the development). Here, I paid especially close attention to the conditions of Altgeld Gardens and the people who live there. I attended Altgeld Murray Local Advisory Council Meetings, CHA Central Advisory Council Meetings, and CHA Board of Commissioners Meetings as well as local community organization gatherings, events, and other spontaneous and/or planned political gatherings on the development. Spending time within the housing development itself, as well as observing CHA meetings and gatherings, allowed me to have greater understanding of the discourses around public housing spaces and the residents they impact, as well as the ways in which the space shifts and changes over time to fit the needs and desires of those in power.

Using my own experiences of conducting fieldwork, I use the following section to expand on the use and need for a black feminist methodology.

Why is black feminist methodological practice necessary?

When I first approached the residents in 2011, I became cognizant of the ways in which academic language consistently impeded my ability to communicate clearly with the individuals that I encountered. Early on, when CHA residents asked me what my study was about (as they assessed whether or not they wanted to participate), I would say something like 'my study is an attempt to understand the way in which black women's political engagement and participation fits within current models of political efficacy and cynicism.' Without exception, the response I received was a blank stare of confusion. Following that confusion, they would then communicate in one way or another that they had no idea what I was talking about. Subsequently, I attempted to find some way to explain my proposed dissertation in a more accessible manner. After many such encounters, I went back to the drawing board to create a recruitment script that was more accessible. Early on in the study, I learned that if I wanted to successfully recruit subjects I needed to avoid words like 'politics,' 'government,' 'efficacy,' and 'cynicism,' not because they triggered a biased response but simply because they consistently caused so much confusion. As I discovered later on in the study, the definitions the residents have for these words, as well as other terminology frequently used by social scientists, are varied. Over a year of participant observation, I never heard the same definition for the word 'politics' twice.

It is these early experiences that are the jumping-off point for the beginnings of the black feminist methodological theory that I develop here. Using Hill Collins's intervention around the single-person narrative and its importance for the political work of feminism, I argue that using the language of respondents in our studies is of foremost importance when studying groups on the sociopolitical margins of our society.

The reality is that the easiest language for respondents to access is the language used in their own communities. While it is impossible for researchers to replicate *every* cultural language pattern of every group that they hope to study, it is possible to simplify the language used in our studies so that we speak *less* and listen *more*. By providing respondents with more opportunities to provide detailed answers within interviews, as well as surveys, we are better able to understand what respondents actually *mean*.

The standard practice of large sample surveys is to use multiple-choice answers that are constructed by the research team designing the survey. Typically, this method is chosen because these data points are easiest to enter into software and subsequently measure the 'condition' that is being analyzed. While this strategy might be more manageable, its actual results are limited and perhaps prevent researchers from getting the fullest and nuanced data available to them.

Instead of beginning with what is easiest, I argue that we should begin with what makes most sense for what we hope to learn. Using a black feminist methodological practice, I prioritize the first-person narrative as a site of political power, as well as methodological honesty. As such, for low-income populations as well as populations of color, surveys that allow for some fill-in-the-blank answers, temperature readings, or multiple-choice questions with an additional fill-in-the-blank option would be most appropriate. Largely because of the reasons that were laid out above: the cultural, educational, and financial privilege held by many researchers often impedes them from being familiar with the language choices of those who live in communities out of their reach. As such, allowing those populations to answer questions around what they consider to be 'political' in their own words makes the most sense when we, as scholars, are attempting to assess their politics. This insight to definitions is important because study after study has shown that marginalized populations are not 'politically active' in a conventional sense (Brady et al. 1995). However, these findings are inconsistent with many anthropological studies that have found otherwise, particularly when the definition of politics is opened up (Pattillo 2007; Scott 1990). The gap between these divergent findings can be attributed to the methodological choices made by researches. For the most part studies that use ethnographic as well as other qualitative method choices that depend on observing populations in their own spaces, tend to find that marginalized populations have a particular type of political engagement that is unique to them (Scott 1990), or at least falls outside rigid definitions of 'political,' while studies that depend on numbers tend to find that marginalized populations are not politically engaged at all (Rosenstone & Hansen 1993). Studies that use mixed-methods, like the Black Youth Project (Cohen 2010), take important steps toward a black feminist methodological practice. By providing individuals or populations the opportunities to speak in their own words as well as respond to a set of survey questions, researchers can get a better sense of whether or not their instruments are adequate measures of the politics of their populations of interest.

What does a black feminist methodological practice look like?

A black feminist methodological practice has four components. First and foremost is the aforementioned centering of the first-person narrative when designing methodological instruments. Second, a black feminist methodological practice would compensate all respondents. Too often, particularly when researchers are conducting qualitative research, they fail to pay respondents, the rationale being that people appreciate the opportunity to talk to someone about their lives. However, this logic is backwards. Whether or not a particular respondent appreciates the opportunity to discuss him or herself is irrelevant. As researchers, we are taking up valuable time that our subject could be using in a number of other ways. By contributing to a study that will ultimately further our research, as well as our careers, we have a responsibility to compensate that person fairly. Black feminism pivots on the belief that every person is inherently valuable and worthy of respect and dignity. In a country where capitalism is paramount, time is a highly valued resource, especially if the community being studied is a low-income community. As such, the way in which to adequately compensate an individual is through some form of monetary payment.

From its beginnings, black feminism has argued that the communities of black women's lives are central to understanding their daily experience (Hill Collins 2000). Such a call for situated knowledge was in contrast to what some mainstream feminists in the 1970s were asking for in their call for separation from patriarchy (Guy-Sheftall 1995). In the late 1970s, into the 1980s, black feminists, as well as voices from the global feminist movement (Sen & Grown 1987), pushed back against this, arguing that in order to understand the politics of marginalized populations, researchers cannot attempt to separate the marginalized population and its individuals from the children, men, and women that they have lived and grown up with their entire lives (hooks 1981). Black feminists firmly believed that 'when and where [they] enter, in the quiet, undisputed dignity of [their] womanhood, without violence and without suing or special patronage, then and there the whole ... race enters with [them]' (Hutchinson & Anacostia Neighborhood Museum 1981). In other words, a black woman's freedom allows for the freedom of the whole race. Therefore, an unwillingness to leave anyone behind is a central keystone of black feminist theory more broadly. As such, the incorporation of respondents' neighborhoods or other lived spaces into the research instrument is the third and particularly critical component of black feminist methodological practice. Using surveys, a researcher might ask respondents about where they live, how they feel about their neighborhoods, and what their experiences within those geographical spaces have been. This method might also include asking about their interpersonal relationships, whether or not they have any friends or family, and what their interactions with those people might look like. While up front these types of questions may not look like they have anything to do with 'politics,' my research makes clear that the way in which an individual lives within their community and the way they relate to the people around them can potentially have a large impact on their expression of citizenship. As political scientists, we cannot simply be concerned with whether or not an individual feels alienated from the state, largely conceived. We also must be concerned with whether or not an individual feels connected to multiple sites of local community. As social network theorists (Sinclar 2012) make clear time and time again, neighborhood, employment, and family can all play a huge role in shaping an individual's politics.

Finally, a fourth core theoretical insight of black feminist theory is intersectionality (Hill Collins 2000). Intersectionality is the idea that each individual has multiple sites of identity, each of which can potentially be privileged or oppressive depending on the particular environment you occupy (Crenshaw 1995). For example, within a wealthy university environment, a young, black, poor, heterosexual janitor may be oppressed on every axis of his identity compared to a white, wealthy, educated female student. But within a mostly black low-income neighborhood, his masculinity, youth, sexuality, and employment status may privilege him over his neighbors. Such a difference in power and based on location, and the impact of this on one's sense of self and the ability to act in given situations, once again, reaffirms why thinking about geographical space and interpersonal relationships in politics, and the act of the political, is critical. Efficacy and cynicism scholars[5] have made clear that political engagement requires a certain level of individual confidence (Verba et al. 1995). In order to participate in the public sphere, a person has to feel that s/he is capable of doing so and has the power and authority to do so. Essentially, an individual's level of confidence can be impacted by the way in which oppression has, or has not, manifested in their lives. For example, the fictitious janitor above may not feel comfortable discussing voting rights with the white female student, but he might organize ways to get his community to voting locations during elections or organize his community to get street lights or a playground. As a result, it is important for scholars to take into account the multiple axes of oppression and privilege when thinking about what the politics of communities on the margins look like. Intersectionality also matters when we begin to think about the various manifestations of political creativity, that is, the extra-systemic political engagement that happens outside of the traditional political sphere. Without understanding the multiple sites of identity within an individual respondent, we can't begin to push and question where, when, and how they think about and engage with what they consider to be the political.

Case study

I met Lisa toward the end of my fieldwork at Altgeld Gardens on Chicago's south side. In her mid-forties, she has lived in Altgeld on and off for most of her life. In 2009, she moved back to assist her ailing mother. After being on the CHA housing waiting list for some time, she was finally offered the opportunity to come back to the development after being away for six years. Her relationship with Altgeld was a mixed one. On one hand, she loved living near her family since she has multiple family members who also live in the development. On the other hand, she described Altgeld as becoming increasingly violent over the

30 years that she'd grown up there. As a result, she has a strong desire to help her community in whatever ways that she can.

Q: When you think about where you most fit, what comes to mind?
A: What comes to mind is actually ... hmm, well, I've always known that I fitted within the community and on a board. More so I could say within my community I should be ... on a board as of, doesn't necessarily have to be considered, like LAC, but as of a board for the community to let the community know that they can come to me and I'm all for them. Anything, you know, my voice is for anything, so ...
Q: So you feel like you should be in some kind of leadership position.
A: Yes, I do.
Q: Are you involved in any groups, volunteer work, or organizations?
A: Yes, at this present time, yes, at my daughter's school. And also I'm with the little, well, we have now with Cheryl Johnson, PCR [People for Community Recovery], with the community, all the politics. Yes, at this present time, yeah.
Q: Why did you get involved in that stuff?
A: Like I said, to try to be part of the community, to do something for the community and people.

In our interview, she mentioned repeatedly that she hopes to be able to leave Altgeld again before her daughter gets much older. But despite her misgivings about the community, Lisa was extremely active in her daughter's school as well as the local environmental justice group run and staffed by women living in Altgeld (PCR). Lisa's high levels of traditional political engagement make her particularly appropriate as a starting point for thinking about the ways in which the language of politics can be diverse, even for those with the most political efficacy, in the strictest sense.

Q: And how did you find out about it [a local community group]?
A: Well, this is just how it happened: well, due to what is that, October, remember we were protesting for the Rosebud Farm? [the local grocery] And like I said, me and a few of the other members got together due to that [being the] only store that's around and ... the outrageous prices. And we were trying to get for the community [involved], you know, we have a lot of parents, mothers that has infants, that has the WIC [Women Infant Child] program and the Rosebud Farm does not accept WIC.

Q: Was the boycott effective?

A: Yes, actually as we speak now it's steady in motion. We been having meetings with them [the grocery owners] so yeah. And also that we did have a little work with them negotiating with us and letting us know that they are going to get the WIC.

Because of Lisa's frequent political activity, I, perhaps naively, assumed that her definition of politics would land toward the traditional end of the spectrum. I expected her to talk about national forms of government like the executive branch, or local government like the mayor's office, alderman, etc. Instead, Lisa very much related her understanding of politics to her everyday experience.

Q: When I say the word politics what do you think of?

A: Hmm ... life. I say life because of politics ... it's all based on that. Your rights, your way of living, you know, what you're obligated for or capable of. You know, what you can put your hand on that's yours. That support and guidance, all of that. It's all in politics. I won't say righteous because there's a lot of crooks in politics. Yeah.

When Lisa was asked to think about her definition of politics, she thought about what she felt politics influenced as well as the personal qualities she imagined politicians should embody. When she answers, 'I say life because of politics ... it's all based on that. Your rights, your way of living,' she's stating that politics can touch every aspect of life. For women living in public housing, this truth is particularly important and real. They are vulnerable to the whims of the state in the way that the wealthy are not. Their homes can be searched at anytime; if they are arrested by the police, they can lose their housing; and they (along with their children) are constantly monitored and asked to check in with state bureaucrats on a regular basis. Thus, for women living in poverty, politics really is about life. Every new piece of legislation passed by local, state, and federal government around social welfare can potentially turn their lives upside down in a way that wealthier Americans couldn't even imagine.

Lisa's interview makes clear how important it is to think about the first and third components of a black feminist methodological practice. First, a researcher should consider how central lived experience is to understanding the respondent's politics and/or other aspects of their social reality. And second, a researcher needs to understand how critical it is to think about the ways in which an individual's neighborhood can shape their perception of the world (and its politics) in unique and unpredictable ways.

When I interviewed Sheila in 2012, she was 30 years old and she'd lived in Altgeld Gardens for four years. She signed up for income-based housing as a younger woman, and years later when she was finally offered an apartment, she took the opportunity and moved in. The rental price in addition to the cost of utilities at her former market-rate apartment were too much for her to handle in addition to taking care of her children. Public housing provided Sheila with the opportunity to care for her children in a way that she wasn't able to on her own. When I spoke to Sheila, she was enthusiastic about the aesthetics of the apartment. She loved that her space had recently been renovated, and she especially appreciated the amount of room that was provided for her and her family. The exterior of her home, however, was another story. As did many of the newer residents, Sheila spoke frequently throughout her interview about how Altgeld has deteriorated over the last 30 years and how the violence at the development constantly worried her. She was concerned about the violence to the point that she sent her daughter to school off the development and didn't allow the daughter to socialize in any way with other children in Altgeld Gardens. An individual's connection to their lived environment, or, more simply, the extent to which someone believes they are a part of their neighborhood community, has a large impact on the shape and form of their political engagement as was evidenced in the case of Sheila and her relationship to the politics of the community. While she was aware of the community work on the development, she refused to participate.

Q: Do you go to CHA meetings?

A: No.

Q: Why not?

A: To be honest with you, because this doesn't feel like a community to me. This feels like what it is. It's you know, they want to say that it's really a community but at the end of the day I don't feel the community vibe. I've lived in a community before and that was a community.

Q: So what does a community feel like?

A: A community feels like people that work together. People that will walk past and pick up a neighbor's garbage. A community feels like you know, did you see that person bust that person's window and did you see that person break into that person's car and stuff like that. That's a community to me; the people who look out for each other in that community. The people who have each other's back in that community. This is not a community.

Q: Ok. So you don't really participate in any ...

A: No, because my car was broke in out here in broad daylight and I know somebody saw it because it was nice outside, it was broad daylight. Yeah, my boyfriend spent the night and somebody stole his license plates off his car.

For Sheila, the perceived unwillingness of her neighbors to look out for her and, by extension, her property made her feel isolated and alienated from the people who lived around her. As a result, she refused to participate in any political activities, like the CHA Board Meeting or the Local Advisory Council Board Meeting (LAC).

It is important to note that Sheila did not feel that she was capable of participating in politics. This fact is not surprising given her level of isolation. She owns and works at a day care, so she is very rarely around other adults, beyond her family, who could possibly shape her political engagement in a meaningful way. When I asked Sheila how she defined politics, she, as did many other respondents, replied with people and places that came to mind as opposed to an actual definition.

Q: So you feel like you're capable of participating in politics?

A: Um, no, I wouldn't get up and just ... you know, no. (Laughs) No, I wouldn't do that but I think I'm pretty smart where I can hold my own if I needed to.

Q: How do you define politics? When I say the word politics what do you think of?

A: I think of Chicago. I think of the president. That's what I think of. I mean Chicago and this politics and it's just ah, it's really ridiculous. So that's what I think of.

Throughout the interview, Sheila mentioned how badly behaved she perceived politicians to be. She frequently mentioned their affairs, dishonesty, and inability to advocate for those who voted them into office. It wasn't surprising, then, that when I asked her for her definition of politics, she almost immediately thought of Chicago's political corruption.[6] As a result, while Sheila considers herself smart enough to vote and to understand day-to-day challenges that come and go, she is doubtful about her ability to navigate her perception of politics as deep and murky waters.

Sheila's case once again brings to the forefront the importance of the first and third components of black feminist methodological practice. The first leg of black feminist methodological practice emphasizes the individual narrative. For Sheila, the narrative and social behaviors she attached to politics had a major part in the way in which she understood the political more broadly. The third component of black feminist methodological practice, the geographical space that the respondent inhabits, came up time and time again throughout my interview with her. Sheila's sense of alienation from her neighborhood was so strong that it eroded any desire she might have to participate in her community. The isolation also became a driver behind her refusal to participate in community and political activities that she was very aware of throughout the development. Through their interviews, and their response to and definitions of politics, activism, and community, both Sheila and Lisa make clear that the four components of a black feminist methodological practice are central to a better understanding of the political and social behaviors of marginalized populations. Such an approach can provide important information about understanding marginalized communities throughout the country.

Conclusion

Feminist methods more broadly, and black feminist interventions in particular, have been largely ignored and/or erased from mainstream academic methodological discussions. However, this erasure has been to the detriment of social science and, in particular, political science. While disciplines like anthropology and sociology have been able to identify some of the unique political behaviors of low-income communities and communities of color (Scott 1990), political science has consistently been missing the complicated and extra-systemic politics of these populations. As minority communities continue to grow over the next 20 years within the United States, political science must understand the importance of how, why, and when they engage in politics and the public sphere, broadly conceived.

Notes

1. Political science is the author's discipline of study.
2. The formal study of women and gender within the academy allows scholars interested in these areas of study to do so without having to fight imbedded systems of power within traditional disciplinary boundaries that might otherwise not see the study of these topics as valuable, or even intellectual.

3. According to the University of Chicago registrar, in spring 2011 only 5.2 percent of the University of Chicago student body identified as black or African American in the Social Sciences Division, and only 4.68 percent in the total student body (University of Chicago 2014).
4. Cheryl is the daughter of Hazel Johnson, the founder of People for Community Recovery (PCR) and is a well-known Chicago environmental activist. After Hazel's death, Cheryl followed in her mother's footsteps, staying within public housing in large part to continue her mother's work. Cheryl now organizes activist actions within the development, provides training workshops, hosts toxic environmental tours, and facilitates activities for local youth.
5. Cynicism and efficacy scholars study the political behaviors of groups by assessing the individual belief in their ability to participate in politics and their relative trust in the government.
6. Chicago has a long history of political corruption. Most recently Illinois governor Rod Blagojevich was found guilty of 17 charges of corruption.

References

Brady, H.E., Verba, S. and Schlozman, K.L. (1995) 'Beyond SES: A Resource Model of Political Participation,' *The American Political Science Review*, 89(2), 271–94.

Cohen, C.J. (2010) *Democracy Remixed* (Oxford University Press).

Crenshaw K.W. (1995) 'Mapping the Margins: Intersectionality, Identity Politics, and Violence Against Women of Color,' in K.W. Crenshaw, N. Gotanda, G. Peller and K. Thomas (eds) *Critical Race Theory: The Key Writings that Formed the Movement* (New York: The New Press).

Dawson, M.C. (1994) *Behind the Mule: Race and Class in African-American Politics* (Princeton University Press).

Guy-Sheftall, B. (1995) *Words of Fire: An Anthology of African-American Feminist Thought* (New York: New Press).

Hill Collins, P. (2000) *Black Feminist Thought: Knowledge, Consciousness, and the Politics of Empowerment*, 10th anniversary edn (New York: Routledge).

hooks, b. (1981) *Ain't I a Woman: Black Women and Feminism* (Boston: South End Press).

Hutchinson, L.D. and Anacostia Neighborhood Museum (1981) *Anna J. Cooper, a Voice from the South* (Washington: Smithsonian Institution Press).

Leighley, J.E. and Vedlitz, A. (1999) 'Race, Ethnicity, and Political Participation: Competing Models and Contrasting Explanations,' *The Journal of Politics*, 61(4), 1092–114.

Liebow, E. (1993) *Tell Them Who I Am: The Lives of Homeless Women* (New York and Toronto: Free Press; Maxwell Macmillan Canada; Maxwell Macmillan International).

Pattillo, M.E. (2007) *Black on the Block: The Politics of Race and Class in the City* (University of Chicago Press).

Rosenstone, S.J. and Hansen, J.M. (1993) *Mobilization, Participation, and Democracy in America* (New York: Macmillan).

Scott, J.C. (1990) *Domination and the Arts of Resistance: Hidden Transcripts* (New Haven: Yale University Press).

Segura, G.M. and Rodrigues, H.A. (2006) 'Comparative Ethnic Politics in the United States: Beyond Black and White,' *Annual Review of Political Science* (9), 375–95.

Sen, G. and Grown, C. (1987) *Development, Crises, and Alternative Visions: Third World Women's Perspectives* (New York: Monthly Review Press).

Sinclair, Betsy (2012) *The Social Citizen: Peer Networks and Political Behavior* (University of Chicago Press).

University of Chicago (2014) 'University Registrar,' *University of Chicago*, registrar.uchicago.edu (accessed 7 April 2014).

Verba, S., Schlozman, K.L. and Brady, H.E. (1995) *Voice and Equality: Civic Voluntarism in American Politics* (Cambridge, MA: Harvard University Press).

Part II
Feminism in Popular Culture

5
Illegible Rage: Performing Femininity in *Manhattan Call Girl*

Katherine Hindle

Introduction

In her book chapter 'Illegible Rage: Post-feminist Disorders' Angela McRobbie (2009) suggests that young women in Western societies are routinely addressed by government and media bodies on the understanding that gender equality has been achieved and that there is no longer any reason for any form of organized feminist movement. Yet, as she argues, this equality appears to have been mysteriously achieved without real change to patriarchal structures in society. Equally mysteriously, women appear to suffer from a new range of normalized pathologies that are understood as simply part of being 'female.' Body issues, self-esteem problems and anxiety about achieving certain markers of femininity such as marriage and motherhood are all understood to some extent to be a part of 'normal' contemporary young womanhood. There are a range of therapies, self-help guides, and forums – such as advice pages in women's magazines that respond to these pathologies in place of feminist critique – which set new norms and values for young womanhood and reinforce young women's beliefs that there are no radical alternatives. As McRobbie states: 'the attributing of normative discontent to young women has become a key mechanism for the production of sexual difference, it provides a vocabulary for understanding the female body-ego as prone to anxiety, as lacking in certain respects, as insufficient to self-esteem' (2009, p. 98). As such, McRobbie considers these forms of disorder to be symptomatic of what she terms, following Judith Butler, 'illegible rage' and demonstrative of the ways in which forming narrowly defined feminine identities is damaging to the young women who perform them.

In this chapter I will attempt to identify the ways in which this illegible rage is present in contemporary popular fiction for women.

I will be focusing particularly on a series of novels written by Tracy Quan. *Diary of a Manhattan Call Girl* was first published in 2001; *Diary of a Married Call Girl* came out in 2005; and *Diary of a Jetsetting Call Girl* in 2008. Kaye Mitchell notes that novels such as these reflect a recent publishing phenomenon, the contemporary erotic memoir. These memoirs, 'featuring pastel colors and suggestive illustrations of the sexually forthright heroines immediately connects them to chick lit' and aims to capitalize on that market (2012, p. 17). The *Manhattan Call Girl* novels can be seen as a hybrid of chick lit and the erotic memoir; the author herself states that the novels are fiction but heavily draw on her real-life experience (Buchwald n.d.). Like a number of titles in the same genre, particularly the best-selling *The Intimate Adventures of a London Call Girl* by Belle De Jour (2005), the *Manhattan Call Girl* novels are marketed on the basis that the author is a former real-life call girl.

This hybrid publishing trend can be understood in the context of what has been referred to by Attwood as the 'sexualisation of culture,' a trend in which sex workers 'are entering the world of mainstream celebrity, writing best-selling books, [and] acting as sex advisors in lifestyle magazines' (2009, pp. xiii–xiv). As Negra points out, 'the female sex worker is becoming one of popular culture's most regular archetypes of paid labor' (2009, p. 100). As Tasker continues, this is a logical progression in the representation of professional women, who are always involved in some sort of sexualized performance (1998, p. 3). The *Manhattan Call Girl* series can therefore be seen as a step further on from single professional women narratives such as *Sex and the City*, in that it develops the theme of female sexuality as a form of empowerment, literally connecting female sexual pleasure with work via a narrative of access to luxury goods, glamorous nightspots and wealthy men, achieved through working in the sex industry. Although third-wave feminists have emphasized the political potential of women's erotic writing in allowing women to define their own sexual subjectivity and tell the truth about their desire, I suggest that, in this instance, this potential is limited as a result of the constraints of the narrative genre of chick lit and the resulting centrality of narrowly defined forms of femininity to female empowerment. Joel Gwynne points out about erotic writing of this type: 'As popular texts produced for mainstream consumption, it is hardly surprising that they espouse conventional regimes framed in discourses of ... empowerment' (2013, p. 27). I argue that although these texts have a veneer of authenticity, there is a tension between this and the requirements of the fictional genre it draws on.

Postfeminism and illegible rage

There is no single agreed definition of postfeminism. However, there seems to be a general consensus amongst scholars that it is a discourse that embraces certain gains thanks to the second wave of feminist activism, such as the right of women to equal pay in the workplace and to conduct sexual relationships outside of marriage. Simultaneously, this discourse distances itself from the rhetoric of second-wave feminism, as the postfeminist woman considers it her right to choose traditional feminine roles and forms of self-presentation. Feminism is not acknowledged as a loss but as something that has done its job and is no longer required. As part of this distancing from feminism, 'femininity' itself is no longer something seen as a social construct, restricting opportunity and inextricably linked to gender-based inequality. As Ferriss and Young (2006) put it: 'Femininity, considered, since the "first wave" led by Mary Wollstonecraft and others, a crippling cultural construction that defined women as fragile and emotional, is now embraced as a choice' (p. 87). Women therefore invest considerable time and money in clothing and grooming routines on the understanding that 'the consumption of products and services, frequently associated with femininity/ sexuality' is part of building an empowered female identity (Genz & Brabon 2009, p. 79).

McRobbie also suggests, however, that young women struggle with the demands of mainstream contemporary femininity, but are encouraged by government organizations and the popular media to see the desire to transform – physically and socially – as empowering. Women understand the gains made by second-wave feminism to be central to their negotiation of power, yet feel overwhelmed by the complex demands that are made of them: to succeed at work while fulfilling the feminine roles of mother, wife, and stylish independent woman, all in accordance with the standards set by consumer culture. Women fear failure in each of these spheres of their lives and this creates body, self-esteem, and anxiety issues.

But why do women fear failure when performing these roles, rather than question their validity? McRobbie draws on Judith Butler's work on melancholia in order to examine the ways in which people come to internalize wider societal norms as their own. McRobbie suggests that young women are aware of feminism but are also aware that in order to count as 'real young women' in society they must conform to gender norms (2009, p. 95). As Butler (1990) points out, subjects internalize wider societal norms as their own, judging their own worth in accordance with the values of the society in which they live. Butler suggests that this is the way in which subjects are formed: through their desire to gain approval, acceptance, and belonging within the wider society in which they live. Those ideals and desires that do not accord with those wider values have to be abandoned if the subject does not wish to risk being seen as abject within their family or society. However, the ideal or desire is retained unconsciously and the subject forms a melancholic relationship with it, in the psychoanalytic sense of melancholia as a loss that cannot be mourned or let go (Butler 1990). McRobbie suggests that feminism is now such an ideal and, although consciously rejected, is preserved in the psyche of young women; and 'this melancholia lurks beneath the surface, threatening to transmogrify into rage' (2009, p. 94). Young women feel constrained and stuck as they have no way to directly communicate this anger, which results from the conditions of modern womanhood and which cause them distress. This anger remains illegible and is directed against the self, causing new forms of female pathology that are debilitating but, importantly, do not threaten the gender hierarchy.

McRobbie argues that 'illegible rage' is evident in a number of texts of popular culture, citing particularly the fashion photograph as a genre aimed at women that expresses, through the performance of femininity, these competing discourses of empowerment and limitation (2009, p. 109). These texts act as a compensatory containment for the illegible rage of the reader who sees her constraint mirrored back at her through the photographs. Both the expression of illegible rage and the recognition of it are unconscious; the photo appears to be a celebration of femininity, not a critique, yet it expresses the reader's unspeakable sense of constraint and ambivalence.

Chick lit and anxiety

Chick lit, like the fashion photograph, is a genre specifically marketed at young women. New areas of anxiety such as the difficulties of combining a career and having children and concerns about leaving marriage too late are central themes of 'chick culture'; for instance, in *Bridget Jones's Diary* (Fielding 1996) the protagonist suggests that: 'As women glide from their twenties to their thirties ... even the most outrageous minxes lose their nerve ... wrestling with fears of dying alone and being found three weeks later half eaten by Alsatians' (p. 20). These are the areas of moral panic that were central to Susan Faludi's seminal text *Backlash* (1992) and Imelda Whelehan (2005) wonders if these moral panics 'dug deeper than some suspected: certainly there is an almost palpable sense of anxiety emanating from many volumes of chick lit' (p. 162). These moral panics appear to spring directly from the anxiety about young women's new position in the workplace and the ways in which this has impacted on the private spheres of home and family. Further, Whelehan notes the way in which these anxieties lead to expressions of ambivalence toward feminism in chick lit, as she points out: 'Second wave feminism could not solve some of the most intimate problems for women – how to conduct heterosexual relationships, how to negotiate self-identity, and how to deal with "power"' (p. 218). Anxiety is therefore a central theme within chick lit and popular media for women, key to the way women are addressed as consumers and also a way in which women understand themselves and each other. Ferriss and Young (2006) note that chick lit celebrates elements of traditional femininity alongside the forms of independence that have resulted from the sexual revolution and women's entry into the professional workplace, and 'in short, they are caught between competing demands to be strong and independent while retaining their femininity' (p. 9).

This seems very close to McRobbie's analysis of the fashion photograph, which she argues 'displays an abundance of tensions which cannot be reconciled' (p. 108). Her argument is that 'they speak of a kind of normative pathology on the basis of the impossibility of femininity in its struggle for autonomy' (2009, p. 108). Can we see this type of 'psychic turbulence' (p. 108) in chick lit? I consider that chick lit, like the fashion photograph, must respond specifically to the needs of a female audience, must 'thus be mediated through the codes of femininity and it must address the nebulous or illegible desires of women' (p. 105). As such, I intend to consider the *Manhattan Call Girl* series of novels, looking particularly at the role of the central character Nancy, to ask what they tell us about the relationship between the requirements of contemporary femininity and the types of female complaint McRobbie identifies.

The loss of feminism

This series follows Nancy Chan, who works secretly as a call girl while engaged and then married to a wealthy investment banker. As a result, Nancy performs two distinct forms of femininity. As a call girl she performs a sexualized form of femininity for her clients, taking on different personas in accordance with their wishes; then with her husband she takes on a traditional 'wifely' persona, in which she performs a more nurturing form of femininity, cooking and shopping. The tension between these performances of femininity and Nancy's sense of 'authentic' self is central to the narrative and leads to all sorts of confusions and near collisions of her separate worlds. This series was extremely successful and has been optioned by Darren Star, the producer of the *Sex and the City* (1998–2004) television series.

The relationship between the series' protagonist Nancy and feminism is a complex one. Nancy appears to reject feminism, and yet feminism as a theme resurfaces frequently throughout the novels and in Tracy Quan's commentary on them. For instance, in a piece written for US website *The Edge*, Quan makes clear that her view accords with that of the postfeminist woman identified in the last section:

> Women of a previous generation said that their own mothers had missed out on ... feminism. Like many women in my cohort, I discovered that my mother was born too early for post-feminism. Of course, post-feminism makes sense only when basic legal and civil rights exist for both sexes ... It makes sense, for the restless privileged daughters of Western feminism, to become moderate post-feminists. (Quan 2012)

Nancy's character appears to take on the view Quan expresses here, and this relationship with feminism is explored in two ways. The first is through Nancy's relationship with her feminist mother; and the second is through the sex worker movement that Nancy becomes involved in through her friend Allison. Nancy's mother appears sporadically throughout the novels, represented as 'the ultimate granola mom [who] can't be bothered with makeup, doesn't tinker with her salt-and-pepper hair' (Quan 2001, p. 141). The mother's lack of interest in her appearance is in contrast to Nancy's heavy investment in hers. Similarly, the feminist women who are part of the sex worker movement are, with few exceptions, unattractive, hairy, and unfashionable. For instance, Roxana, the head of the NYCOT (New York Council of Trollops) sex workers' rights group greets Nancy 'dressed in an oversize tie dyed t-shirt' which rode up to reveal her 'unkempt pubic hair' (p. 58). This painting of the feminist as abject is a common way of representing feminists in chick lit (see for example Gerhard 2005) and demonstrates that the performance of femininity represents a major divide between feminism and postfeminism within the novels. This divide is further reflected in the way in which feminists are represented as humorless and fanatic throughout the novels.

However, as Imelda Whelehan asks:

> If feminism is in demise or young women have moved beyond the need for such a gender-specific politics, then why does it emerge so frequently with these writers, so often embracing the confessional form, feeling the need to defend themselves against some invisible critic? (2005, p. 218)

Why is it, if feminism is so redundant, that this series of novels seemingly returns to it so frequently? What Whelehan observes is that chick lit often seems to be in a dialogue with feminism (see Fielding 1996; Pearson 2002). Despite Nancy's desire to have nothing to do with feminism it keeps reappearing, both when talking about her mother and through the activities of feminist activists, threatening to expose her double life and lose her clients. Such texts, Whelehan suggests, are haunted by the ghost of feminism and seem to evoke its spirit for no other reason than to denounce it again.

Is it helpful to think about this strained relationship between feminism and contemporary womanhood in chick lit as melancholic? Young women in chick lit express hate toward the object – feminism – that was once valued and now lost, maintaining, as does the melancholic, that to have lost such an object is not a loss at all. For Nancy the loss is double, for she not only rejects her mother's feminist values as an adolescent, preferring to get her guidance on young womanhood from fashion and teen magazines, but also literally rejects her mother by running away from home at 14. Nancy becomes sensitive during her adolescence to the ways in which normative femininity is celebrated in mainstream media and, seduced by the images she sees in fashion magazines and *Playboy*, Nancy repudiates feminism in response to these values. Once she has run away, she builds identities that are the antithesis of her mother's values and for which she repeatedly states her preference. However, I argue that in this series of novels Nancy, in indirect and opaque ways, expresses her discontent with the demands and limits of her new identities in ways that are recognizably symptomatic of illegible rage.

Nancy undertakes a wide range of expensive and time-consuming grooming practices and considers her decision to take on this work as a choice. She expresses pleasure in many aspects of the creation and performance of her two feminine roles, particularly shopping for designer clothes and the admiration that her carefully groomed and disciplined body receives from her clients and her husband. Yet McRobbie suggests that there is a connection between the types of ideal and sexualized images of femininity that Nancy enjoys and certain forms of female pathology. She states: 'Female body anxieties are intricately tied up with the need for social approval and more generally with the high value which society places on spectacularly coded styles of feminine beauty and sexuality at the expense of other capacities' (2009, p. 118). Gill (2007) also suggests that contemporary femininity is constructed as a bodily property and that femininity is now 'defined in advertising and elsewhere in the media as the possession of a young, able-bodied, heterosexual "sexy" body' (p. 91). It is not surprising that Nancy herself seems to feel more attractive just anticipating the approval she will receive when preparing and dressing her body to see a client; she says she feels 'like a superhero, sprouting magical powers' (Quan 2005, p. 7). We can see, with Nancy's superhero analogy, how clothes, makeup, accessories, and gym passes can be sold to women not just as a way of improving their appearance, but as sources of empowerment. Robert Goldman (1992) considers this form of address to be effective because women experience fear as a result of this emphasis on appearance:

> There is a mundane psychic terror associated with not receiving 'looks' of admiration – i.e. of not having the other validate one's appearance. A similar sense of terror involves the fear of 'losing one's looks' – the quite reasonable fear that ageing will deplete one's value and social power. A related source of anxiety involves fears about losing control over body weight and appearance. (p. 90)

Nancy experiences these anxieties at various points in the novels, but such feelings are normalized. What Goldman's account reveals is a psychological dimension to femininity in contemporary culture that is key to the ways women are addressed as consumers and subjects. I consider this type of anxiety about one's looks symptomatic of women's illegible rage and argue that it has become normalized in popular culture. As such it is one of the factors which lead to anxiety being understood as a normal female psychological state. Equally, Nancy experiences an extreme anxiety in these novels that is treated within the narrative as a normal part of womanhood. Anxiety about bodily appearance and male approval are literally linked to worth as Nancy's bodily appearance directly relates to her value on the erotic marketplace. Therefore when Nancy paints the call girl world as one where she and her friends talk constantly about diets and grooming regimes, this is both 'ordinary' women's talk and attending to business. When Nancy puts on six pounds in weight she states: 'I can get away with some fluctuation without alienating my regulars, but I might be approaching the limit' (Quan 2005, p. 7). This sense of bodily appearance that must be maintained for the approval of a man is replicated with her husband, who, one evening, compares her cooking to his mother's. That evening when he 'places an affectionate hand' (p. 54) under Nancy's camisole, rather than initiating sex, she wonders if 'the six pounds is taking its toll after all' (p. 54). Nancy throws all the biscuits and bread out of the kitchen in a fit of near hysteria. She is afraid that she has lost control of her performances of femininity and complains to her therapist:

> Everyone thinks I'm some kind of overweight, paranoid housewife ... could I have become, in less than a year of marriage, the total embodiment of everything that causes men to see hookers in the first place? That's so not fair. (pp. 58–9)

Nancy's response is to self-berate rather than critique the social norms. This tendency to complain about the impossibility of feminine ideals and then endorse those ideals by trying to achieve them is typical of the melancholic and an expression of Nancy's illegible rage. Nancy is in a double bind: in trying to conform to the ideal she suffers low self-esteem because her body and behavior cannot be manipulated as she would like, not least because of the contradictions inherent in contemporary ideals of femininity. If she does not try to conform or even chooses to critique these ideals she fears being labeled undesirable and losing the status and opportunities for approval and affection that her femininity promises.

This extreme anxiety about the body, and its relation to sexual attractiveness and rejection, reflects the ways in which women's attitudes to their body are deeply tied up with feelings of social acceptability and self-esteem. Nancy only feels sexually acceptable if her body appears a certain way and, if it changes, she fears sexual rejection, which will have severe consequences for the stability of her financial and emotional life. This relationship between celebration of the body and anger and disappointment with it when it fails to conform demonstrates that pleasure experienced through the body is often anxious. It perhaps would be more accurate to describe it as relief when the body has conformed, a happiness that her hard work and vigilance has paid off rather than an experience of pleasure in her own body. These worries about maintaining control over appearance and maintaining her performance of femininity are related to deeper concerns about the stability of her relationship, and extend beyond bodily appearance. Nancy does not express her anxiety about motherhood directly to her husband, deciding to go on the pill instead of telling him she does not want to get pregnant. When challenged about this, Nancy admits to her therapist:

> I know that's really old school and kind of not what my mom and all her granola friends think, but look at them! Their marriages didn't last! They were always demanding equal time, complaining about having to take some man's name. I'm letting my husband have his way, and he's happier for it. (Quan 2001, p. 259)

Nancy suggests here that her mother, a feminist, lost her husband through openly voicing her own desires and needs. Fearing the failure of her marriage, Nancy does not want to risk her husband's disapproval and do the same. Nancy feels that she must maintain her performance of ideal femininity in order to ensure her husband's interest and the stability of her marriage. As Radner (1993) points out for the postfeminist woman: 'the work of ... new femininity must be maintained or he can leave you at any time' (p. 59). Nancy recalls the circumstances of her parents' divorce and how her mother struggled financially afterwards; and Nancy's fear of pregnancy is related to this memory and the fact that issues surrounding motherhood, work, and autonomy remain problematic for her contemporaries. Nancy believes that she is vulnerable if she becomes a mother, as she fears she will not be able to earn her own money as a result of the changes to her body that motherhood will bring. Furthermore, she feels she could not trust her husband to stay with her. The instability of modern relationships may mean potentially being left with sole responsibility for childcare with a considerably lower standard of living; or, if her marriage survives, having to give up her work as a prostitute in order to care for the infant.

As McRobbie suggests, this anxiety comes from the fact that young women are routinely addressed as beneficiaries of a feminist struggle for equality which has been achieved, yet simultaneously new conditions for women are being set (2009, pp. 72–82). One of these new conditions is that women are asked 'to come forward as willing subjects of economic capacity, while also undertaking to retain their traditionally marked out roles in the household, rather than radically challenge the division of labour in the home, as feminists did with noticeable effect from the mid-1970s onwards' (McRobbie 2009, p. 81). Again we can see that the new conditions of womanhood are associated with new anxieties that are symptomatic of illegible rage, but understood as simply being part of ordinary womanhood in popular culture.

A lack of intelligibility

Nancy derives her sense of power and independence from her skilled performances of femininity; literally as a prostitute able to charge a high hourly rate for the use of her body and her ability to please her clients and then, also, in order to maintain a sense of power and invulnerability in her marriage. This causes her considerable anxiety because Nancy has desires (and a body) that sometimes contradict the very narrow requirements of this performance. This is partly because she attempts to perform two roles simultaneously, and this causes incoherence as the requirements come to contradict each other. But it is also because there is another, inner persona which contradicts these performances. These desires and the anger that results from not having the cultural permission to express them means that this sublimated anger 'becomes privatised or even illegible for the reason that the critique of masculinity would return complaining women to the camp of the repudiated feminist' (McRobbie 2009, p. 68).

Nancy therefore has an anxious persona which is synonymous with the 'authentic' (within the terms of the fiction) persona that narrates the novels. Many commentators have noted this anxious persona as a characteristic of chick lit generally. As Harzewski (2011) says: '"Neurotic" is a label often applied to the chick lit protagonist by media commentators to characterize her conflicting needs and wants' (p. 130). In writing in the first person, often in diary form, the reader is offered 'closer insight into the heroine's personal life and psychological dilemmas ... chick lit provides the fiction of an "authentic" female voice bewildered by the contradictory demands and mixed messages of heterosexual romance and feminist emancipation' (Genz & Brabon 2009, p. 86).

The *Manhattan Call Girl* novels are similarly written in diary form, a diary that Nancy keeps on the recommendation of her therapist (for an argument that therapy is itself melancholic, see Frosh 2012). The diary gives us access, as Genz and Brabon suggest, to a fictional 'authentic' voice that sits between the performances of femininity that mark Nancy's interaction with the social world. Through the asocial space of the diary, Nancy relates her private thoughts and also the content of her regular sessions with her therapist. It is in this space that Nancy attempts to resolve some of her conflicts between the contradictory demands of the feminine personas that she performs.

This confessional mode of writing gives voice to Nancy's illegible rage. The 'authentic' persona carries out a form of indirect critique of the requirements of Nancy's performance of femininity. Through the trope of the secret diary, while she is compliant and subservient to her husband and her clients, she is able to undermine that subservience by demonstrating to the readers her superiority and detachment from the men in her life. Also, by using it to express the difficulties she experiences and in recounting the content of her appointments with her therapist, the reader can see reflected back at her the difficulties of her own life. In this way readers can enjoy the triumph of Nancy's successful performances of femininity and the sense of success in social terms they give her; but then commiserate with her when this need to maintain the appearance of ideal femininity causes her pain and anxiety. As both Gill (2007) and Whelehan (2005) have noted, the recognition of female readers of the private sentiments of the protagonists of chick lit are central to their appeal. But this also acts as a form of containment, because it confirms for them that their feelings are a normal part of being female, and also that there is no other alternative.

Nancy's many contradictions are evident throughout the novel. The impression we get as a reader of her diary (rather than as a witness of her performances) is of an incoherent person, expressing desires for safety and to be looked after while asserting her desire for independence, expressing love for her husband and then referring to him as her 'corporate sponsor' (Quan 2001, p. 11), suggesting that her ambition has always been to prostitute and then revealing that she started to prostitute because she was a teenage runaway in an abusive relationship and needed to find some independence to leave her boyfriend. This level of contradiction creates a sense of instability that is also illegible. She can never fully speak her desires and therefore she can never fully stabilize as a coherent person. This instability results from the social requirement that Nancy provide a coherent feminine identity to the world within a strict set of rules.

The entire series therefore seems to revolve around a crisis of feminine identity. Nancy has several identities which she uses with her clients and her husband, but this series of facades gives Nancy a sense of intangibility, a ghostly presence in that she is a constant presence but never quite materializes. She is Nancy at home checking her emails, then Nancy disappears and she is a college student called Sabrina for a session with a client, then Sabrina disappears as she becomes Suzy for another client, who again disappears, and she reappears as a different Nancy, a domestic goddess who gets pleasure from cooking for her husband; and then she is gone as well. She has an air of unreality which she deliberately cultivates, calling this mysteriousness her 'feminine mystery' (Quan 2005, p. 121). But what does this mean in terms of illegible rage?

This lack of ability to manifest is a repeated theme in thinking about contemporary femininity. Radner (2010) points out that the figure of the girl so central to representations of modern femininity connotes an identity that is not yet fixed. The girlhood that is celebrated in popular culture representations of women, whatever their actual chronological age, means that women are always in the 'process of becoming,' repeatedly constructing and deconstructing their identities and never quite making it into womanhood (Radner 2010, p. 9). Griggers (1990) also points out that women are invited, through the fashion press, to create different looks and personas and as a result are required to forfeit the idea of being a '(unified) social self' (p. 98). Griggers argues:

> [O]ne cannot forget the cumulative effect on historical women of the whole spectrum of representation and the possible permutations of their combinations: when she is the 'natural' can she also be the working professional? the desiring subject? the power dresser? the mother? (p. 98)

In these novels we see Nancy asking herself all these questions: can she be sexy and a wife? A call girl and mother? What boundaries should she put in place to stop the performances disrupting each other? In her attempt to work these things out, Nancy discovers the project is impossible; she ends up bemoaning the difficulties of coping with the demands of her personas to her therapist. As Jane Ussher (1997) points out, young women 'know what a girl *should* do if she wants to play the game – they have learnt the rules ... But this doesn't mean that they believe in what they are doing or that the outward appearance ... reflects who they are' (p. 25). Nancy's distress, however, demonstrates the limits of playing out these roles knowingly or ironically. Nancy cannot ensure her performance is interpreted as she wishes. Further, Nancy's attempt to simultaneously perform her different personas is not something she always has control of; the desires and behaviors bleed into each other and into her sense of authentic self.

'Compensatory containment'

Here I would like to return to McRobbie's contention that the fashion photograph acts as a 'compensatory containment' (2009, p. 115) for the illegible rage of the consumer of the image. As I set out above, this is because the fashion image speaks to both the desires and the anxieties that result from the consumer's own difficulties with the demands of modern femininity. It stimulates and speaks to women's desire for freedom and autonomy while at the same time mirroring back to the reader her own sense of constraint and anxiety. Following McRobbie's argument here, I propose that just as the fashion photograph provides a cultural outlet for the expression of these tensions, the genre of chick lit and specifically the *Manhattan Call Girl* novels also represent such an outlet. A mechanism for this outlet I would like to touch upon before concluding is the use of humor.

Whelehan (2005) has noted the use of generally self-deprecating humor in chick lit, and asks whether the humor 'rather ineffectively disguises ... the rage underpinning it' (p. 219). What Whelehan observes here is the way in which chick lit protagonists often appear to recognize the difficulties inherent in performing femininity, but express their anxiety through humor at their own expense. Although Nancy is not necessarily self-deprecating, the novels are full of humorous little asides that diffuse tension and highly improbable plot coincidences that give the books a sense of farce. For instance, on one occasion she talks about her father's second wife, who suspects Nancy is a prostitute. When visiting her father, she arrives with some expensive Louis Vuitton luggage. Her stepmother asks her where she got it, and Nancy lies and tells her that it was on sale. Nancy diffuses the tension in this moment by concluding the story by saying as an aside to the reader: 'Louis Vuitton *never* goes on sale – but this is what I mean about my parents. Neither one has a clue about the most basic facts of life!' (Quan 2001, p. 187). This is a joke characteristic of the chick lit protagonist in an anxious moment. There is an extreme self-consciousness in the frivolity of this type of humor, as if even the protagonist knows she is not as silly as she pretends to be. The frothiness that the narrative voice often lapses into and the mock reverence she uses to discuss fashion accessories are themselves part of the narrative conventions of chick lit. McRobbie points us to the contemporary woman who adopts the air of being 'foolish and bewildered in order to navigate the terrain of hegemonic masculinity without jeopardizing her sexual identity' and we can see Nancy in this description (2009, p. 67). This extends to the conventions of the marketing of the novels with their pastel covers which form an identity for the genre as 'silly' and 'fun,' when the issues that are raised within the novels are often serious. In this way it provides a compensatory containment for the anxiety of the reader, resolving their anxiety without challenging the dominant order.

At the beginning of this chapter I set out to explore what the *Manhattan Call Girl* series of novels could tell us about the relationship between the requirements of contemporary femininity and the types of female complaint McRobbie identifies. For young women who are required to give up feminism, it is in these texts that they can find a type of critique on the conditions of contemporary femininity, without suffering the social stigma of being associated with a movement that openly critiques the existing social structure. As a result such expressions remain opaque but valuable to the feminist scholar in understanding the restricted conditions in which young women are able to voice their discontent, thinking the problems they face are as a result of their own inadequacies rather than inflexibility on the part of society. Quan's novels speak to the contradictory requirements of narrowly defined contemporary femininities and the appearance of coherence they demand, and some of the difficulties young women encounter in trying to maintain them.

References

Attwood, F. (2009) *Mainstreaming Sex: The Sexualization of Western Culture* (London and New York: I.B. Tauris).

Buchwald, L (n.d.) 'A Conversation with Tracy Quan,' https://www.randomhouse.com/boldtype/0901/quan/interview.html.

Butler, J. (1990) *Gender Trouble: Feminism and the Subversion of Identity* (New York: Routledge).

De Jour, B. (2005) *The Intimate Adventures of a London Call Girl* (London: Weidenfeld & Nicolson).

Faludi, S. (1992) *Backlash: The Undeclared War Against American Women* (New York: Doubleday Books).

Ferriss, S. and Young, M. (2006) 'Chicks, Girls and Choice: Redefining Feminism,' *Junctures: The Journal for Thematic Dialogue*, 6, 87–97.

Fielding, H. (1996) *Bridget Jones's Diary* (London: Picador).

Frosh, S. (2012) 'Hauntings: Psychoanalysis and Ghostly Transmissions,' *American Imago*, 69(2), 241–64.

Genz, S. and Brabon, B.A. (2009) *Postfeminism: Cultural Texts and Theories* (Edinburgh University Press).

Gerhard, J. (2005) 'Carrie Bradshaw's Queer Postfeminism,' *Feminist Media Studies*, 5(1), 37–49.

Gill, R. (2007) *Gender and the Media* (Cambridge: Polity).

Goldman, R. (1992) *Reading Ads Socially* (London and New York: Routledge).

Griggers, C. (1990) 'A Certain Tension in the Visual/Cultural Field: Helmut Newton, Deborah Turbeville, and the *VOGUE* Fashion Layout,' *Differences: A Journal of Feminist Cultural Studies*, 2(2), 76–104.

Gwynne, J. (2013) *Erotic Memoirs and Postfeminism: The Politics of Pleasure* (New York: Palgrave Macmillan).

Harzewski, S. (2011) *Chick Lit and Postfeminism* (Charlottesville: University of Virginia Press).

McRobbie, A. (2009) *The Aftermath of Feminism* (London: Sage).

Mitchell, K. (2012) 'Raunch Versus Prude: Contemporary Sex Blogs and Erotic Memoirs by Women,' *Psychology & Sexuality*, 3(1), 12–25.

Negra, D. (2009) *What a Girl Wants? Fantasizing Reclamation of Self in Postfeminism* (Abingdon: Routledge).

Pearson, A. (2002) *I Don't Know How She Does It* (London: Chatto & Windus).

Quan, T. (2001) *Diary of a Manhattan Call Girl* (London: Harper Perennial).

Quan, T. (2005) *Diary of a Married Call Girl* (London: Harper Perennial).

Quan, T. (2008) *Diary of a Jetsetting Call Girl* (London: Harper Perennial).

Quan, T. (2012) 'After Postfeminism, What's Next?,' *The Edge*, www.edge.org/response-detail/10702 (accessed 10 August 2013).

Radner, H. (1993) 'Pretty is as Pretty Does: Free Enterprise and the Marriage Plot,' in J. Collins, H. Radner, and A. Preacher Collins (eds) *Film Theory Goes to the Movies* (London: Routledge), 56–76.

Radner, H. (2010) *Neo-Feminist Cinema: Girly Films, Chick Flicks, and Consumer Culture* (London: Routledge).

Sex and the City (1998–2004) (Television series) (New York: HBO).

Tasker, Y. (1998) *Working Girls: Gender and Sexuality in Popular Cinema* (London: Routledge).

Ussher, J.M. (1997) *Fantasies of Femininity: Reframing the Boundaries of Sex* (New Brunswick, NJ: Rutgers University Press).

Whelehan, I. (2005) *The Feminist Bestseller* (Basingstoke: Palgrave Macmillan).

6
Empowered Vulnerability?: A Feminist Response to the Ubiquity of Sexual Violence in the Pilots of Female-Fronted Teen Drama Series

Susan Berridge

Introduction

This chapter emerges from a striking observation: in stark contrast to male-fronted or ensemble-based teen series, female-fronted programs commonly feature representations of sexual violence in their initial episodes. This recurring trend occurs in US and British teen series spanning a 15-year period, including *My So-Called Life* (1994–95), *Buffy the Vampire Slayer* (1997–2003), *Veronica Mars* (2004–7), *Hex* (2004–5), and *The Vampire Diaries* (2009–present). However, although much contemporary feminist scholarship engages with many of these female-fronted series, their ubiquitous representations of sexual violence have been largely overlooked. This omission is surprising given the pervasive anxiety that surrounds the sexualization of young girls in contemporary popular culture more widely. Instead, feminist teen television scholarship tends to focus on autonomous viewing pleasure and the representation of individual heroines in isolated programs (particularly *Buffy*), making it ill-suited to say anything broader about men, masculinity, and gender relations. More importantly, the relentless focus on isolated heroines means that the more urgent goals of feminism – such as eradicating gendered inequality and male violence against women – slip from view. This chapter addresses this critical neglect, interrogating how sexual violence functions narratively and ideologically in these series' pilots.

The teen drama series offers a particularly conducive genre from which to examine the depiction of sexual violence, concerned as it is with issues of sexuality as well as vulnerability as teenage characters negotiate the transition from childhood to adulthood. The liminal teenage period is portrayed as a particularly vulnerable stage and teenage characters' fallibility and vulnerability, including their sexual vulnerability, is a prominent and recurring generic theme. What this chapter is interested in exploring is how this vulnerability is gendered and sexualized in significant ways. In particular, by highlighting the pervasiveness of representations of sexual violence in the opening episodes of female-fronted teen series, I hope to provide a challenge to postfeminism's insistence that feminism is no longer relevant or necessary. Indeed, I argue that the presence of sexual violence in these pilots suggests that feminism, and particularly female sexual vulnerability, is an unavoidable context for female-fronted programs.

Heroine TV

Writing in 1997, Charlotte Brunsdon identifies an area of feminist television scholarship as textual studies of 'heroine television' (p. 34). Using predominantly female-fronted sitcoms as examples – such as *Kate and Allie* (1984–89), *Designing Women* (1986–93), and *The Golden Girls* (1985–92) – she argues that 'these shows are all, in some fundamental way, addressing feminism, or addressing the agenda that feminism has made public about the contradictory demands on women' (1997, p. 34). In relation to feminist teen television scholarship, specifically, several scholars argue that female-fronted teen series incorporate the tensions and contradictions between femininity and feminism as part of their narrative logic and, in doing so, foreground the performative nature of gender identity and, specifically, girlhood (Bavidge 2004; Braun 2007; Pender 2002). There is a consensus across this work that these programs are, therefore, particularly well suited to critique issues of gender inequality. However, despite this consensus, at the center of these debates remains a persistent emphasis on the heroine in isolation, making the work ill suited to say anything broader about gender relations and urgent feminist issues such as male sexual violence against women. Indeed, in relation to feminist media studies more broadly, Karen Boyle notes that this critical focus on deconstructing female characters means that issues of men, masculinity, and violence remain unexplored (2005, p. 38).

Instead, feminist television scholarship on teen drama series has tended to focus quite narrowly on whether individual teenage characters (usually heterosexual females) constitute appropriate role models for young viewers, frequently justifying this concern with an underlying assumption that these viewers are more susceptible to televisual imagery and thus in need of guidance on how and what to watch (see for example Vint 2002). Feminism and femininity are often viewed as mutually exclusive in this work and, thus, the heroine is typically categorized as a positive or negative role model according to whether she subverts or conforms to feminine stereotypes (Pender 2002). Ultimately, the central question of this work becomes: is this female character a good or bad feminist?; a question which is often answered by analyzing the character's appearance (Pender 2002).

As there is no common consensus on what a feminist identity entails, the persistent emphasis of contemporary feminist criticism on the feminist credentials of individual female television characters can seem rather pointless and circuitous. An array of different feminisms exist and terms such as 'post' and 'third-wave' feminism can be interpreted in vastly different ways depending on the individual scholars' political beliefs (see Genz & Brabon 2009 for an example of the different definitions of postfeminism). Generational difference is also central to these debates (Modleski 1999). Although there is no common agreement on what post- and third-wave feminism entails, both share a similar differentiation from second-wave feminism. Brunsdon (2006) explains that second-wave feminism often becomes the 'other' of postfeminist women, who falsely demonize this earlier generation for repressing all sense of difference between women and for being excessively hostile (p. 43). In her anthology of third-wave feminism and television, Merri Lisa Johnson similarly invokes this idea of the second-wave generation as essentialist and humorless, positing a version of second-wave feminism that is characterized by self-restraint and 'flawless self-abnegation,' in contrast to a version of third-wave feminism that is characterized by self-indulgence and autonomous pleasure (2007, p. 8). While it can be interesting and informative to interrogate one's own viewing pleasure, there is danger of this work becoming overly insular if it fails to connect these personal analyses with wider feminist concerns about the relationship between gender, sexuality, and power. Indeed, the rejection of the so-called 'victimizing' tendency of second-wave feminist criticism by many post- and third-wave feminist scholars in favor of an emphasis on women's pleasure means that televisual representations of sexual violence remain largely unexplored (Boyle 2005, p. 40).

The exceptions to this are the book-length studies by Lisa M. Cuklanz (2000), Sujata Moorti (2002), and Sarah Projansky (2001) on screen representations of rape. These scholars provide useful precedents when examining representational patterns of sexual violence across a number of texts. Each of these authors applies textual analysis across a range of depictions of rape in order to identify central recurring trends in these depictions, examining the potentials and limitations of these narratives in facilitating a feminist discourse on male sexual violence against women. All three authors note the tendency of fictional representations to foreground female experiences of rape and its aftermath, condemn the rapist, and challenge rape myths.

However, all three also observe the limitations of fictional formats in presenting feminist perspectives on violence against women, arguing that these rape narratives rarely critique the patriarchal social structures that contribute to gendered inequality and violence. Projansky directly relates these limitations to the intersection of postfeminism with these narratives, arguing that 'like most post feminist discourses, these rape narratives generally absorb and alter what feminism is, suggesting in the process, that feminism is no longer necessary' (2001, p. 94).

In this chapter, I will develop their work by broadening my definition of sexual violence. While the feminist attention to onscreen depictions of heterosexual rape is both important and necessary, there is also value in considering other forms of sexual violence in order to make connections between a range of abusive behaviors. Liz Kelly explains that, 'the continuum of sexual violence ranges from extensions of the myriad forms of sexism women encounter everyday through to the all too frequent murder of women and girls by men' (1988, p. 97). Drawing on interviews with a volunteer sample of 60 women, Kelly creates female-centered definitions of sexual violence, based on their experiences. These experiences range from more 'minor' and less physical incidents such as male leering, menacing staring, whistles, the use of innuendo, and obscene phone-calls to more physical and sexually explicit incidents such as pressurized sex, coerced sex, rape, and incest. Kelly argues that it is important to broaden definitions of sexual violence in order to challenge 'common-sense' understandings of this abuse that 'reflect men's ideas and limit the range of male behavior that is deemed unacceptable to the most extreme, gross and public forms' (1988, p. 138).

Her use of the term 'continuum' is not to imply that some forms of sexual violence are more significant than others, but rather to indicate that there is a direct relationship between different forms of male sexual abuse against women. She explains that incidents of sexual violence that may appear more 'minor,' such as flashing, rely on the pervasive threat of further male sexual assault, thus creating a sense of generalized fear in women that in turn operates to reassert men's sexual dominance (1988, p. 97). What links different forms of sexually abusive behavior, then, is fear, specifically the victim's perceptions of what may happen next. By emphasizing this fear, Kelly is able to consider forms of male sexual behavior that women have experienced as violating or abusive, but may not have defined explicitly as violent, thereby challenging dominant, patriarchal notions of what sexual violence is.

Kelly's notion of a continuum of male sexual violence against women is helpful to this chapter as it offers a way to challenge dominant definitions of sexual violence and, in turn, allows me to consider connections across a range of sexual violence representations. In particular, my emphasis on the relationship between this abuse and pilot episodes fits well with Kelly's continuum, as situating these representations in relation to broader series' frameworks enables me to highlight representational patterns across several different forms of abuse, while still retaining a sense of their specificity. Throughout this chapter, then, I will use the term 'sexual violence' to describe a range of sexually abusive behaviors, including rape, attempted rape, sexual assault, sexually motivated murder, and sexual harassment.

Pilots

Pilot episodes serve a particular function in the broader context of teen drama series, at once establishing the series' similarity to and difference from other teen programs. As Jason Mittell explains, 'for a television series, a pilot is the primary site for establishing intrinsic norms for the ongoing series, and making clear connections to the relevant external norms of genre, narrative, mode, and style' (2009). The presence of sexual violence in the pilots of female-fronted teen series, then, suggests that an engagement with feminist norms is an 'intrinsic norm' of these types of programs. In what follows, I explore this pattern in more depth, but firstly I want to outline other 'norms' of *My So-Called Life*, *Buffy*, *Veronica Mars*, *Hex*, and *The Vampire Diaries* as established in their pilot episodes in order to then consider how these intersect with representations of sexual violence and alter how these depictions are framed.

The recurring feminist critical argument that female-fronted teen series offer a particularly conducive site for critiquing gendered norms and inequalities is inextricably linked to the centrality of a female narrative perspective (Bolte 2008; Braithwaite 2008). All five series establish this female perspective through the amount of screen-time and space the heroines are afforded. *Veronica Mars* and *My So-Called Life* further reinforce a female point of view through their respective heroines' voice-overs, which are more prominent in their pilot episodes than at any other time. In relation to *Veronica Mars* specifically, Andrea

Braithwaite argues that, 'intimate in tone, these confessional moments frame the audience's entry into the conditions young women face as they navigate and interrogate their personal and professional relationships' (2008, p. 140). It is through her voice-over that Veronica (Kristin Bell) directly critiques hegemonic constructions of gender and gendered romance, cynically declaring in the show's opening line that 'I'm never getting married.' While this romantic scepticism could be attributed to the series' noir hybridity, it is notable that a similar cynicism is conveyed through the voice-over of Angela (Claire Danes) in the pilot of *My So-Called Life*, commenting on gendered inequalities as she walks down a school corridor.

Further, Caralyn Bolte suggests that the ability of female-fronted series to critique hegemonic gender norms is linked not only to the centrality of a female perspective, but to an *exiled* female perspective, noting that the position of Buffy (Sarah Michelle Gellar) and Veronica on the margins of the diegetic in-crowd of their schools affords them a particularly credible and powerful space from which to expose and critique 'the underpinnings of social, gender and class dynamics' (2008, p. 99). The same argument is applicable to the heroines of *My So-Called Life*, *Hex*, and *The Vampire Diaries*. Cassie (Christina Cole), the heroine of *Hex*, for example, also exists on the margins; she is frequently ignored by her classmates and spends a lot of time on her own. Her isolation is heightened at the end of the series' pilot when her best friend, Thelma (Jemima Rooper), dies. Similarly, Elena (Nina Dobrev), the protagonist of *The Vampire Diaries*, occupies an exiled position when she is distanced from her peers after she is suddenly orphaned, following a car crash.

Notably, almost all teenage protagonists, regardless of whether they are male or female, occupy an initial outsider status within their high school and are often bullied. Yet, while male protagonists are bullied because of their lower class (see Ryan (Benjamin McKenzie) in *The O.C.* (2003–7) or Lucas (Chad Michael Murray) in *One Tree Hill* (2003–12) for examples), female protagonists are harassed on the basis of their gender and sexuality. In the pilot of *Hex*, Cassie and Thelma are routinely subject to verbal sexual abuse which teachers do little to prevent. The opening of *Buffy* also explicitly renders the high school a sexually threatening space. The pilot opens on a visibly nervous teenage female, dressed in school uniform, and a slightly older male breaking into the school at night. Highlighting the series' central subversion of gender expectations, this opening plays on the expectation of female sexual vulnerability when the frightened female suddenly reveals herself as a vampire and kills the previously cocky male. The rest of the episode continues to draw on the threat of sexual violence. For example, Buffy is followed by a shadowy man as she walks alone down a dark street to the local nightclub. She continually glances over her shoulder, resonating with Kelly's (1988) findings that females experience a generalized fear of sexual violence (although, as Buffy is a vampire slayer, she soon turns the tables on her stalker and ambushes him).

Later in the episode, after taking Buffy's advice to 'seize the day,' her friend, Willow (Alyson Hannigan), leaves the local nightclub with a slightly older male whom she has been flirting with. Unbeknownst to her, he is a vampire. At this point, the threat of sexual violence is reconfigured as a narrative concerning Buffy's personal identity. Throughout the pilot episode, Buffy fights against her destiny as a vampire slayer, complaining that she wants to do normal, teenage things. Yet, upon seeing Willow in danger, she realizes that she has no choice but to help. It is Buffy's perspective that the viewer is aligned with as she frantically searches for Willow. The camera then cuts to the man taking Willow on a 'shortcut' through a graveyard. Her increasing fear is captured in facial close-ups and by her stammering dialogue. She shrieks as he pushes her roughly into a crypt. Shortly after, two other vampires join them. Suddenly Buffy enters and a climactic battle ensues. Sexual violence, here, operates to emphasize to Buffy that she must embrace her destiny as slayer in order to protect the people she cares about as well as to establish a sense of (sexual) threat that will run through the entire series.

Like the pilot of *Buffy*, sexual violence in the opening episode of *The Vampire Diaries* operates to highlight the series' horror/teen generic hybridity by creating suspense, tension, and a general climate of (sexual) danger. Halfway through the episode, Vicki (Kayla Ewell), a female teenage character, is sexually assaulted by her boyfriend whilst at an exclusively teenage party held outdoors in the woods. As they kiss against a tree, he becomes increasingly rough and tries to physically force her to have sex despite her loud protests. She manages to escape and walks off into the woods. Suspense is heightened by eerie non-diegetic music as a long-shot captures Vicki walking alone through the dark, fog pooling around her. The camera suddenly cuts to a facial close-up, highlighting her fear as she glimpses a shadowy figure following her. The previous scene creates mystery here: is the figure her pushy boyfriend or is it a vampire – the presence of which in the town has already been hinted at earlier in the episode? The music rises suddenly in pitch and volume as the scene fades to black. Shortly afterwards, Vicki is discovered by the series' heroine, Elena, and her brother barely conscious and covered in blood. From then on, Vicky is largely forgotten and the narrative is reframed as a story about Elena. The episode ends with a suggestion that Elena is the real point of interest for the vampires in the town.

In both these pilot episodes, sexual violence functions to establish a dangerous climate in which female sexual vulnerability is stressed. While this could be attributed to these particular series' horror/teen generic hybridity, it is notable that sexual threat is also stressed in the opening episodes of *My So-Called Life*, *Hex*, and *Veronica Mars*. In these pilot episodes, representations of sexual violence act as a reminder of female characters' age-related vulnerability. Patterns cut across all five series; in each, female characters – usually the protagonist or a close female friend – are physically sexually attacked by males at night in settings that are largely devoid of adult presence, such as exclusively teenage parties or clubs (*Veronica Mars*, *Hex*) or directly outside these spaces in more isolated areas (*Buffy*, *The Vampire Diaries*, *My So-Called Life*). Significantly, with the exception of *The Vampire Diaries* example mentioned above, this vulnerability is heightened in relation to *single* females, suggesting that in these programs sexuality outside the context of a monogamous, romantic relationship is a dangerous space for young women. The victim is typically single at the time of the attack, and in *Hex*, *Buffy*, and *My So-Called Life*, the attack occurs after she has been flirting with the perpetrator. Moreover, in *My So-Called Life* and *Hex*, the attack also follows the female character attempting to act older than her age, by drinking alcohol and/or dressing in revealing clothing, thus functioning as a warning to young (female) viewers about the perils of this kind of behavior.

The 1994 pilot of *My So-Called Life* provides a clear example of this. In this episode, Angela lies to her parents and goes to an over-21s nightclub with her new friends Rayanne (A.J. Langer) and Rickie (Wilson Cruz), changing on the way into a tight, revealing outfit. After being denied entry to the club, the friends sit in the car park, drinking alcohol. It is here that Rayanne is sexually assaulted by an older, male stranger who pushes her roughly against a car and kisses her without her consent. The actual moment in which Rayanne is sexually assaulted occupies only ten seconds of screen-time. A rapid series of tight close-ups capture her struggle as she tries to fight off the man, her teeth gritted and eyes tightly shut, before Angela intervenes and the man throws Rayanne to the ground. The scene is all the more poignant and shocking because this is the first time that Rayanne appears vulnerable. Up until this point, she has been self-assured and cocky. The perpetrator leaves after some police officers intervene although, notably, the man is not arrested.

The narrative then diverts away from the sexual assault to highlight the theme of budding romance. As Rayanne and Angela get into the police car to be driven home, Jordan (Jared Leto), the boy that Angela has a crush on, notices her and calls her name. This is the first time in the program that he has properly acknowledged her and the moment is marked by upbeat non-diegetic music and Angela's broad smile as she stares back at him. This moment between Angela and Jordan diverts attention away from the sexual assault and from Rayanne. Indeed, there is little emphasis in these pilot episodes on the emotional aftermath of the assault on the victim. Significantly, Rayanne suffers from alcohol-induced amnesia, allowing the program to ignore this issue altogether.

The sexual assault does, however, have a profound effect on *Angela*, highlighting to her the dangers of acting older than her age. As she returns to her warmly lit house, she begins to regress. She stares at her reflection in her bedroom mirror before harshly wiping off her lipstick, indicating a rejection of the adult life she previously craved. The camera then follows her down the hall to her parents' bedroom where she climbs into bed with her mother and cries. The two women are framed together as her mother gently strokes Angela's hair and comforts her. Here, sexual violence is framed as a young woman's personal experience, rather than a wider social or political issue. Yet, notably, the episode privileges Angela's, not the victim Rayanne's, reaction.

At the end of the pilot, an individualized understanding of sexual violence is privileged. In the final scene, Rickie and Rayanne boast to their school peers, uncorrected by Angela, about the events of their weekend. Rayanne appears completely unphased, again illustrating the lack of emphasis on the victim's emotional aftermath. The violent nature of Rayanne's assault is erased here, with Rickie using the language of a normative, non-abusive dating ritual to describe their encounter with the men. This assimilation of sexual violence into dating discourse resonates more widely with teenage culture and experiences of intimate relationships, in which, studies have revealed, sexual abuse is common (Chung 2007). Yet by framing sexual violence in this way, it becomes divorced from the broader gendered sexual inequalities underpinning this abuse.

The sexual violence narrative in *Veronica Mars* similarly focuses on the heroine's personal identity. Through Veronica's flashbacks, the pilot establishes two overarching sexual violence narratives that will span the following two seasons. The first concerns Veronica's best friend's murder, which is later revealed to be sexually motivated, and the second involves Veronica's rape at a classmate's party. The viewer is aligned with Veronica's point of view as she walks through the party, with classmates looking at her scornfully. A shot of her taking a drink is accompanied by her voice-over informing the viewer that the drink was laced with a date-rape drug. From this point, the party's diegetic pop music is replaced by an ethereal, non-diegetic soundtrack. The viewer is aligned with Veronica's literally and figuratively fuzzy point of view as she wanders outside past a hot-tub full of students who stare and laugh at her. As she collapses on a sun-lounger, the scene fades to black.

The music links the previous scene with the next, which opens with a close-up of Veronica opening her eyes and then an overhead shot as she gets out of bed. Sunlight streams through the window behind her, indicating that it is the next morning. The camera cuts to a close-up of a pair of white pants, discarded on the floor, indicating that Veronica has been raped. This is reinforced by a close-up of Veronica's face registering a tear rolling down her cheek. Her cynical voice-over is conspicuously absent here, in keeping with the series' norms more widely in which her narration disappears at highly emotional moments. The close-up fades into the next image as Veronica walks away from the house, her voice-over explaining that, 'I'm no longer that girl.'

Sexual violence in the pilot of *Hex* is also framed as an issue related to the heroine's self-identity. Echoing the *My So-Called Life* example, Cassie is sexually assaulted after she decides to go to a nightclub alone, dressed in a revealing, tight outfit. After being verbally harassed by her classmate, Leon (Jamie Davis), she escapes to a deserted, dimly lit corridor only for him to follow her. The camera cuts quickly between tight facial close-ups of the two, with more than a shot per second, as Cassie struggles against Leon's attempts to kiss her. A sudden extreme close-up of her eye, accompanied by a piercing scream, is followed by a close-up of an overhead electrical box blowing up, sending sparks flying and plunging Cassie and Leon into darkness. The close secession of shots indicate that Cassie's telekinetic powers, which have been hinted at previously, are the cause of the explosion. This reading is reinforced by an extreme facial close-up of Cassie looking incredulous at what she has done. The scene lasts just ten seconds before Cassie is able to escape and runs back to the boarding school where she lives.

In a series of shot/reverse shot close-ups, Cassie tearfully recounts the evening's event to her female best friend. Their dialogue is significant, reinforcing that in these pilots sexual violence is primarily framed as a personal issue for the protagonist.

CASSIE: Leon tried to ...
THELMA: What?
CASSIE: I dunno, he tried to ...
THELMA: What?
CASSIE: It's not that ... I touch things.

She then proceeds to tell Thelma about her powers. As this extract demonstrates, Cassie's dialogue diverts attention away from Leon's actions to focus on her new-found powers. Thus, sexual violence is framed as an issue about Cassie's personal identity, specifically her telekinesis, rather than a broader social problem relating to dominant constructions of gender and sexuality.

It is important to note that the liminal space between childhood and adulthood is figured as a dangerous stage in male-fronted series and is also signaled by violence in their pilot episodes. Yet, significantly, this violence is not sexually threatening in nature. Instead, the violence takes place between the protagonist and another male character (typically a jock) and is often instigated by the protagonist's disgust over how the jock treats his girlfriend. Thus, it operates to define the male protagonist as virtuous, only using violence in the service of protecting others and, in doing so, highlighting his sensitivity toward female characters (Ryan in *The O.C.*, Lucas in *One Tree Hill*, Clark (Tom Welling) in *Smallville* (2001–11)), in contrast to aggressive, selfish, and sexist jocks, who use violence to assert their power (Luke (Chris Carmack) in *The O.C.*, Nathan (James Lafferty) in *One Tree Hill*, Whitney (Eric Johnson) in *Smallville*). Notably, these protagonists are the same males who go on to protect and defend female victims from sexually violent men in sexual violence narratives occurring later in the series. These scenes are aesthetically different to scenes of sexual violence in the pilots of female-fronted series. Instead of connoting danger and threat, the scenes emphasize excitement, adrenaline, and even glamour. Although the violence, as in *Hex* and *The Vampire Diaries*, takes place outdoors at night and is marked by fast-paced editing and alternating long-shots and close-ups, it is accompanied by fast, upbeat pop music and followed immediately by scenes that emphasize humor. Indicating this lack of danger, following a fight involving Ryan in the pilot of *The O.C.*, his friend jokily remarks, 'it was like *Fight Club* or something'.

This comparison indicates that feminism and feminist concerns such as sexual violence are an unavoidable context for female-fronted series. Although, in these pilots, sexual violence is inextricably linked to the heroine's personal identity, the specific context – a context that repeatedly stresses a cynicism surrounding gender norms and hegemonic romantic ideals and emphasizes gendered bullying – affects how these sexual violence representations are framed, potentially challenging an understanding of this abuse as an isolated problem of an otherwise functioning patriarchy. Interestingly, these differences are not just predicated on the gender of the protagonist, but on her sexuality also. The broader research project of which this analysis comes out of also included analysis of *Sugar Rush* (2005), a British teen series with a lesbian protagonist. Interestingly, although this series features a rape narrative toward the end of season one, the pilot episode is devoid of representations of sexual violence. This suggests a direct connection between hegemonic constructions of gender, sexuality, and power. An additional finding reveals that the positioning of sexual violence storylines in pilot episodes is not unique to drama series with *teenage* heroines, but occurs more widely in programs fronted by female adults, including *True Blood* (2008–present), *Tru Calling* (2003–5), *Bones* (2005–present), and *The Closer* (2005–12). While it is beyond the scope of this chapter, this would be an interesting avenue to explore further as it suggests that female sexual vulnerability is not solely tied to youth.

Conclusion

Importantly (and obviously), these pilot episodes do not exist in vacuums. Indeed, as Mittell (2012) notes, pilot episodes are often atypical from the ongoing series as they must accomplish numerous tasks: gathering a cast and crew, establishing a production routine, and making an argument for the program's longer-term viability to both network executives looking for a hit show and prospective viewers at home. Nevertheless, pilot episodes play an important role in establishing the premise of series more widely. Regardless of their exceptionality, the presence of sexual violence in the pilots of five female-fronted teen drama series is striking. This enduring and pervasive pattern suggests that an engagement with feminist concerns is an unavoidable context for these shows. As Diane Negra and Yvonne Tasker note, 'contemporary popular culture is produced, in part at least, in response to feminism. That is, feminism forms an important part of contemporary culture' (2007, p. 5).

This is not to say that these programs consistently privilege a feminist reading, however. As demonstrated by the examples in this chapter, sexual violence is frequently framed as a personal issue for the heroine, rather than a broader social problem. With the exception of *Veronica Mars* and *Hex*, which feature the heroine herself as the victim of the sexual attack, the aftermath on the victim is rarely explored. Furthermore, perpetrators are typically marginal male characters who disappear shortly after the attack takes place and, as such, are not held accountable for their actions. However, unlike male-fronted or ensemble-based teen drama series, as I have shown, teen series fronted by heterosexual heroines regularly foreground feminist concerns, including sexual violence, in a way that makes it difficult to simply transform these issues into something else or to see them as isolated aberrations of an otherwise functioning patriarchy. In turn, this suggests a challenge to postfeminism's relentless insistence that feminism is now redundant and unnecessary.

The tendency of contemporary feminist scholarship to focus on viewing pleasure and the (elusive) feminist credentials of individual televisual heroines has meant that depictions of sexual violence have been widely overlooked. It is certainly not wrong to reflect upon our viewing pleasure, but it does mean that the more urgent goals of feminism, which to me involve challenging male sexual violence against women, are in danger of becoming lost (Boyle 2005). The pervasive presence of sexual violence in the pilot episodes of female-fronted teen drama series spanning a 15-year period and different national contexts (as well as the lack of critical attention paid to these representations) suggest that feminist television scholarship needs to engage with and interrogate these portrayals. While sexual violence representations are not reflective of reality, they are generative and productive and, as such, have the capacity to inform and educate. Thus, as a feminist scholar, I believe that it is vitally important to study depictions of feminist issues as a means of affecting change.

References

Bavidge, J. (2004) 'Chosen Ones: Reading the Contemporary Teen Heroine,' in G. Davis and K. Dickinson (eds) *Teen TV: Genre, Consumption and Identity* (London: BFI), 41–53.

Bolte, C. (2008) '"Normal is the Watchword": Exiling Cultural Anxieties and Redefining Desire from the Margins,' in S.M. Ross and L.E. Stein (eds) *Teen Television: Essays on Programming and Fandom* (Jefferson, NC and London: McFarland), 93–113.

Bones (2005–present) (Television series) (US: Fox).

Boyle, K. (2005) 'Feminism Without Men: Feminist Media Studies in a Post-Feminist Age,' in J. Curran and M. Gurevitch (eds) *Mass Media and Society*, 4th edn (London: Hodder Arnold), 29–45.

Braithwaite, A. (2008) '"That girl of yours – she's pretty hard-boiled, huh?": Detecting Feminism in *Veronica Mars*,' in S.M. Ross and L.E. Stein (eds) *Teen*

Television: Essays on Programming and Fandom (Jefferson, NC and London: McFarland), 132–49.

Braun, J. (2007) 'Passing Notes and Passing Crushes: Writing Desire and Sexuality in *My So-Called Life*,' in M. Byers and D. Lavery (eds) *Dear Angela: Remembering My So-Called Life* (Lanham, MD: Rowman & Littlefield), 107–19.

Brunsdon, C. (1997) *Screen Tastes: Soap Opera to Satellite Dishes* (London: Routledge).

Brunsdon, C. (2006) 'The Feminist in the Kitchen: Martha, Martha and Nigella,' in J. Hollows and R. Moseley (eds) *Feminism in Popular Culture* (Oxford and New York: Berg), 41–56.

Buffy the Vampire Slayer (1997–2003) (Television series) (US: The WB/UPN).

Chung, D. (2007) 'Making Meaning of Relationships: Young Women's Experiences and Understandings of Dating Violence,' *Violence Against Women*, 13(12), 1274–95.

The Closer (2005–12) (Television series) (US: TNT).

Cuklanz, L.M. (2000) *Rape in Prime Time: Television, Masculinity and Sexual Violence* (Philadelphia: University of Pennsylvania Press).

Designing Women (1986–93) (Television series) (US: CBS).

Genz, S. and Brabon, B.A. (2009) *Postfeminism: Cultural Texts and Theories* (Edinburgh University Press).

The Golden Girls (1985–92) (Television series) (US: NBC).

Hex (2004–5) (Television series) (UK: Sky One).

Johnson, M.L. (ed.) (2007) *Third Wave Feminism and Television: Jane Puts it in a Box*. London and New York: I.B. Tauris.

Kate and Allie (1984–89) (Television series) (US: CBS).

Kelly, L. (1988) *Surviving Sexual Violence* (Cambridge: Polity Press).

Mittell, J. (2009) '"These Questions Need Answers": Narrative Construction and the *Veronica Mars* Pilot,' *Just TV*, 10 August, http://justtv.wordpress.com/2009/08/10/the-questions-needanswers-an-essay-on-the-veronica-mars-pilot/ (accessed 21 September 2009).

Mittell, J. (2012) *Complex TV: The Poetics of Contemporary Television Storytelling* (Pre- Publication edition. MediaCommons Press).

Modleski, T. (1999) 'Introduction: Feminist Criticism Today: Notes from Jurassic Park,' in *Old Wives' Tales: Feminist Re-Visions of Film and Other Fictions* (London and New York: I.B. Tauris), 1–12.

Moorti, S. (2002) *Color of Rape: Gender and Race in Television's Public Spheres* (Albany: State University of New York Press).

My So-Called Life (1994–95) (Television series) (US: ABC).

Negra, D. and Tasker, Y. (2007) 'Introduction: Feminist Politics and Postfeminist Culture,' In Y. Tasker and D. Negra (eds) *Interrogating Post-Feminism: Gender and the Politics of Popular Culture* (Durham, NC and London: Duke University Press), 1–25.

The O.C. (2003–7) (Television series) (US: Fox).

One Tree Hill (2003–12) (Television series) (US: The WB/CW).

Pender, P. (2002) '"I'm Buffy and You're ... History": The Postmodern Politics of *Buffy*,' in R.V. Wilcox and D. Lavery (eds) *Fighting the Forces: What's at Stake in Buffy the Vampire Slayer* (London: Rowman & Littlefield), 35–44.

Projansky, S. (2001) *Watching Rape: Film and Television in Postfeminist Culture* (New York University Press).

Smallville (2001–11) (Television series) (US: The WB/CW).

Sugar Rush (2005) (Television series) (UK: E4).

Tru Calling (2003–5) (Television series) (US: Fox).

True Blood (2008–present) (Television series) (US: HBO).

The Vampire Diaries (2009–present) (Television series) (US: The CW).

Veronica Mars (2004–7) (Television series) (US: UPN/The CW).

Vint, S. (2002) '"Killing Us Softly?" A Feminist Search for the "Real" Buffy,' *Slayage: The Online Journal of Buffy Studies*, 5 April, www.slayage.tv (accessed 24 June 2008).

7
Against Conformity: Families, Respectability, and the Representation of Gender-Nonconforming Youth of Color in *Gun Hill Road* and *Pariah*

Natalie Havlin and Celiany Rivera-Velázquez

Introduction

In 2011, the Sundance Film Festival featured two films portraying queer youth in New York City. Directed by Rashaad Ernesto Green, *Gun Hill Road* (2011) was marketed as 'the story of a family in transition' featuring 'a young man exploring his sexuality in an intolerant and judgmental world and his exploration's impact on his relationship with his parents and himself' ('About the Film' 2011). Set in the Fort Greene neighborhood in Brooklyn, Dee Rees's *Pariah* (2011) tells the story of Alike, a 17-year-old African American woman who 'is quietly but firmly embracing her identity as a lesbian' and is 'especially eager to find a girlfriend' as she navigates her parents' strained marriage ('Story' 2011).

Since the films' premieres at Sundance in 2011, critics and audiences have celebrated *Gun Hill Road* and *Pariah* as groundbreaking coming-of-age narratives depicting queer and questioning[1] youth of color who struggle to balance their parents' expectations with the sense of freedom that gender and sexual exploration brings (Arnold 2012; McLeod 2012). In this essay, we examine *Gun Hill Road* and *Pariah* as films countering the historic erasure of Latina/o and black queer and gender-nonconforming[2] youth and their families from mainstream media as well as feminist and LGBTQ histories of New York City. Feature films depicting Latina/o and black communities and scholarship on queer media have largely situated representations of Latina/o and black queer sexuality and gender nonconformity at the periphery (Coleman & Cobb 2007;

106

Keeling 2007; La Fountain-Stokes 2011; Wlodarz 2004). With the exception of the documentary *Paris is Burning* (1990), most coming-of-age films about queer youth in New York, from *All Over Me* (1997) to *Dorian Blues* (2004), have focused on white LGBTQ subcultures and figured Manhattan as the defining locale of urban queer cultures. Likewise, mainstream feminist and LGBTQ political projects in the greater New York area have historically privileged whiteness and cis-gender identities in LGBTQ and women's struggles for equality and empowerment, rendering invisible (within hegemonic frameworks) the concerns and activism of queer and transgender Latina/o and black cultural workers (see Cohen 1997; Cruz-Malavé 2007; Hill Collins 2004; Isoke 2013; Johnson & Henderson 2005; Manalansan 2005; Retzloff 2007). Recent independent documentaries about queer youth of color in New York City such as *The Aggressives* (2005), the youth-produced film *Fenced OUT* (2007), and *Dreams Deferred: The Sakia Gunn Film Project* (2008) have brought more visibility to urban queer Latina/o and black youth subcultures and activism by LGBTQ youth of color in Manhattan and Newark, New Jersey. *Gun Hill Road* and *Pariah*, however, are the first feature films to center Latina/o and black gender-nonconforming and queer youth as protagonists in narratives that not only dramatize elements of the urban realities in long-standing Latina/o and black communities in the Bronx and Brooklyn, but also spotlight intergenerational family relationships as shaping queer youth's lives in the neoliberal landscape of the boroughs of New York City.

Gun Hill Road and *Pariah* bring Latina/o and black gender-nonconforming youth to the screen as agents of their own futures, humanizing gender-nonconforming youth in the cinematic sphere while also demonstrating the continuing need for feminist and queer political projects to simultaneously challenge gender policing, sexism, homophobia, racism, and economic hierarchies in urban locales. Women of color feminist theorists and practitioners from Audre Lorde (1984) to Chela Sandoval (2000) have historically deconstructed the co-constitutive production of gender, sexuality, race, ability, class, and nation within global systems of capitalism and colonialism. The related critical lens of queer of color critique and the emerging fields of black queer studies and Latina/o queer studies have drawn on women of color feminism to bring an analysis of gender and the material histories of racialization and capitalism to the study of sexuality within queer studies and LGBTQ studies (see Hames-García & Martínez 2011; Hong & Ferguson 2011; Johnson & Henderson 2005; Muñoz 1999). As we discuss the impact of the films' circulation of representations of

Latina/o and black gender-nonconforming youth as protagonists, we draw on women of color feminism theory and queer of color critique to argue that *Gun Hill Road* and *Pariah* also demonstrate the limits of using visibility as a model for empowerment within a sociopolitical system that renders queer and gender-nonconforming youth of color and their families hypervisible. With growing urban economic inequality occurring in concert with the expansion of the punitive policing paradigms that disproportionately criminalize Latina/o and black communities, the consequences of not conforming to hegemonic class, sexual, and gender norms are increasingly greater for Latina/o and black men, women, and youth (Cohen 2004; Gilmore 2007). By highlighting the day-to-day survival strategies and the differential consequences of visibility for queer and gender-nonconforming youth of color in *Gun Hill Road* and *Pariah*, we pinpoint the simultaneous operation of misogyny, homophobia, gender policing, transphobia, racism, and economic exploitation in the everyday struggles of not only gender-nonconforming youth of color, but also their broader families and social networks. We critically analyze the films' scenes of generational conflict to link the internal power dynamics among family members to the broader socio-historical landscape of post-Guiliani policing paradigms and the increasing economic vulnerability of Latina/o and black communities in rapidly gentrifying neighborhoods in Brooklyn and the Bronx.

Studies of generational conflict within narratives about racialized groups have historically simplified the complex context and influence of economic, gender, sexual, and racial hierarchies on the interpersonal relationships and political positions within families and communities. Speaking to this, Lisa Lowe (1996) writes: 'the reduction of the cultural politics of racialized ethnic groups ... to first-generation/second-generation struggles displaces social differences into a privatized familial opposition' (p. 63). While our focus on generational conflict in *Gun Hill Road* and *Pariah* has the potential to reproduce a singular narrative about interpersonal conflict as solely located in domestic relations, we argue that it is crucial to read the films' narrative focus on the violent relationships among parents and queer youth as linked to the broader structural economic, sexual, gender, and other social hierarchies. Our aim is not to reinforce a focus on generational conflict as the sole framework to understand the films. Rather, we read the narratives of domestic generational violence in the films as opportunities to trace the differential consequences of visibility and the broader stakes of institutional and social pressures on Latino and black youth and adults in a world where men and women are valued differently, based on notions of 'proper' gender performance. In this sense, our methodology builds on Aisha Durham's (2007) important clarification that narratives of generational conflict – whether in cultural production or feminist theory – can misread practices of critique. In her work, Durham explains that hiphop feminism and black feminism offer correctives to white feminism's emphasis on conflict among different generations of women. Black feminism, Durham clarifies, develops out of the 'rejection of stereotypes rather than a rejection of the mother (2007, p. 118). Following Durham, we argue that *Gun Hill Road* and *Pariah* offer complex portrayals of parental gender roles, particularly the performance of hypermasculinity and respectable femininity, by indexing the economic and institutional pressures of the criminal justice system and religious organizations on Latino and black parents.

Reading *Gun Hill Road* and *Pariah* together, we also encourage a consideration of strategies for building queer alternatives to heteropatriarchy – a hierarchical social system that both naturalizes heterosexuality as compulsory and privileges masculinity and men in cultural, legal, and religious spheres[3] – that support healing for both queer and heteronormative people from the violent cycles of self-enforced and state-enforced gender and sexual norms. In her theorization of the production of social value, Lisa Marie Cacho has identified how literary and political narratives aiming to humanize or revalue communities of color and queer subjects can, at times, reinscribe the social hierarchies that produce inequality and dehumanize particular groups. She explains that narratives ranging from fictional stories of queer Latina self-discovery to discourses valorizing immigrant Latino families as not 'criminals' demonstrate how 'practices of revaluation may unwittingly depend on an/other's criminalization' (Cacho 2011, p. 72). In our reading of *Gun Hill Road* and *Pariah*, we join Cacho (2011) in calling for queer critiques of family violence and cultural nationalism to 'reimagine and reinvent' the family and, in particular, criminalized Latino masculinities and pathologized black femininities in order to intervene against the 'state violence and abandonment' directed at black and Latina/o communities (p. 78). To elucidate the potential for re-narrating generational conflict among gender-nonconforming youth and parents, we conclude by examining two glimpses of alternative family structures and masculinities in *Gun Hill Road*. In our analysis of these alternatives, we consider how we can build queer alternatives to heteropatriarchy that support healing from the violent cycles of state-enforced gender and sexual norms.

Gender-nonconforming youth and self-determination

'Coming to the stage ... from the B X!'
[La Bruja, a Bronx-based poet and spoken word artist, raises her arms
in an X shape while a crowd of visibly queer youth are participating
in a call-and-response that welcomes Vanessa onto the stage]
'Please welcome
the one, the only:
Vanessa!'

Within the first ten minutes of *Gun Hill Road*, we watch as the main
queer character 'Michael' establishes her preferred gender identity as
'Vanessa' through a spoken word performance, as she is called onto
the Camaradas stage. Camaradas is one of the best-known stages for
the celebration of Puerto Rican and Nuyorican (New York Puerto Rican)
traditions and culture in the Upper East Side of Manhattan (also referred to
as 'El Barrio') (Dávila 2012, p. 78). The contrast between Michael and
Vanessa is sharp. Michael projects an uncomfortable energy whenever
he has to 'butch up' and perform masculinity around his Puerto Rican
family. Vanessa, on the other hand, unravels in front of audiences
that do not really know her in the personal realm but get to see her
as she prefers: an attractive young woman. She recites: 'Brown and bone
structure ... / bent to your likeness. / I like this. / Living in the mirror /
with peace of mind. / Make like a mirror / and turn me lovely. / Face to
face / and say you love me.' When Vanessa coquettishly expresses her
desire to be seen and loved in this spoken word piece, we see her at
her happiest and most in-control point in the whole film.

In this section we analyze how *Gun Hill Road* and *Pariah* present the
complexity of the development of queer identities. Both films bravely
portray struggles with gender nonconformity and experiences of sexual
exploration among black and Latina/o youth. Through representing the
process of everyday self-fashioning, queer urban wanderings, dating,
and sexual exploration, both films humanize the process of queer self-
definition as inherently valuable. Viewers get a glimpse of the economies
of queer youth: where they go (Camaradas in El Barrio, the Christopher
Street piers, queer and straight dance clubs, and underneath parks'
bleachers); what they do (change clothes in the school's bathroom, go
to Tamar-Kali concerts, and listen to new music-sharing headphones);
and what they buy (premanicured acrylic nails, and strap-on dildos) –
precisely in the way we imagine these things may have happened
late in the first decade of the 2000s. Both films rely on an aesthetic

and cultural verisimilitude to draw the geographic contours of queer youth of color culture in the Bronx, Brooklyn, and two locations – El Barrio and the Christopher Street piers – in Manhattan.

The portrayal of Vanessa in *Gun Hill Road* as a youth publicly articulating her gender identity and sexual desire in spoken word pieces and public social scenes presents gender expression and sexuality as an everyday element of youth self-definition and exploration. Vanessa presents herself as confident in her gender expression and identity as she engages in self-fashioning. In her introductory poem at Camaradas, Vanessa explains that she is 'Living in the mirror / with peace of mind.' While she affirms her self-reflection in her spoken word performance, the film's characterization of Vanessa takes place through sequences detailing Vanessa's makeup routine and scenes depicting an underground beauty clinic where she obtains a silicone injection in her buttocks. We interpret Vanessa's use of silicone injections as one of the film's most tangible moments of portraying Vanessa as engaged in a process of self-fashioning and exploration. At the underground beauty clinic, she takes a step further into her transition despite all the family factors at home that may be interpreted as mechanisms to dissuade, deter, or stall the process of Michael becoming Vanessa.

Critics such as Lilliana Ramos-Collado (2013), in talking about an underground Puerto Rican beauty clinic portrayed in the film *La Aguja/ The Needle* (2012), describe underground beauty clinics as spaces that enable the process of personal reinvention. Furthermore, the person who administers the treatments at the beauty clinic is seen as a 'contemporary, self-styled shaman who, like *santeros* in the *botanicas*, administers ointments, potions and other substances to diverse people' who urgently seek to change what they perceive as a battered, aged body in need of cosmetic support (Ramos-Collado 2013). As viewers of *Gun Hill Road* learn about the unsafe processes through which many transwomen without medical insurance go through in New York City and around the world, the filmmakers encourage viewers to sympathize with whatever measures Vanessa has to take to become the woman that she sees in herself (see also Namaste 2000, p. 129).

As *Gun Hill Road* establishes Vanessa as both secure in her identity and exploring how she wants to perform femininity, the film also presents teen sexuality as part of her sexual everyday element. Vanessa's sexual experimentation with Chris, a slightly older straight-identified young man, is presented as one of these opportunities that a girl looking for a guy should not miss. Here we see Chris, an 'open-minded straight guy,' who would not mind getting into sexual situations with Vanessa as long as her 'stuff' (read: penis) is not part of the sexual interaction. As their interaction develops over a few weeks, the audience comes to find out that there is a difference between Vanessa's and Chris's expectations of their relationship. While Vanessa desires sexual experimentation with this straight guy, she is also interested in developing other kinds of romantic and emotional intimacy. Vanessa wants to date and potentially occupy public space as a romantic couple. Chris only seems to be comfortable with having sexual interactions with Vanessa in private. Even in the compromised circumstances of her relationship with Chris, Vanessa maintains control and agency. In the beginning of their relationship, Chris offers her financial resources for acquiring hormones and silicon injections. While it is unclear if Vanessa accepts money from Chris, she accepts her relationship with Chris as enough for a time. The incompatibility of Vanessa's desire for a public relationship and Chris's interest in private meetings, however, come to a boiling point when Chris does not 'stand up' and claim Vanessa as his date when some other guys go by and 'holler' at her. After Chris suggests that Vanessa is not his 'real' girl and does not stand up for her, Vanessa abandons Chris and ends the relationship.

Throughout the process of dating and self-definition in *Gun Hill Road*, we see a story that is rarely seen in other films depicting transpeople: that of an empowered transwoman negotiating a romantic relationship and expressing desire. Vanessa's decision to leave an unsatisfying relationship displays a level of feminist self-confidence that rarely appears in conventional romance narratives. Her character's commitment to self-determination models an alternative to common representations of transwomen and cis-gendered women as sublimating their interests to the desires of others. Not only is this film a more positive representation of transwomen than most mainstream films, but it also offers a corrective to popular media representations of the experiences of Puerto Rican queer subjects living in New York City. In particular, this film contrasts the portrayal of Puerto Rican transwomen living in New York City in the 1980s and 1990s. In salsa songs like 'El Gran Varón' (1989) (which roughly translates as 'The Great Son'),[4] written by the Venezuelan Omar Alfanno and popularized by the Bronx-born Puerto Rican Willie Colón, the lyrics recount a story about a man who becomes a transwoman upon her migration from Puerto Rico to New York and ends up dying from complications related to AIDS. Although this popular radio song is generally remembered as a sympathetic attempt to tackle Latina/o American machismo and make a queer theme visible, it has been critiqued as a text because it lacked the critical punch necessary to destabilize larger myths and dichotomies about gender and nation. *Gun Hill Road* enters this media conversation about the wellbeing of transwomen in the city to present gender nonconformity as still an uphill battle. Yet the film certainly offers a more optimistic portrayal of a transwoman who determines her own path. *Gun Hill Road* counters the pessimism of popular narratives like 'El Gran Varón' to celebrate transwomen's identity and sexuality as a healthy expression of self-determination.

Like *Gun Hill Road*, *Pariah* portrays a teenager exploring gender expression and intimacy. The film opens with Alike's experiment with performing masculinity as a means of self-definition in a black queer club. Alike and her best friend, Laura, who is also masculine-presenting, are at a lesbian club. There Laura provides a skill-share role-modeling session of how to pick up femme-presenting women at the club. Alike's experimentation with masculinity at the club introduces how her gender and sexual exploration emerges as a strategy of both survival and desire. As Kara Keeling (2003) argues, butch–femme gender presentation in working-class black lesbian spaces not only enables the 'survival of communities,' but also operates as a 'source of erotic tension and fulfillment, and as a set of personal gender choices and expressions' (p. 42). The fact that the film demonstrates different aspects of Alike's experimentation with becoming a black/lesbian/masculine woman presents this particular coming-of-age experience and Alike's desire as valuable and recognizable.

Lesbian youth experimentation is often informed by many 'what if' questions such as: What happens after a lot of kissing and making out? How can one actually have sex with a woman? Penetrative sex? What do you mean you can fuck someone with your fingers? How do you go down on a woman properly? Do I need to get a strap on and how do I make sure that I am working it properly? Because we know that queer women who are questioning their sexuality engage in these conversations, we were actually not surprised that one of the first funny and sympathetic lesbian moments in the film occurs when Alike is trying on a strap-on dildo that she asked Laura to purchase for her. Not only is Alike upset about the fact that the strap-on dildo represents a super-light-skinned penis, which deeply contrasts with the color of her own skin, but the tension of the scene is accentuated, of course, by the awkwardness of Alike's younger sister's interruption while the dildo is strapped on Alike's body. In front of her sister and even Laura, Alike appears to feel shame for both 'having' to explore these 'tools' for more 'efficient' lesbian sex and the fact that these are 'tools' produced as a result of the commercialization of certain sex toys for women who have sex with women. Alike ultimately rejects the dildo as a phallic white symbol. The staging of the scene suggests that not knowing how to perform 'lesbian' in bed and playfulness would have been as embarrassing for Alike as whipping out a white penis. It is not a coincidence that Alike's symbolic gesture of rejecting mainstream definitions of lesbian sex happens as she develops a very flirty friendship with another young woman, Bina – organically, on her own terms, and in the absence of any 'tools.' In fact, we also observe a shift on her gender presentation – from a butch or aggressive (AG) – or someone who identifies as a 'women and/or female and present themselves as masculine or male' (Keeling 2009, p. 573) to one of fluid masculinity as she begins to develop a relationship with Bina, a young woman with a middle-class feminine aesthetic. Alike's shifting gender presentation develops the broader characterization of Alike as a queer subject-in-process. Rather than depicting the experience of coming out and sexual exploration as just a before and after moment, the narrative movement between Alike's experimentation with black masculinity, sex tools, and intimacy with Bina portray Alike as engaging in an ongoing trial and error process of seeing what works and what does not.

Although the bi-curious Bina ultimately breaks Alike's heart, Alike learns that there is more than one way to 'be' and display butch swagger and confidence. Her sexual experimentation with Bina also leads to her articulation of a lesbian identity in spite of her mother Audrey's attempts to enforce gender and sexual normativity by restricting Alike's access to her friends and her clothing choices. Audrey bans Alike's queer friend Laura from visiting and polices Alike's gender presentation by forcing her to wear a pink sweater to church as opposed to a button-down shirt. Audrey clearly idealizes more feminine churchgoing girls. Even as Audrey polices Alike's gender expression and friendships, *Pariah* ultimately depicts Audrey's efforts as having a limited effect on Alike's gender and sexual exploration. As a result of Audrey encouraging Alike to develop a friendship with Bina, the daughter of a church friend, Alike experiences her first sexual encounter with a woman. After joining Bina at a Tamar-Kali concert and visiting the Christopher Street piers where Alike and Bina run into Laura, Alike goes home with Bina and stays overnight. Laying side by side on Bina's bed, Alike and Bina nervously giggle, and Alike responds to Bina's touch with a kiss. The scene closes after an extended sequence of Alike and Bina passionately embracing each other.

While providing a representation of queer youth intimacy and sexual desire, the scene also illustrates how Alike acts on her desire and moves out of the purview of her mother. From the underground show by Tamar-Kali, a Brooklyn Afro Punk singer and songwriter, to the Christopher Street piers where queer youth of color from across New York City and New Jersey regularly hang out, the film presents Alike's movements and urban landscape as expanding beyond her mother's tightly regulated domestic and religious spaces. The matter-of-fact presentation of Alike's and Bina's sexual exploration in the style of a recognizable lesbian trope – that of the sexual interactions that simply emerge from women's intimacy – points to the paradoxical nature of parents wanting to enforce gender binaries and gender segregation among their children. It also points out parents' naiveté in not being able to recognize how they facilitate non-heterosexual experiences, which in this case is especially poignant since Alike meets Bina as a result of Audrey's efforts to fit in with her church. In a sense, what the parents do not know or even cannot imagine cannot be punished.

Youth resiliency in *Pariah* and *Gun Hill Road*

When comparing *Pariah* to *Gun Hill Road*, a key confluence in the narratives is the representation of the main queer characters experiencing sexual intimacy with people who appear to be 'straight' in their everyday life. Both of the people who become intimate with Alike and Vanessa are curious about the experience of being with these gender–nonconforming people. Alike meets Bina at church while Vanessa meets her lover Chris at a poetry reading in a straight Latino bar in East Harlem. In other words, these films portray how the logic of traditional cultural institutions seen as 'safe' bastions of heteronormativity and places to enforce heterosexuality can facilitate queer relationships. The actual interactions among perceived straight individuals and questioning and queer people flip upside-down the meaning of making fellowship.

While both films reveal queer desire within seemingly normative spaces and relationships, the films' sympathetic portrayal of youth's sexual and gender experimentation hinges on critical characterizations of the attempts by parents to enforce social norms. Both of these films have scenes in which the youth are physically and verbally attacked by their parents because of their disapproval of the children's self-expression of gender. In *Gun Hill Road*, for example, Vanessa's father Enrique forcefully cuts her long hair while telling her, 'I fucking love you. I'm not going to let you do this to yourself. Be strong. Be strong.' This is by far one of the most traumatic moments for Vanessa as she continues to say that 'I'm not pretty anymore.' Vanessa's mother consoles Vanessa following Enrique's violent actions and tells Vanessa that she is indeed beautiful. Later Enrique again attempts to force Vanessa into masculinity by paying for a Latina sex worker to 'initiate' Vanessa into heterosexuality. Following a scene where Enrique forcibly takes Vanessa to the sex worker's apartment and a sequence of close-ups of Vanessa crying while the sex worker reaches for Vanessa's pants zipper, the film cuts to shots of Vanessa desperately crying and gasping for air in the shower at her mother's apartment. Like other women who have also experienced a sexual assault, Vanessa seems to try to wash off the violence of the externally enforced rape. The sympathetic and stark composition of the scenes underscores the trauma Vanessa experiences as a result of the non-consensual sexual experience that her father forced. In the immediate scene following the shots of Vanessa in the shower, she runs away from home. The trauma and sexual violence initiated by Enrique signals his effort to discipline Vanessa's feminine gender identity, gender expression, and sexual desire for men. Vanessa's self-exile following her experience of sexual violence links generational conflict to parents' violent enforcement of normative gender and sexual codes. Enrique's violent attempts to force Vanessa into masculinity encourage viewers to understand parental violence through gender and sexual policing as a commonplace in trans youth's lives. The film also portrays Vanessa as a survivor of sexual violence who decides to abandon a violent home at any cost. As Vanessa walks alone at night, she is faced with the real danger of being homeless in the streets of New York City. The film depicts a common reality of the difficult domestic and institutional barriers to self-determination and safety that trans youth regularly negotiate (see Lowrey & Burke 2010; Stanley 2011). Vanessa's decision to risk homelessness in order to escape Enrique's violence encourages viewers to empathically identify with Vanessa and condemn parental violence against trans and queer youth.

In *Pariah*, parental violence also emerges as Alike confidently expresses her gender and sexual identities. Following her sexual exploration with Bina and rejection the following morning, Alike falls asleep to the sound of her parents arguing on the first floor of the brownstone. Waking from the increasing anger evident in her parents' voices, Alike and her sister descend downstairs, and Alike attempts to intervene in her parents' argument. With Alike's arrival, Audrey turns from demanding that Arthur account for his absences from home, to accusing Arthur of not addressing Alike's masculine gender expression. Audrey demands that Alike needs to confess to Arthur where she hangs out, admit that Laura is her girlfriend, and state that she's a 'nasty ass dyke.' Arthur counters Audrey by entreating Alike to tell her mother that her accusations are false. When Alike does not respond, Audrey rushes at Alike, demanding that she 'say it, say it' and pins her against the wall of the foyer. Alike looks at both Audrey and Arthur and forcefully responds to her mother's face: 'I'm a lesbian; yeah I'm a dyke.' Screaming, Audrey throws Alike to the ground, and Arthur pulls Audrey off her. Following a final shot of Alike curled on the foyer floor crying, the film cuts to Laura comforting Alike at her sister's apartment, indicating that Alike left her parents' home and her mother's violence.

Pariah closes with Alike refusing to return to a violent home and boarding a bus to Berkeley, California, to enroll in an early college program. For Alike, living with Audrey is untenable because of her violent efforts to enforce normative femininity and a heterosexual identity. However, the film does not present the exile of queer youth as an explicit parental ultimatum. Instead, Alike's exile is an act of self-determination. The closing sequence of *Pariah* underscores Alike's agency. Cutting between shots of Alike reading aloud a poem to her sympathetic English teacher and shots of Arthur packing her clothes in preparation for her journey to California, Alike's reading of the poem closes with a stanza about her decision to leave: 'My spirit takes journey / my spirit takes flight / could not have risen otherwise / and I am not running / I am choosing.' Alike's powerful 'I am not running / I am choosing' encourages readers to understand Alike as an agent rejecting Audrey's violent enforcement of heteropatriarchy. In doing so, the film also shifts the trajectory of the generational conflict narrative which structures the majority of the film. The closing scene of *Pariah* and Alike's poem suggest that queer youth can only survive as agents by choosing to leave the heteropatriarchal family. Parental punishment tactics do not stall the queer characters' process of queer self-definition (or, at least, not for long). Alike emerges as resilient in the face of parental violence.

Beyond queer youth: heteropatriarchy as familial violence

As Alike's departure for college marks the violence directed at masculine of center teens, the secondary plot of Arthur's infidelity illustrates how straight-identified characters do not necessarily conform to the heteropatriarchal ideals that queer youth are measured against. Arthur, for example, pursues an extramarital affair while pretending to be faithful to Audrey. While the film does not forestall viewers from sympathizing with Audrey for Arthur's infidelity, its portrayal of Arthur as physically protecting Alike, and supportive of her decision to leave

New York, places his non-monogamy as having a parallel impact to the rupture of the heteronormative family as Alike's gender expression and articulation of lesbian sexuality. Arthur's supportive relationship with Alike further situates Audrey as both the antagonist to Alike's queer self-expression and physical safety, and the primary figure enforcing a heteropatriarchal configuration of the family. It is also clear that Audrey's adherence to compulsory heteropatriarchy negatively impacts her as well. In the scene in which Audrey requires Alike to change from a button-down shirt into a pink sweater and skirt before leaving for church, viewers learn the extent to which Audrey has internalized both religious and social values of respectability and social uplift. Audrey's requirement that Alike and her sister Sharonda wear feminine clothes to church arises out of her desire for social recognition from her co-workers and members of the congregation as a responsible mother. Outside church, Audrey's anxious and performative exchange with Bina's mother indicates that Audrey believes the performance of gender normativity and heteronormativity by her daughters will provide her entrance to the Fort Greene middle- and upper-class social circles which she aspires to join.

Audrey's idealization of normative class, gender, and sexual behaviors at the expense of her relationship with Alike presents the social values of respectability attached to social norms as harmful to queer youth. Respectability, as described by Evelyn Brooks Higginbotham (1993), has historically developed as a discursive strategy deployed by black women to offer a model of self-worth that countered white supremacist logics that ascribed valuelessness to blackness and perpetuated sexual stereotypes about black women. In Higginbotham's foundational study of black women's social movements in the 1920s, black women historically focused on conduct and morals to claim respect and facilitate 'racial uplift' in order to both critique white supremacy and facilitate self-representation (Higginbotham 1993, pp. 194–5). Hazel Carby (1999), Lisa Thompson (2009), Sandra L. Barnes and Mia Smith Bynum (2009), and Shayne Lee (2010) have also identified respectability discourses within twentieth- and twenty-first-century black social institutions, particularly within black religious spaces. Respectability discourses emerge when ideals about sexual decorum and appropriate modes of normative gender expression, particularly black femininity, converge with the social and political efforts by black communities to achieve economic mobility and create positive images of black communities.

A desire for upward mobility and the church community's potential critical evaluation of Audrey's daughters as not respectable provide rationales for why Audrey seeks recognition through the performance of heteronormativity and femininity. Yet, the film also depicts Audrey as lacking friends at work and turning to Arthur as the sole source of emotional and social recognition. Arthur's absence, because of his affair, and his critical appraisal of Audrey's desire for upward mobility contribute to Audrey's desperate search for social recognition through the performance of respectability. Audrey's internalization of heteropatriarchal values and the daily impossibility of finding recognition through performing heteropatriarchy ultimately prove to be emotionally traumatic for both Audrey and Alike.

The characterization of Audrey as driven to enforcing heteropatriarchal norms because of her failed search for social and romantic recognition in normative social and labor structures adds a complex layer to the film's critique of Audrey's violent relationship with Alike. As the film frames Audrey's violence toward Alike as a consequence of Audrey's loneliness and Arthur's lack of emotional engagement, the film allows viewers, particularly viewers who recognize Audrey's struggle, to rationalize her actions even while sympathizing with Alike's struggle for self-definition. Yet Audrey's pursuit of respectability also indexes the traumatic effects of performing heteropatriarchy within a social and economic system built on pathologizing black women and men as non-normative. Her character illuminates what Roderick Ferguson (2004) describes as a key contradiction of late capitalism: the increasing social value ascribed to the heteropatriarchal family even as the drive for profit has historically produced a mobile low wage and an incarcerated labor pool structurally unable to support immediate or extended families compliant with heteropatriarchy or the social valuation of whiteness (p. 17). As the social recognition of black and Latino populations becomes more intertwined with the participation in low- or no-wage labor sectors that disrupt heteronormativity, the logic of white supremacy that values heteropatriarchy and the desire for profit simultaneously renders black and Latina/o populations valuable and disposable. As Ruth Wilson Gilmore (2002) explains, personhood in the United States has been structured by processes such as racism that organize a 'hierarchy of human and inhuman persons that in sum form the category of "human being"' (p. 16). In the United States, Latinas/os, African Americans, Asians, and indigenous peoples historically have been subject to legal and social categorization as inhuman within a system that values whiteness, property ownership, and Christianity. In this context, performing heteronormativity is both compulsory and impossible for populations historically pathologized as non-normative.

The characterization of Audrey illuminates the seemingly impossible task of finding personal and social value in heteropatriarchal social structures and a racial order that devalues black women. The conflict between Alike and Audrey occurs as a result of Audrey's investment in heteropatriarchal values and both experience trauma as a consequence of compulsory heteropatriarchy. In one sense, the film's portrayal of heteropatriarchy as untenable for all of the characters – Alike, Audrey, and Arthur – provides an opportunity to build a radical critique of intergenerational conflict narratives. The failure and violence of heteropatriarchy in the film indicate that we need not only to support queer youth, but also to support healing among heterosexual parents as well. Just as queer youth of color need support and space to heal from the violence of white supremacist and heteropatriarchal institutions, straight-identified people and more broadly families of color need support in challenging social norms and economic practices that structure urban communities' everyday struggle to survive.

The concluding scenes in *Pariah* open up the potential for Alike to begin healing, yet an intergenerational resolution remains beyond the narrative of the film. Alike begins a new journey as she travels to the University of California, Berkeley. The film validates Alike's pursuit of healing and self-determination, yet leaves off-screen any resolution of Audrey's relationships with Arthur or Alike. The film humanizes Audrey by exposing the emotionally traumatic consequences of heteropatriarchal codes for black women, yet it does not represent or suggest a way forward for Audrey to build a supportive relationship with Alike or work through the violence that she experiences as a result of internalizing and performing compulsory heteropatriarchal values. *Pariah* leaves audiences with hope for Alike's future and stasis for Audrey and Arthur. In this way, the film ultimately validates queer youth and non-normative gender expression through the static representation of Audrey's investment in heteronormativity and her commitment to disciplining youth sexuality and gender expression.

Gun Hill Road traces a parallel trajectory of validating queer youth through a portrayal of a parent deeply invested in heteropatriarchy. Unlike *Pariah*'s portrayal of Audrey, however, *Gun Hill Road* more visibly presents Vanessa's father Enrique's efforts to conform to heteropatriarchy through hypermasculinity as a result of the structural and interpersonal violence of the prison industrial complex. The opening sequence of the film shows Enrique lunging toward another man in prison with a razor yelling 'fucking faggot – don't ever touch me – fucking puta.' As the prison guards pull Enrique off the man and chide him for breaking his record of 'good behavior,' Enrique stays silent. While the film does not clarify the off-screen events that prompt Enrique to attack the man, subsequent scenes depicting Enrique's discovery that the man has been released from prison and his violent attack on the man in an alley in the Bronx suggest that Enrique experienced either sexual violence or felt sexually threatened while in prison. The subplot of Enrique's violent attack against the man frames Enrique's investment in forcing Vanessa to perform heteronormativity and hypermasculinity. The juxtaposition of the opening scene of Enrique's violent reaction to homosexuality and Enrique's ensuing violence toward Vanessa follows the trajectory of hegemonic homosexual panic narratives. Homosexual panic narratives describe stories and legal testimony that posit that the perception of unwanted homosexual sexual advances creates a momentary 'psychological condition' that 'causes' a person to attack the person they perceive as making sexual advances (see Kahan 2013, p. 188; Adams et al. 2007). As Eve Sedgwick (1990) explains, the acceptance of homosexual panic's logic in legal circles and medical psychology continues to legitimate antigay violence as acceptable (p. 19).

While it is unclear whether Enrique's anxiety about homosexuality and his violence result from an experience of sexual violence, unwanted sexual advances, or other interactions that may have occurred while incarcerated, the film's portrayal nonetheless implies that his violent actions toward both Vanessa and the man whom he met in prison derive from a combined fear of homosexuality, potential trauma from sexual violence, and fear of others seeing him as homosexual and/or gender non-normative. Moreover, Enrique's homophobic violence and hypermasculine gender expression occur in tandem with his efforts to navigate the limited economic and social opportunities for Puerto Rican men convicted of felonies. Under New York State law, parole rules frequently require people who have been incarcerated to find a permanent residence and employment or face re-incarceration (New York State 2010). After his parole officer reviews Enrique's arrest record spanning 1995 to 2010 and reminds Enrique that any violation of parole – lack of 'gainful employment,' an incident of police contact, or a positive drug test – will send Enrique back to prison, Enrique initially finds employment as a line cook at a Bronx restaurant. Yet as a result of the manager's disrespectful treatment, Enrique quits the job despite its impact on his parole status. The film's representation of the employment conditions faced by people who have been incarcerated in New York State frames Enrique's investment in hypermasculinity as a strategy for claiming social value within a neoliberal urban landscape that encourages heteropatriarchal values while simultaneously dehumanizing and exploiting men of color who perform heteropatriarchal masculinities and sexualities. As the film rationalizes Enrique's violence by linking his hypermasculinity to his violent anxiety about queer sexuality, and the structural racism of the prison industrial complex, *Gun Hill Road* stops short of envisioning a way for *both* Vanessa and Enrique to survive social and state violence. The film portrays Enrique's violent homophobia as a rational result of his experience of the violence of the prison industrial complex, and the closing scene where the New York Police Department arrest Enrique for breaking parole further indicates that challenging the status quo has violent consequences for men of color.

Rewriting queer tragedy: transformative futures

Gun Hill Road and *Pariah* figure the rupture of the heteropatriarchal family as a necessary precondition of queer futures, particularly the survival of gender-nonconforming youth of color. In the films, the conflicts between queer youth and parents committed to heteropatriarchy are only resolved through the expulsion of either the queer youth or the parent enforcing heteropatriarchy. *Pariah* leaves Alike's future open-ended and reflects the very real and often necessary need for queer youth of color to remove themselves from violence. Yet the resolution of the conflict within the heteropatriarchal family through the self-exile of the queer child forecloses the possibility of reworking straight femininity and Audrey challenging the impossible gender and sexual expectations she experiences and transfers to Alike. *Gun Hill Road*, in contrast, closes with the New York Police Department arresting Vanessa's father for violating parole, effectively removing Enrique from Vanessa's life. Just as *Gun Hill Road* cuts short the possibility that Enrique may change his violent performance of heteropatriarchy and hypermasculinity, the conclusion of *Pariah* precludes any potential shift in Audrey's aspirations for respectability. In representing the survival and self-determination of queer youth of color as linked to the removal of a hostile parent or the self-exile of queer youth, *Gun Hill Road* and *Pariah* suggest that the violence and interpersonal cost of heteropatriarchy is so great that transformation or healing seems unimaginable or structurally impossible. A liberatory, healing, or reconciliatory future for queer youth and their given families does not emerge as a possibility in either film.

At the same time that *Gun Hill Road* and *Pariah* foreclose intergenerational relations and a reimagining of normative gender investments, we would like to conclude with a consideration of two brief scenes in *Gun Hill Road* that gesture toward alternative masculinities and family formations inclusive of gender-nonconforming youth of color. Neither Vanessa's mother's lover Hector, nor Enrique's friends, perform hypermasculinity or enforce heteronormativity to the same degree as Enrique. For example, Hector supports Vanessa's gender expression and provides her a place to stay following Enrique's attempt to force Vanessa into compulsory heterosexuality. Even Enrique's close friends approach Vanessa with less hostility than Enrique. After Vanessa refuses to attend a Yankees game with Enrique, his friend Tito asks 'what if that's [Vanessa's] life – that's him' and urges Enrique accept that Vanessa will not follow Enrique's model of masculinity. Later Tito again counters Enrique's performance of hypermasculinity and violence by pulling Enrique away from beating his enemy from prison. Surrounded by other modes of masculinity, Enrique's hypermasculinity emerges as only one response among many possibilities.

While Enrique's friends perform self-secure masculinities, *Gun Hill Road* briefly gestures toward the possibility that Enrique may change. In the exchange following Vanessa's decision to stay with Hector after running away from home, Enrique apologizes to Vanessa acknowledging that he 'made a lot of mistakes' and 'never meant to hurt' Vanessa. Yet as he encourages Vanessa to make her own decisions, Enrique explains to her that 'You're my son. My boy. My baby boy ... I just want you back home son.' Surrounded by other men who have sheltered Vanessa from his violence, Enrique's acknowledgment of his violence despite continuing to address Vanessa as his son illustrates how his investment in gender norms operates as a choice that Enrique makes rather than an innate reaction or the sole approach to navigating the systemic criminalization of Puerto Rican men and the heteropatriarchal values that men of color are measured against.

The fleeting visions of alternative masculinities and family configurations in *Gun Hill Road* reveal the potential for developing inclusive intergenerational relationships that recognize different vulnerabilities to violence within urban communities of color. *Gun Hill Road* ultimately joins *Pariah* in falling short of exploring in-depth alternative masculinities and family configurations inclusive of queer youth. The narrative trajectories of both films stop short of envisioning a way for *both* gender-nonconforming youth and their parents to survive social and state violence. Yet in our discussion of the parallel plot trajectories of *Gun Hill Road* and *Pariah* and the moments of queer self-definition, we hope to have highlighted how these films offer a critical opportunity to consider the ways in which queer and gender-nonconforming youth are not only at odds with systems of compulsory heteropatriarchy, but also the structures of normative gender identities, white supremacy, and economic exploitation. From our close reading of the films, we hope to have elucidated how the patterns and practices of intergenerational relations could be positively affected by a deep questioning of the ways in which gender-nonconforming youth and women and men of color are measured against heteropatriarchal and racialized norms. Compulsory heterosexuality and patriarchal family structures, we learn from the films, can negatively impact both gender-nonconforming youth and families of color.

In closing, the cinematic narratives of *Gun Hill Road* and *Pariah* speak to the potential of a feminist and queer politics of visibility that takes into account the differential consequences of visibility within a het-eropatriarchal system that values whiteness and reinforces economic inequality through capitalism and ongoing US settler-colonialism. The films have the potential for shifting the everyday realities encountered by gender-nonconforming youth by offering an opportunity for view-ers who are parents to understand the potential damage they could be doing to their children for not accepting them as they are. The everyday relevance and emancipatory potential of these films for queer audiences on the other hand is that they portray experiences that queer audiences can potentially relate to. The film reflects those moments when your mom doesn't reply to 'I love you' because you are a lesbian. Or the moment when your father's actions have gone past the point of recon-ciliation. The film leaves queer audiences with an impossible desire for reconciliation among queer youth and parents in the timeframe of the film. Yet we know that reconciliation is a lifelong process and requires a commitment by both parents and youth.

On a broader scale, these films have enduring relevance for feminist and queer political projects for empowerment and social justice. *Gun Hill Road* and *Pariah* realistically capture the feelings of displacement that can only be amended by queer subjects centering their own life narratives *while also* addressing the structures that cause harm within their own lives and in the lives of their families. As such, making queer and gender-nonconforming youth visible through cinema does not necessarily lead to concrete social change or the immediate expan-sion of feminist and LGBTQ political projects. The films can only catalyze self-reflection and dialogue that will require action beyond the screen. Positive change would require a collective reevaluation of social structures – the prison industrial complex, compulsory monogamy and heteropatriarchy, and class structures – that enact violence on urban communities of color and facilitate interpersonal conflict within and outside our given families. Collective healing for both queer youth and parents would not only require reconciliation, but also the transformation of social structures through feminist and queer political projects that simultaneously challenge gender policing, sexism, homophobia, racism, and economic hierarchies. From placing *Gun Hill Road* and *Pariah* in conversation, we hope that our reading of the films reveal the potential and necessity for developing inclusive intergenerational relationships that recognize different vulnerabilities to violence within urban communities of color.

Notes

1. 'Queer' is an umbrella term to refer to all LGBTQ people, as well as an identity which advocates breaking binary thinking and seeing both sexual orientation and gender identity as potentially fluid. While it has been reclaimed as a unifying, celebratory, and neutral term among many LGBTQ people today, historically it has been derogatory and can still be viewed negatively by some. 'Questioning' is an identity for people who are uncertain of their sexual orientation and/or their gender identity. Usage of these words depends on various factors, including national and social location, socioeconomic status, education, language, etc.
2. We use 'gender nonconforming' as an umbrella identity shared by the two main characters because both teenagers' gender characteristics and behaviors fall outside (or in between) traditional masculine or feminine binaries.
3. For the purpose of this chapter we understand 'heteropatriarchy' as a social system that reflects the dominance of men in cultural, legal, and religious spheres as well as references the privileges afforded to heterosexual people based on the assumption that everyone is, or should be, straight. Heteropatriarchy sustains modes and means of political and financial gain that encourage intolerance against groups of people who are not generally valued by the majority of the society. For example, only heterosexual couples can legally marry the person they love in many parts of the world. LGBTQ issues are not included in school curricula. Around the world, very few countries have laws to prohibit employment discrimination against people because of their sexual orientation or gender identity. LGBTQ people are rarely represented in TV shows and movies, ads, songs, magazines, and entertainment in a wide variety of roles. LGBTQ people cannot assume automatic recognition of a spouse as health care decision-maker in medical emergencies – amongst other countless examples.
4. The axiom 'palo que nace dobla'o, jamás su tronco endereza' (or 'a bent sapling will never straighten its trunk') was popularized as a signifier of 'twisted' gender and sexual manifestations through the salsa song 'El Gran Varón,' written by the Venezuelan Omar Alfanno and popularized by the Bronx-born Puerto Rican Willie Colón. Popularized in 1989, the song tells the story of a

macho-raised guy who becomes a transvestite and later dies of AIDS, alone and in the diaspora. While this song is generally remembered as a sympathetic attempt to tackle Latina/o American machismo, it has been critiqued as a text because although it made a queer theme visible, it lacked the critical punch necessary to destabilize larger myths and dichotomies about gender and nation.

References

'About the Film' (2011) *Gun Hill Road*, www.gunhillroad.com/about-the-film. html (accessed 14 February 2013).

Adams, M., Bell, L.A. and Griffin, P. (eds) (2007) *Teaching for Diversity and Social Justice*, 2nd edn (New York: Routledge), Appendix I.

The Aggressives (2005) (Documentary) (New York: Seventh Art Releasing).

La Aguja/The Needle (2012) (Documentary) (Puerto Rico).

All Over Me (1997) (Film) (New York: Baldini Pictures, Medusa Pictures, and Slam Pictures).

Arnold, A. (2012) 'Best of Cine Festival: Mosquita y Mari,' *Chicano Channel Magazine*, http://chicanochannel.com/magazine/2012/03/best-cinefestival-mosquita-y-mari (accessed 12 March 2013).

Barnes, S.L. and Smith Bynum, M. (2009) 'Black Mother–Daughter Narratives about Sexuality: The Influence of Black Religious Symbolism on Attitudes and Behaviors,' in J. Battle and S.L. Barnes (eds) *Black Sexualities: Probing Powers, Passions, Practices and Policies* (New Brunswick, NJ: Rutgers University Press), 357–76.

Cacho, L.M. (2011) 'If I Turn Into a Boy, I Don't Think I Want Huevos: Reassessing Racial Masculinities in *What Night Brings*,' *GLQ*, 18(1), 71–85.

Carby, H. (1999) 'The Quicksands of Representation: Rethinking Black Cultural Politics,' in H.L. Gates (ed.) *Reading Black, Reading Feminist: A Critical Anthology* (New York: Meridian Books), 76–90.

Cohen, C.J. (1997) 'Punks, Bulldaggers, and Welfare Queens: The Radical Potential of Queer Politics?,' *GLQ*, 3(4), 437–65.

Cohen, C.J. (2004) 'Deviance as Resistance: A New Research Agenda for the Study of Black Politics,' *DuBois Review*, 1(1), 27–45.

Coleman, R.R. Means and Cobb, J. (2007) 'No way of seeing': Mainstreaming and Selling the Gaze of Homo-thug Hip-Hop,' *Popular Communication*, 5(2), 89–108.

Cruz-Malavé, A. (2007) *Queer Latino Testimonio, Keith Haring, and Juanito Xtravaganza: Hard Tails* (New York: Palgrave Macmillan).

Dávila, A. (2012) *Culture Works: Space, Value, and Mobility Across the Neoliberal Americas* (New York University Press).

Dorian Blues (2004) (Film) (New York: Daydreamer Films).

Dreams Deferred: The Sakia Gunn Film Project (2008) (Documentary) (New York: Third World Newsreel).

Durham, A. (2007) 'Homegirl Going Home: Hip Hop Feminism and the Representational Politics of Location' (Doctoral Dissertation) ProQuest (accessed 2 March 2013).

Fenced OUT (2007) (Documentary) (New York: FIERCE).

Ferguson, R. (2004) *Aberrations in Black: Toward a Queer of Color Critique* (Minneapolis: University of Minnesota Press).

Gilmore, R.W. (2002) 'Fatal Couplings of Power and Difference: Notes on Racism and Geography,' *The Professional Geographer*, 54(1) (February), 15–24.

Gilmore, R.W. (2007) *Golden Gulag: Prisons, Surplus, Crisis, and Opposition in Globalizing California* (Berkeley: University of California Press).

Gun Hill Road (2011) (Film) (New York: SimonSays Entertainment and A Small Production Company).

Hames-García, M. and Martínez, E.J. (eds) *Gay Latino Studies: A Critical Reader* (Durham, NC: Duke University Press).

Higginbotham, E. (1993) *Righteous Discontent: The Women's Movement in the Black Baptist Church, 1880–1920* (Cambridge, MA: Harvard University Press), 194–5.

Hill Collins, P. (2004) *Black Sexual Politics: African Americans, Gender, and the New Racism* (London and New York: Routledge).

Hong, G.K. and Ferguson, R.A. (eds) (2011) *Strange Affinities: The Gender and Sexual Politics of Comparative Racialization* (Durham, NC: Duke University Press).

Isoke, Z. (2013) *Urban Black Women and the Politics of Resistance* (New York: Palgrave Macmillan).

Johnson, E.P. and Henderson, M.G. (eds) (2005) *Black Queer Studies: A Critical Anthology* (Durham, NC: Duke University Press).

Kahan, B. (2013) 'The Walk-In Closet: Situational Homosexuality and Homosexual Panic in Hellman's *The Children's Hour*,' *Criticism*, 55(2) (Spring), 177–201.

Keeling, K. (2003) 'As "Ghetto Heaven": Set It Off and the Valorization of Black Lesbian Butch–Femme Sociality,' *Black Scholar*, 33(1), 33–46.

Keeling, K. (2007) *The Witch's Flight: The Cinematic, the Black Femme, and the Image of Common Sense* (Durham, NC: Duke University Press).

Keeling, K. (2009) 'Looking for M – Queer Temporality, Black Political Possibility and Poetry from the Future,' *GLQ*, 15(4), 577–9.

La Fountain-Stokes, L. (2011) 'Gay Shame, Latina- and Latino-Style: A Critique of White Queer Performativity,' in M. Hames-García and E.J. Martínez (eds) *Gay Latino Studies: A Critical Reader* (Durham, NC: Duke University Press), 55–80.

Lee, S. (2010) *Erotic Revolutionaries: Black Women, Sexuality and Popular Culture* (Lantham, MD: Hamilton Books).

Lorde, A. (1984) *Sister Outsider: Essays and Speeches by Audre Lorde* (Freedom, CA: Crossing).

Lowe, L. (1996) *Immigrant Acts: On Asian American Cultural Politics* (Durham, NC: Duke University Press).

Lowrey, S. and Burke, J.C. (eds) (2010) *Kicked Out* (Ypsilanti: Homofactus Press).

Manalansan, M. (2005) 'Race, Violence and Neoliberal Spatial Politics in the Global City,' *Social Text*, 84–5 (Fall–Winter), 42–55.

McLeod, K. (2012) 'Pariah' Recap: First Reactions to the Groundbreaking Film,' *GLAAD*, www.glaad.org/blog/pariah-recap-first-reactions-groundbreaking-film (accessed 3 February 2013).

Muñoz, J.E. (1999) *Disidentifications: Queers of Color and the Performance of Politics* (Minneapolis: University of Minnesota Press).

Namaste, V. (2000) *Invisible Lives: The Erasure of Transsexual and Transgendered People* (University of Chicago Press).

New York State (2010) *Parole Handbook*, https://www.parole.ny.gov/intro_handbook.html (accessed 20 January 2013).

Pariah (2011) (Film) (New York: Focus Features).

Paris is Burning (1990) (Documentary) (New York: Miramax Films).

Ramos-Collado, L. (2013) 'The Needle, a Film by Carmen Oquendo-Villar and Jose Correa-Vigier,' *e-misférica*, 10(1), http://hemisphericinstitute.org/hemi/en/e-misferica-101/ramos-collado (accessed 13 March 2013).

Retzloff, T. (2007) 'Eliding Trans Latino/a Queer Experience in US LGBT History: José Sarria and Sylvia Rivera Reexamined,' *Centro Journal*, 19(1), 140–61.

Sandoval, C. (2000) *Methodology of the Oppressed* (Minneapolis: University of Minnesota Press).

Sedgwick, E. (1990) *Epistemology of the Closet* (Berkeley: University of California Press).

Stanley, E. (2011) 'Fugitive Flesh: Gender Self-Determination, Queer Abolition, and Trans Resistance,' in E. Stanley (ed.) *Captive Genders: Trans Embodiment and the Prison Industrial Complex* (Oakland, CA: AK Press), 1–11.

'Story' (2011) *Focus Features*, www.focusfeatures.com/pariah/synopsis (accessed 20 February 2013).

Thompson, L. (2009) *Beyond the Black Lady: Sexuality and the New African American Middle Class* (Urbana: University of Illinois Press).

Wlodarz, J. (2004) 'Beyond the Black Macho: Queer Blaxploitation,' *The Velvet Light Trap*, 53(1), 10–25.

8
Women, Gender, and the Financial Markets in Hollywood Films

Micky Lee and Monika Raesch

Introduction

In *Boiler Room* (2000), a group of loud, young stockbrokers sit at a bar teasing and joking. One of the jokes is about a feminist submitting to the man: 'why did the feminist cross the road? To suck my balls.' This joke illustrates a popular belief that the financial industry is a male-dominated environment. In *The Associate* (1996), a middle-aged, old-fashioned secretary vents to an African American female executive that Wall Street is a sexist place. She says, '[t]he women's movement, it didn't make it to Wall Street.' The executive replies by saying that her achievement is not a result of affirmative action, but of hard work and talent. The financial market is assumed to be a place where anyone – men and women, wealthy and poor – can succeed if one is hard-working, persistent, and money-minded. Given the two contradictory beliefs about the industry, we apply a feminist political economic perspective to analyze how the financial industry is represented in Hollywood films. This approach examines a gendered production, distribution, and consumption of goods and resources. It also critiques how ideology is used to stabilize the unbalanced power relation between the two genders (Lee 2011).

This essay explores what kinds of gender relations are found in fictional films produced in the US on the financial markets from the 1980s. While many Hollywood narratives mention the financial industry, only a few films are centered on the financial industry; this may imply the audience is not interested in stories that take place in the financial world.[1] Prior to the 2008 financial crisis, the American middle class may have thought that the financial markets were too abstract to understand. But the crisis, and its subsequent impact on the average North American, radically reduced the trust that the general public places in financial institutions, while also slowly recognizing how financial markets work. Incidents such as Bernard Madoff's Ponzi Scheme and the collapse of financial institutions like the Lehman Brothers brought to the public consciousness that many fictional characters in movies actually exist in real life. The market has a human face, and is not just an abstraction any longer.

Similarly to Hollywood audiences who ignore the impact of larger financial institutions on their everyday lives, feminists have also ignored these enterprises in their theorizing and interventions. There are few studies on women, gender, and the financial markets (Assassi 2009), and even fewer from a communication perspective. Two bodies of literature are found in women's and gender studies. The first body of literature looks at women investors in eighteenth- and nineteenth-century England (a representative volume is Laurence et al. 2009). In this literature, the financial markets are seen to have liberated women. Capitalism in eighteenth- and nineteenth-century England is believed to have brought along the separation between the public sphere from the private one, and that between communal property from private property (Assassi 2009). The rise of the property concept turned women into a 'thing' that could be owned by men. Despite the fact that speculative activities were seen as a female vice (Freeman et al. 2009), women investors as a group made more money than men did (Carlos et al. 2009). Because women investors had to consult experts and newspapers for advice and information, they participated in the public sphere that was denied to them (Assassi 2009).

The second body of literature looks at the gender nature of global finance and argues that global finance is gender-biased. According to this body of literature, few women occupy decision-making positions; global investment worsens the unbalanced power relation between men and women; high-risk, speculative activities are associated with male traits; and inefficient resource allocation negatively impacts women (Porter 2005; Van Staveren 2002).

In the field of communication, Lee (2014) examined popular books on investment for women and found that women are asked to solve the problems they face in a patriarchal household (for example, the fear of financial hardship after divorce) by participating in a patriarchal market. At times, the market is characterized as masculine, at other times as gender-neutral. Lee further critiqued that popular books are commodities which are produced for money-making purposes. At a macro level, transnational corporations, financial institutions, and households mutually maintain a gendered production, distribution, and consumption of goods and resources. By buying investment books, women who have few financial assets subsidize wealthy households through the latter's ownership of stocks.

Continuing a feminist political economic critique of popular media, Hollywood films are examined in two ways: first, films are representations of gender roles and gender relations in both the household and the financial industry – what are women's roles in relation to men's in the family and in the workplace? Genre is also of utmost importance in gender portrayal. For example, comedy is described as a society's 'collective unconscious' (Belton 1994, p. 135). This light-hearted genre permits the discussion of taboo and sensitive topics without serious undertones (Tasker 1998). For instance, the long-running TV show *Friends* (1994–2004) showed the growing acceptance of a homosexual lifestyle, and by the time *Will and Grace* debuted in 1998 one homosexual had become the main character. Further, the reality television genre has made gay lifestyle a piece of background information about the contestants. One of the most famous is Pedro Zamora in *The Real World* season three (1994), who also brought attention to the sensitive subject matter of being HIV positive. Contestants' gayness does not have a bearing on their ability to succeed in various settings. The more socially acceptable a subject matter becomes, the less it is joked about. A formerly taboo subject matter can then be seriously discussed in the drama genre.[2]

Second, a feminist political economic approach views films as commodities: what kinds of genres, narrative conventions, and images ensure box office success? Hollywood, aka 'The Dream Factory,' is a major entertainment industry, both domestically and globally. It produces pictures to make profits. If a movie flops at the box office the industry will not produce a similar film in the near future in order to avoid another 'miss' and low profit returns. In contrast, successful films may turn into franchises, through sequels, like *Sex and the City* or *Twilight*. In addition, audiences may be drawn to films that are similar to those that they have liked in the past. This dynamic triangle describes the relation between the consumer (the cinema audience), the industry (Hollywood), and the text (the films).[3] The symbiotic relationship between the industry and the audience – illustrated by which films are being produced – provides insights into a dominant ideology of how gender in the financial industry is viewed over time. Since the 1970s, Hollywood has catered to a male audience (Kramer 1998) because of young men's presumed consuming power, and this may constrain the possibilities of gender roles and relations based on the triangle we've introduced above.

For this essay, films released from 1980 to 2012 were examined. Films released prior to 1980 were excluded because they were not readily available for rental. Also, the American public did not view the financial markets as an exciting place prior to the 1980s (Lowenstein 2004). The list was compiled by consulting recommendations in film sites and financial publications such as imdb.com and savingadvice.com. In addition, searches were conducted at the DVD rental site Netflix with the keywords 'financial market' and 'Wall Street.' Only films that show the financial markets as a workplace were included. The financial markets are those where titles are traded (stocks, commodities, mortgages, derivatives). As the selected films span three decades, the analysis makes visible an evolving treatment of the financial industry and the men and women involved. Out of the 15 titles, two are HBO made-for-TV films (*Working Tra$h* and *Too Big to Fail*). Because both received Hollywood funding and/or major distribution, they can be considered together with the theatrical releases. The independent film *Pi* is discussed in the Notes for contrast. All films were directed by men. Both authors watched the films in separate settings to ensure individual investigation and compared notes thereafter to determine whether individual observations were shared.

In the following section, we first explore gender difference in five common themes deduced from the films. The next section focuses on the roles, professions, and narrative functions that women play in the films. The two films *Working Girl* and *The Associate* are compared and contrasted to illustrate how women's narrative functions work. Lastly, we examine gender roles in relation to film representations of the financial markets in three time periods.

Gender difference in five common themes

Five common themes are found in the 15 films. There is no gender difference in the two themes 'festivities' and 'success through hard work and talent'; both women and men can achieve the American Dream. Gender difference exists in the three themes: 'the New York City skyline'; 'deception'; and 'living up to a father's dream.' Specifically, gender difference exists in *how* the two genders achieve the American Dream and what the dream means to them.

Theme 1: festivities

A significant number of films select the Thanksgiving or Christmas holiday seasons as the timeframe for the narratives. Both holidays are associated with family and joy, hence provide a backdrop for 'feel-good' films.

In *The Associate* (1996), a comedy, the story takes place partially during the holiday season. Laurel Ayres (Whoopi Goldberg) represents the holiday spirit well: as a kind and open-minded person, she selected tenants from various backgrounds, including a drag queen. Like Santa Claus, she does not trick others for a living, yet she is forced to pretend to be somebody else in order to have businessmen believe in her. When she gives a speech disguised as a man in the climactic scene of the film, she receives applause, and the men who previously rejected her as a business partner are honored to be in her presence. In this case, Laurel turns the festive season into a metaphor for her character's place in the financial system (this plot twist will be analyzed further under 'Theme 5: deception').

Trading Places (1983) is a typical comedy that uses Christmas to create commentary upon its characters. Two rich, elderly businessmen who are brothers perform a Christmas miracle by switching the places of two people: a highly paid employee, Louis Winthorpe III (Dan Aykroyd) – who enjoys an upper-class lifestyle – and a con man, Billy Ray Valentine (Eddie Murphy), who pretends to be homeless. The brothers bet on one dollar to prove the nature vs. nurture theory. For Billy, this story truly is a miracle. For his counterpart though, it is a nightmare. However, it will eventually end as a nightmare for the two businessmen as well because Louis and Billy decide to get even with them when the bet is discovered. The festive season adds to the drama and bad/good luck of the respective characters: the brothers do not represent a 'giving' spirit, instead they exploit others for their own enjoyment. This film aims to reassure the audience that good persons are rewarded and bad ones are punished; social status and wealth do not matter.

In contrast, in two drama films that were released after the 2008 crisis, festivities are used to show ugly human nature beneath the glittering surface. For example, *Arbitrage* (2012) celebrates the birthday of its main character, Robert Miller (Richard Gere), during the film's exposition. This permits the introduction of his family to the viewers and creates the idea that we are seeing a well-functioning, happy family clan. This impression is turned upside down a few scenes later, when it becomes clear that Miller has a mistress. In another example, *Wall Street: Money Never Sleeps* (2010), a pregnancy is used to comment on the price of blood relations. An occasion that should make future parents and grandparents happy is instead used by the parents-to-be to pressure Michael Douglas's character, Gordon Gekko, into certain actions.

The contrasting functions that the celebrations play within the respective narratives implicitly point out it is personality traits that determine whether characters are antagonistic or protagonistic. Thus, festivities are not used to comment on gender roles – instead, they are used to point out who the good and bad people are, hence persuading audiences to take sides.

Theme 2: success through hard work and talent

The American Dream is further reinforced through the protagonists' humble background. Against the odds of not having an elite education and not coming from a wealthy family, the leads succeed, if not surpass, those from a privileged background. There is no apparent gender difference in the quest for the American Dream, but the path to success is gendered (as will be shown in Theme 5).

Almost all male and female leads are graduates of state colleges and non-Ivy League schools.[4] If they graduated from an Ivy League school, they either attended with a full scholarship (Daniel Seaver (Bryan Greenberg) in *The Good Guy*) or were in the 'wrong' discipline for a financial job (such as Peter Sullivan (Zachary Quinto) who was trained as an engineer in *Margin Call*). The leads who came from a wealthy background and attended elite colleges are shown in a bad light; they are seen as spoilt, arrogant, and out-of-touch elites. Gordon Gekko (Michael Douglas) in *Wall Street*, a City College of New York graduate, speaks for the underdogs-who-turned-top-dogs: 'now all these Ivy league Schmucks are sucking my kneecaps.' Along with holiday miracles (Theme 1), the from-rags-to-riches story suggests that one's background is not as important as one's hard work and morality.

Theme 3: the New York City skyline

In contrast to the above two themes, gender differences are present in the remaining themes. The representation of New York City relates to the gender of the protagonists. Eleven of the 15 films incorporate NYC skyline shots (or the equivalent if the story takes place in a different city. For instance, *The Pursuit of Happyness* (2006) opens with the San Francisco skyline). In general, the financial district skyline of Lower Manhattan in the opening of the film is followed by a scene on Wall Street. In contrast, films that use the financial industry as a backdrop do not incorporate a skyline prominently as this would mislead audiences. For example, *The Good Guy* (2009) is the story about Beth Vest (Alexis Bledel) who is looking for Mr Right and falling for a young Wall Street hot shot. The financial markets show her boyfriend's character, not hers.

Gender difference is noticeable in the usage of the skyline: while both men and women are connected with the skyline, it functions as a metaphor for women's hopes and dreams in the two films in which women play the protagonists (*The Associate* and *Working Girl* (1988)). *Working Girl* opens with a shot incorporating the Statue of Liberty, which represents the American Dream – Tess McGill's (Melanie Griffith) hope to make it in the financial markets. In contrast, in movies with a male lead, the skyline is devoid of such hopeful symbolism and is instead used to present the harsh business world; this is accomplished by the choice of weather and lighting, which signal to the audience that not everything is sunshine. Even when the skyline is shown during a beautiful early morning, as in the case in *Wall Street* (1987), the shot suggests that Wall Street men begin a hard-working day very early. A different meaning of the NYC skyline is found in *Working Tra$h* (1990), which centers on two working-class protagonists. The skyline is juxtaposed with the working-class neighborhood where Ralph (George Carlin) and Freddy Novak (Ben Stiller) live. The meaning created via the cut shows different, seemingly unrelated classes. While connecting women with 'hope' makes them the emotional gender, men are portrayed to be less emotional even if they are hungry for promotions and wealth, thus implying that men are more efficient in the Wall Street work environment.

Theme 4: living up to a father's dream

Fathers' dreams, patrilineality, and father figures are present in many films. In contrast, none of the films emphasizes mothers' dreams, matrilineality, and mother figures. The desire to gain a father's approval is so strong that it leads men to make the wrong decisions. For example, Seth Davis (Giovanni Ribisi) from *Boiler Room* works for a phony investment firm to gain his father's respect. Seth's illegal trading activities nearly cause his father to be indicted by the FBI. Seth redeems his guilt by opting to go to jail rather than making his father lose his judgeship. Bud Fox (Charlie Sheen) in *Wall Street* also redeems himself by helping the SEC indict his boss Gekko who liquidates the aviation firm where Bud's father works.

Living up to a father's dream changes one's fate: Laurel in *The Associate* sets up her own firm by mortgaging the six-apartment house that her father left her. In *Other People's Money*, living up to his violinist father's dream helps Lawrence Garfield (Danny DeVito) – a greedy, heartless investor – to gain a woman's love.

Patrilineality is so important that men need to threaten in order to maintain it. *Wall Street: Money Never Sleeps* shows a softened Gekko who hopes to reunite with his estranged daughter Winnie Gekko (Carey Mulligan) by befriending her boyfriend Jake Moore (Shia LeBeouf) and urging him to: 'try harder [to reunite me and Winnie]. Then you both will have a father.' After the relationship is rekindled between father and daughter, Gekko lies to have Winnie give him her money, flees to London, and launches his business. He only returns the money to Winnie after Jake shows him an ultrasound baby scan. The grandchild in Winnie's womb is the hostage for whom Gekko must pay a ransom to be a grandfather. Like Gekko, Chris Gardner (Will Smith) in *The Pursuit of Happyness* loses his savings, rental apartment, and wife, but he insists on keeping his son even though he could not provide for both of them. He threatens his wife to not 'take my son away from me.'

If the characters do not have an onscreen biological father, they seek a father figure, usually their male bosses. Peter Sullivan (Zachary Quinto) in *Margin Call* continues his former boss's unfinished project, which makes him a hero after unveiling the firm's financial crisis.

The only instance where a mother has a meaningful talk with a daughter is that between Ellen Miller (Susan Sarandon) and Brooke Miller (Brit Marling) in *Arbitrage*. The mother asks the daughter, who believes that 'I have to trust [her dad],' to think for herself. Yet the daughter does not heed the advice. In the last scene, she calls the father a mentor and a friend even though she discovers his fraud. Female approval is rarely present because it is deemed irrelevant to the narrative.

Theme 5: deception

Many narratives suggest that deception is necessary for one to become a successful financial professional. There are three kinds of deception. The first type of deception is justifiable because the protagonist is forced to deceive for a 'good' reason that the audience supports. Deception does not negatively impact the likeability of the character. In contrast, the second and third kinds of deception are usually used by the antagonists or characters who are a blend of both good and bad. A bad person's deception will further strengthen the audience's disliking of that character. A significant gender difference exists regarding the functions of deception, with women only committing the first two types.

The first function of deception is used by the underdog characters because it is the only possible way for them to succeed. These characters are good-at-heart, hard-working, yet are not rewarded for their honest work because of their gender and class. Their failed attempts result in the audiences' support of a deception because they have been treated unfairly. Both female leads – Tess in *Working Girl* and Laurel in

The Associate – have to utilize this form of deception because their male bosses, colleagues, and partners will not take them seriously otherwise. Deception eventually humiliates both women in front of a crowd before they achieve their goals. In *Working Tra$h,* working-class men who deceive are indicted.

However, as these three films are comedies, indictment and humiliation are taken lightly. Given that comedy hints at taboo subjects, these films discuss the marginal role of women and suggest that men are at fault for gender discrimination. In contrast, a likeable deceiver in a drama, such as Bud in *Wall Street,* gets indicted for insider trading but is nonetheless redeemed as he does it naively and without bad intentions. No equivalent female example can be found in existing titles in the drama genre, again pointing at the marginalization of women via omission.

The second function of deception encapsulates the actions of such characters who could succeed without deceiving others, yet choose to engage in such behavior nonetheless. It is their intentional choice to get ahead by deceiving others, such as Katharine Parker (Sigourney Weaver) in *Working Girl.* She deceives her male colleagues by presenting Tess's idea as hers while lying to Tess that her idea is not viable. As she is already in a position of power, she is using Tess's idea to further her career, yet should come up with her own or be honest about the origin of the ideas so that the right person receives credit for them. In *Wall Street: Money Never Sleeps,* Gekko could have used the royalties from writing a successful book to launch his business, yet he deceives his daughter and future son-in-law into giving him money (though he later returns the money). Will Smith's character, Chris Gardner, in *The Pursuit of Happyness* lies about his living situation without any repercussions. Instead, the audience is asked to sympathize with his 'white lies.'

These examples illustrate that men can get away with deception or receive a milder form of punishment although the type of deception they engage in is sometimes severe. Men also regain trust from both the public and the family, such as in the case of Gekko. Female deception is rooted in desperation due to their marginal position. While the audience roots for Tess, we can understand on some level why Katharine behaved the way she did. Despite their deceptions being more innocent, women have to pay for their deeds via humiliation at the hands of men. Katharine will eventually lose the trust and respect of her male colleagues and her lover, all to Tess.

The third function of deception only applies to men. It is used by the antagonists who see deception as the norm. These characters willingly deceive others and have no moral quandaries about it. The consequences depend on how wealthy the man is: *The Good Guy*'s Tommy Fielding (Scott Porter) is a successful stockbroker. He is shown being abandoned by his girlfriend and has no money in his wallet at the end of the film. His punishment, however, is only temporary because he has other girl-friends lining up, and he still has his well-paying job. Jeremy Irons's character John Tuld in *Margin Call* makes close to $100 million a year. His deception not only goes unpunished but is rewarded by being given a bigger bonus. Additionally, men's immoral behaviors are pointed out privately, usually between them and another person, thus preventing them from public humiliation. This stands in contrast to the treatment of the female characters. The message is that men, including the antago-nists, can get away with illegal, morally and ethically inappropriate behavior. This illustrates male privilege in the financial world. Women cannot use this kind of deception because they are suggested to be the weaker gender: they are not strong enough to make it in this tough busi-ness world, are too 'good' to behave like bad guys, and are not smart enough to get away with such behavior (after all, Katharine gets caught in public in *Working Girl*). Omitting a gender from a certain kind of behavior also creates negative connotations about this sex.[5]

Women's roles, professions, and narrative functions

This section surveys women's roles, professions, and representation, which illustrate their relations to men in the household and the work-place. It further discusses the five narrative functions carried out by the female characters. Their functions are very limited when compared to those of male characters.

Women's roles and professions

The female leads often play the roles of girlfriends, secretaries, and professionals in both the financial and non-financial industries. Other women's roles include wives, mistresses, daughters, neighbors, prosti-tutes, strippers, board members, and manual workers. The female leads are most often the girlfriends of the male leads who work in the financial industry. The professions of the girlfriends matter little because they are rarely shown in the workplace (except if they are the secretaries). They are related to men in the household more often than those in the work-place. For example, Winnie in *Wall Street: Money Never Sleeps* is shown in her office only once while she is there talking to the boyfriend who visits. In contrast, the boyfriend is shown in his workplace while his relationship with his colleagues and bosses is explicated. The girlfriends are usually sexualized; they are shown engaging in sexual activities and wear sexy outfits ranging from lingerie to tight work clothes. In *The Associate*, Frank's girlfriend is an extra. She only appears once in red lingerie urging her boyfriend to unwrap her like a Christmas present. There is no indication before or after that he has a girlfriend.

In contrast, the female leads are less often the wives. The wives are represented as middle-aged, sexually less or not attractive, and not shown engaging in sexual acts. Some wives are frustrated because of the husbands' financial woes (*The Pursuit of Happyness, Boiler Room*, and *Working Tra$h*). Others are supportive of their men's efforts to save a company (*Other People's Money*) or to solve a global financial problem (*Too Big to Fail*). The only wife that is sexual is 60-year-old Ellen in *Arbitrage*. She wears shirts that show cleavage. But when she attempts to seduce her husband at his birthday party, he claims that he needs to go into the office, instead sneaking off to see his mistress who is a much younger woman.

Somewhat surprisingly, not all secretaries are sexualized. When they are, they play the girlfriends of the male leads (such as Abbie Halpter (Nia Long) in *Boiler Room*) or they are extras with no names. When they are not sexualized, they play reliable, boring, and sexually unattractive 'office wives' (Marcellus 2011) who plan their male bosses' schedule. As one of them reaffirms to her boss: 'you can rely on me, sir' (*Other People's Money*).

The female leads often play professionals in the financial and non-financial industries. Highly successful investment bankers and lawyers are sexualized; they use their sex and body to consolidate power and to make more money – usually from men. Katharine (*Working Girl*) is a highly paid business executive who has the right background, wealth, and power, yet she had to strip down to white-laced lingerie to seduce Jack Trainer (Harrison Ford) – a man of a lower social and financial status than she is. When a financial professional is non-sexualized, it is because she is middle-aged and African American (Whoopi Goldberg in *The Associate*). This will be elaborated in the next section.

The three films that are critical of the 2008 financial crisis may appear to have more 'progressive' female roles, yet the leads have to be nice-looking and professional at the same time. Sarah Robertson (Demi Moore in *Margin Call*), the chief risk management executive of a financial firm, has long hair, is impeccably made up, and wears form-fitting clothing. Similarly, Michele Davis (Cynthia Nixon) in *Too Big to Fail* is more slender and younger than the real Assistant Secretary of the Treasury of Public Relations and Director of Policy Planning at the time of the crisis. Brooke in *Arbitrage* dresses innocently (always in white and with neckline covered), almost like a daddy's little girl. In addition, the three high-ranking female professionals are seen as dispensable in the workplace: Sarah is used as a scapegoat blamed for the company's problem despite warning her boss about the firm's looming problem. Michele appears to be clueless and naively asks her male colleagues how she could explain the bailout package to the press. Brooke asserts herself to be a partner of her father's firm, but the father tells her that she is only an employee.

Prostitutes and strippers are pervasive in the films. They rarely have a name and some of them do not even have a face – only their body parts are highlighted. They exist to show male bonding and a male-dominated industry. In *Margin Call*, Peter and a colleague search for their recently fired boss in the streets of New York City. Unbeknownst to others, they end up in a strip club. The only female lead who plays a prostitute (Ophelia (Jamie Lee Curtis) in *Trading Places*) is portrayed as a business-minded woman who plans to quit her profession after making enough money. She is not shown doing her 'trade' because her role is mostly as the girlfriend of the male lead. Few women are board members. When they are, the lone woman or two sit among a sea of men in the boardroom. In *Too Big to Fail*, the two female board members have no names, dialogue, or close-up shots. When one woman gets to say one word, 'yes,' she is not shown on camera, which emphasis is on the CEO of Lehman instead.

In addition, few female leads are manual workers. Linda (Thandie Newton), Chris's wife in *The Pursuit of Happyness*, works at a laundromat. She has to work two shifts because her husband does not provide for the family. However, she is unfavorably portrayed as someone who is not supportive of her husband because she does not 'dare to dream.' Essentially, she is an unsympathetic character even though she is an object of misogyny.

Five narrative functions of the female characters

Narrative function describes the role that a character occupies in a story. Hollywood produces formulaic storylines and therefore predictable sets of characters. Linda Seger suggests four character functions in narrative films: 'storytelling function'; 'helping to reveal the main characters'; 'revealing a theme'; and 'adding color and texture' (1992, pp. 122–5). Characters must fulfill at least one of these; otherwise they can be cut, as they do not serve a purpose within the plot. As becomes apparent, women in financial films rarely have storytelling functions;

they are mostly to support the main male character and the story's larger purpose.

Five narrative functions are deduced from the financial films. The first one is to reassure the male leads, meaning assisting to show more sides to the main character. In *Trading Places*, Ophelia rebuilds Winthorpe III's self-esteem. In *The Associate*, before leaving the firm after having been passed over for a promotion, Laurel supports her male colleagues in their new positions.

A second narrative function is to reaffirm positive male action, thus pointing out men's greatness. Penelope (Kristin Holby) and Ophelia – Winthorpe III's first and second girlfriends respectively – take on these roles in *Trading Places*. Penelope first celebrates her fiancé's success. But when he falls from grace, she channels her supportive, loving feelings toward another hot shot. The change of heart also suggests that women are attracted to men's power and wealth as opposed to their personalities. These women also imply that women are easily blinded by power and wealth. In *Wall Street*, Darien Taylor (Daryl Hannah) is designed to point out the greatness of Gekko and Bud. She supports them by being a listener, investing in artwork for them, and redecorating their houses, thus literally adding 'color and texture' on several levels.

The third narrative function is to create conflicts with other women, implying a theme that women are difficult to get along with each other, unlike men who bond easily over drinks in bars and strip clubs. In *The Associate*, Laurel, at first, does not think highly of assistant Sally Dugan (Dianne Wiest). Sally has to prove her computer knowledge and loyalty before Laurel trusts and confides in her. Katharine and Tess's relationship falls apart entirely in *Working Girl*. They represent the stereotypical females who fight over the same romantic partner and the same male patron.

The fourth narrative function is to look pretty: in every film there are extras who, regardless of being secretaries or stockbrokers, are very well groomed and wear extremely form-fitting clothes. They embody the notion of sexiness at the time. Their function is to be looked at by the male characters in the narratives as well as by the (male) cinema audiences. They are the eye candy in the male-dominated financial world. This reinforces John Berger's (1972) observation that 'men act and women appear.'

The fifth narrative function is to betray and/or ruin the male leads. In *Corporate Affairs* (1990), Jessica Pierce (Mary Crosby) aims to destroy Simon Tanner's (Peter Scolarli) career. Her motivation is to take a personal revenge (a previous failed love relationship) in a professional setting, suggesting again the theme that the female gender is weak and is governed by emotions. In *Boiler Room*, Abbie is used as a pawn (controlled by male FBI investigators) to ruin Seth and his colleagues.[6] Lastly, *Arbitrage* illustrates that supporting and ruining someone occupy the opposite ends of a spectrum. A woman can move from one end to the other, as in the case with Sarandon's character Ellen. Her shift on the slide makes her more powerful and unpredictable, thus suggesting the saying 'a man is nothing without his woman by his side.' This also illustrates the evolution of female characters from unequivocally supportive of their men to self-determining the fates of themselves and their children.

Except the fifth function (to betray and to ruin), all other narrative functions imply that the female characters are weak and they are not in control of their own destinies. Using Seger's model, they do not hold the 'storytelling function' which would provide them with power in the story.[7] The functions are connected via dependency on the male characters: a woman is nothing without the man in the household and in the workplace; therefore, the man needs to be supported and encouraged (this also applies to Tess and Laurel, even as lead characters in their respective films). If a man loses a job, so will his female personal assistant; and his wife (and mistress) will also lose their financial support. The fifth function (to betray and to ruin) may imply that women could be strong, yet women are likened to a disorder and a chaos in an otherwise rule-based male world.

Working Girl and *The Associate*: how race, age, and sexual attractiveness matter

Working Girl and *The Associate* are the only two films where the female protagonists drive the story, are given a storytelling function (that is, their actions lead to consequences). Therefore, it is worthwhile to provide some analysis here to determine the nature of gender representation in such a context by connecting to the five themes and narrative functions discussed earlier. In the two films, the characters face obstacles in advancing their careers in the financial industry, but the ways in which they overcome the difficulties are different because *how* they succeed is determined by their ethnicity, age, and sexual attractiveness.

Working Girl's Tess (played by Melanie Griffith) is white, sexually attractive, and younger (30-year-old). As a secretary, she wears heavy makeup and short skirts. Her appearance makes her a target of sexual harassment, but it helps her to draw attention from Jack, a potential business partner, who exclaims: 'she dresses like a woman' and 'you surely are pretty.' While the character attracts Jack, the body of Griffith is used to sexually allure the (male) audience. In one scene, she wears black lingerie and looks at herself in a mirror while both her boyfriend *and* the audience look at her. In another scene, she gets dressed in front of two mirrors, which reflect every angle of her body (Function 4: to be looked at), this for the benefit of the (male) theatre audience.

When Tess pretends to be her boss when pitching an idea to Jack, a potential business partner, she does not tone down her sexuality. Instead she switches from a working-class, unprofessional look to a 'simple, elegant, impeccable' look of an upper-middle-class woman who flaunts her body in designer dresses. Tasker (1998) suggested that cross-dressing is about gender as well as class. She wrote: 'for women in cinema, cross-dressing is almost always about status' (p. 26). She adds that to working-class women, femininity is a costume, a form of parody. Once Tess gains confidence in the new persona, she competes with her boss for men and business (Function 3: to create conflicts with other women).

In contrast, Laurel in *The Associate* has no family or love life. It is not apparent if she has had any lover in the past. Her sexuality is unstated because she is not shown as having intimacy with either men or women. Her lack of conventional femininity (such as long, straight hair, form-fitting clothing) may be interpreted as empowering because she does not use her sex to sell her talent. However, both Laurel and Goldberg are denied to be a sexual being in the first place. Playing a romantic and sexual role is not an option for Goldberg if she wants to be successful in Hollywood. Akin to Goldberg's marginalized position in Hollywood, Laurel's status as an African American woman in the financial industry is also marginalized by her befriending a freak (a drag queen neighbor), a geek (a computer company owner), and a loser (an old-fashioned, middle-aged secretary who is belittled by her boss).

Ironically, Laurel's lack of sex life changes when she pretends to be an old, white, and wealthy man, Cutty, who cannot fight off beautiful, younger, accomplished women who literally chase Cutty for sex. One of them throws herself at Cutty/Laurel in a hotel room, and eventually claims to carry Cutty's baby, giving Laurel a family that she does not have. Later in the film, Laurel discloses in public that Cutty is indeed a woman in disguise (Theme 5: deception). Once her deception is made public, she shuts herself in her apartment and is reluctant to go to the church to light a candle for her deceased father, thus rendering herself to be a lone soul during the holidays (Theme 1: festivities; Theme 4: living up to a father's dream).

Although both *Working Girl* and *The Associate* show how females overcome obstacles to advance their career in the financial industry, the two characters cannot be interchanged; that is, Laurel could not be Tess and vice versa. If Laurel, a 40-year-old black woman, were a secretary in a trading firm, she would be in a dead-end career. She would not turn heads and have a white man falling in love with her. Essentially, there would be no story. If she were shown living in a black community, her career struggle would be interpreted as a race problem rather than a gender problem. This would alienate the majority of the audience, which is not what Hollywood, as a money-making industry, desires. On the other hand, if Melanie Griffith played a high-ranking executive, she would not need a male disguise to have her chance at success. It would also be unconventional for her to not have a lover in the film.

Both films are at times critical of the white male-dominated financial industry: the male characters are blatantly sexist and are often less smart and less hard-working than the women. This once again shows male privilege in the financial profession. By showing the male characters as such, it is harder for critics to denounce the many gender and racial codified images in the films because those images can be dismissed as a criticism of a male-dominated financial industry. In fact, those images are used to keep the audience in a comfort zone – that is, although the leads are women and they achieve the American Dream (Theme 2: success through hard work and talent), they do not challenge white, male norms.

A younger, white woman has to use her sexuality on screen while an older, black woman has to be denied any sexual agency or romance. Because the audience has difficulty seeing Goldberg as a woman (Tasker 1998), the producers would rather show a rich, white businessman (Laurel's disguise) kissing another man than a black woman kissing a white man. However, the plot twist is easily mistaken as Hollywood taking a liberal stance toward homosexuality and race. The conservative, all-white, all-male club members are first disgusted by the same-sex kiss. When Laurel slowly removes her gloves, wig, and mask, the members turn their disgust from the display of homosexuality to her gender and race. The same-sex kiss is casually brushed aside as a non-issue. The black servers first applaud Laurel for her courage in crashing the all-male club as a *black woman* (not as a man kissing another man), then the members follow. The film director could have chosen Laurel to first reveal her gender and race, then her kissing a white man. By not doing so, the director first avoided showing Goldberg as a sexual being, second, reduced the same-sex kiss to a side note that does not need to be worked into the narrative. In addition to being denied sexuality, Goldberg's blackness is also toned down by her not living in a black community, by not having black friends, by not doing 'ethnic' things, and by her fluency in white male norms, such as demeanors and leisure activities.

Discussion: women, gender, and the financial markets in Hollywood films

Have there been changes in the gender representation in financial films? The answer is a resounding yes. Because a feminist political economic approach decenters the media of communication (Mosco 2009), films are not seen as a self-contained entity. Gender representation in films is influenced by the changing nature of the financial markets and is constrained by the genre.

Films on the financial industry can be categorized into three distinct periods differentiated by genres. The first period (1980s and 1990s) is dominated by comedy; the second and the third periods partly overlap with the second starting from the early 1990s, and the third starting after the 2008 financial crisis. Drama and thriller are popular genres in both periods but the financial industry is essential to the narrative in the third period. Because films follow established narrative conventions, gender roles are used to achieve specific goals. There has been an expansion of women's roles and professions in the third period, but the changes in men's roles are more remarkable. Thus, men are the focal point in all three periods.

In the first period, the financial industry is non-essential to the narrative, it only provides an excuse for an excessive amount of money and sex. From 1983 (when *Trading Places* was released) to 1996 (when *The Associate* was released), the Dow Jones Index rose sharply from 770 to 5000 (source: stockcharts.com). Easy money and holiday miracles manifest the 'feel good' nature of comedy. How else is it easier to be wealthy than being a black con man who is given a lavish, upper-middle-class lifestyle overnight (*Trading Places*)? Or janitors finding insider trading information in trash cans (*Working Tra$h*)? In the world of excess, women's bodies are a form of currency. In *Wall Street*, Gekko defines for Bud that a successful man can 'afford a girl.' Later on, he adds, 'I gave you Darien! I gave you your manhood! I gave you everything!' In *Other People's Money*, talking about business is the same as talking about sex. Lawrence proposes a romantic dinner date every time lawyer Kate Sullivan (Penelope Ann Miller) wants to talk about business. She however plays along with Lawrence's sexual harassment by being a seducer. Business talk is in the guise of sex talk, and vice versa. From a male perspective, both business and sex can be sold and bought.

In the second period, from the 1990s onwards, the financial industry is evil, greedy, and dark. Similar to film noir of the 1950s, men's money (*Boiler Room*) and honesty (*The Good Guy*) are at risk in the dangerous financial markets. Also similar to film noir, women are the *femmes fatales* (such as Abby in *Boiler Room*). Interestingly, money is a *femme fatale* as well because it causes a man's downfall. In *Wall Street: Money Never Sleeps*, speculative activities are said to be 'the mother of all evil.' Further, Gekko asks his future son-in-law Jake what he thinks about money: 'What about money? Do you like her? She lies there in bed at night with you, looking at you, one eye open. Money's a bitch that never sleeps. And she's jealous. And if you don't pay close attention, you wake up in the morning, and she might be gone forever.' The men have a mutual understanding of why money is a female.

The third period commenced after the 2008 financial crisis when the Dow Jones Index plummeted to 6500 from a height of 14,000. The financial market is essential to three out of the five films released (*Margin Call*, *Too Big to Fail*, and *Arbitrage*). Films in this period are introspective of the financial crisis; they attempt to find out what went wrong yet harbor no hope for morality and fairness. Unlike films in the first two periods, the good people are not always rewarded and the bad ones not necessarily punished. The endings are also more ambiguous, given that no satisfactory solution has yet been found and audiences are still living the aftermath of the collapse that the films are discussing.

Women's roles and professions are more expansive in this period, yet they are still the sexy secretaries in tight short skirts, the strippers, the supportive wives, and the *femme fatale*. There are a few high-ranking women professionals. However, these characters are rendered insignificant as the story develops; their actions are inconsequential. Brooke, after discovering her father's fraud, takes no action thereafter (*Arbitrage*). It becomes apparent that while women's roles have evolved they still cannot gain real power and control by themselves without men. This weakens the storytelling function of women's characters, unlike comedy in the 1980s and 1990s where women's storytelling function could be used to comment on taboo issues. Only in an ensemble cast, such as Moore's character Sarah Robertson in *Margin Call*, can a woman share a storytelling role.

The most remarkable change in gender representation in the third period (after the 2008 crisis) is that the male leads exhibit different characteristics than those in the first two periods. They are more vulnerable, morally failing, and do not redeem themselves. Against the now weaker sex, women are allowed to judge men, to determine their fate, and to guard morality. However, this does not mean that women are getting more empowered; it only means that men are failing their manhood. Similar to films made in the 1930s during the Great Depression, masculinity is in crisis, but women's lives are shown less disrupted than men's lives (Gilmour 1998). The opening scene of *Margin Call* shows two women marching into a conference room to fire a high-paying veteran male employee. In the same film, Kevin Spacey's character Sam Rogers has to betray his conscience: even though he disagrees with his boss, he has to submit because he needs the money. In the last scene, he emotionally digs a grave for the dead (female) dog while his ex-wife tells him he trespasses on her property.

The case of the failing man is the most obvious in *Arbitrage* in which Gere's character Miller is yelled at by his male business partner, wife, mistress, daughter, and even a young, black man with a criminal record. He says 'I'm sorry' more than any male characters in other financial films. His daughter, in Miller's opinion, is a capable, moral, young woman while the son is a fool. Although he is able to get away with two major crimes, his wife forces him to choose between handing over his wealth to the daughter or going to jail. The film ends without a definite answer of what Miller chooses. However, in an earlier confrontation with his daughter, he explains why he commits fraud: 'I'm a patriarch, that's the role. I'm going to play it.' Although women's roles are more complex in the third period, the patriarch still takes center stage, because it is a role that has to be played in Hollywood films.

Notes

1. The MPAA provides an overview of the number of Hollywood films released each year, ranging from 455 to 638, in the time period 2002–11.
2. The drama *Philadelphia* (1993) illustrates societal acceptance of the HIV virus and a homosexual lifestyle. The movie grossed almost $77.5 million at the US box office alone (the international markets added almost another $130 million) (boxofficemojo.com). With a production budget of $26 million, the film was a critical and commercial success that illustrated that audiences desired to learn more about the previously taboo subject matters. In contrast, when heartthrob actor Rock Hudson died in 1985, a homosexual lifestyle was a taboo, and only recently is this part of his life more openly discussed, most notably in the documentary *Rock Hudson: Dark and Handsome Stranger* (2010).
3. The dynamic triangle is also referred to as the 'rhetorical triangle' and is a modification of the traditional version that included Logos (Text), Ethos (Author), and Pathos (Audience).
4. In US higher education, Ivy League colleges are elite, top-tier institutions. Some have suggested that only the graduates from three places (Harvard

University, Yale University, and Princeton University) have a chance to get an investment job.

5. Marcy Dawson (Pamela Hart) in *Pi* is assisted by two male colleagues, suggesting that even though she is the boss, she cannot handle the situation without male assistance. The same message is sent in *Too Big to Fail* when the chief female PR officer, Michele Davis (Cynthia Nixon), requires the assistance of her male colleagues to formulate a public statement.

6. *Pi* uses a female character in a similar way; Marcy Dawson (Pamela Hart) has to track down and intimidate Maximillian Cohen (Sean Gulette). When she does not succeed by herself, she is accompanied by male colleagues.

7. The exceptions are Tess and Laurel in the respective comedies, *Working Girl* and *The Associate*.

References

Arbitrage (2012) (Film) (US: Lionsgate).
Assassi, L. (2009) *The Gendering of Global Finance* (New York: Palgrave Macmillan).
The Associate (1996) (Film) (US: Buena Vista Pictures).
Belton, J. (1994) *American Cinema/American Culture* (New York: McGraw-Hill).
Berger, J. (1972) *Ways of Seeing* (London: BBC/Penguin).
Boiler Room (2000) (Film) (US: New Line Cinema).
Carlos, A.M., Maguire, K. and Larry, N. (2009) 'Women in the City: Financial Acumen during the South Sea Bubble,' in A. Laurence, J. Maltby, and J. Rutterford (eds) *In Women and Their Money: Essays on Women and Finance* (London: Routledge).
Corporate Affairs (1990) (Film) (US: Concorde Pictures).
Freeman, M., Pearson, R. and Taylor, J. (2009) 'Between Madam Bubble and Kitty Lorimer: Women Investors in British and Irish Stock Companies,' in A. Laurence, J. Maltby, and J. Rutterford (eds) *Women and Their Money: Essays on Women and Finance* (London: Routledge).
Gilmour, H. (1998) 'Different, Except in a Different Way: Marriage, Divorce, and Gender in the Hollywood Comedy or Remarriage,' *Journal of Film and Video*, 50(2), 26–39.
The Good Guy (2009) (Film) (US: Roadside Attractions).
Kramer, P. (1998) 'Women First: "Titanic" (1997), Action-Adventure Film and Hollywood's Female Audience,' *Journal of Film, Radio, and Television*, 18(4), 599–619.
Laurence, A., Maltby, J. and Rutterford, J. (ed.) (2009) *Women and Their Money: Essays on Women and Finance* (London: Routledge).
Lee, M. (2011) 'A Feminist Political Economy of Communication,' *Feminist Media Studies*, 11(1), 83–7.
Lee, M. (2014) 'A Feminist Political Economic Critique of Women and Investment in the Popular Media,' *Feminist Media Studies*, 14(2), 270–85.
Lowenstein, R. (2004) *Origins of the Crash: The Great Bubble and its Undoing* (London: Penguin).
Marcellus, J. (2011) *Business Girls and Two-Job Wives: Emerging Stereotypes of Employed Women* (Cresskill, NJ: Hampton Press).
Margin Call (2011) (Film) (US: Lionsgate).

Mosco, V. (2009) *The Political Economy of Communication,* 2nd edn (London: Sage).

Other People's Money (1991) (Film) (US: Warner Bros. Pictures).

Pi (1998) (Film) (US: Live Film & Mediaworks Inc).

Porter, T. (2005) *Globalization and Finance* (Cambridge: Polity).

The Pursuit of Happyness (2006) (Film) (US: Columbia Pictures).

Rock Hudson: Dark and Handsome Stranger (2010) (Film) (Germany: Florianfilm GmbH)

Seger, L. (1992) *The Art of Adaptation: Turning Fact and Fiction into Film* (New York: Holt).

Tasker, Y. (1998) *Working Girls: Gender and Sexuality in Popular Cinema* (New York: Routledge).

Too Big to Fail (2011) (TV Film) (US: HBO).

Trading Places (1983) (Film) (US: Paramount Pictures).

Van Staveren, I. (2002) 'Global Finance and Gender,' in A. Schoste and A. Schnabel (ed.) *Civil Society and Global Finance* (London: Routledge).

Wall Street (1987) (Film) (US: 20th Century Fox).

Wall Street: Money Never Sleeps (2010) (Film) (US: 20th Century Fox).

Working Girl (1988) (Film) (US: 20th Century Fox).

Working Tra$h (1990) (TV Film) (US: Fox Network).

9

Gladiator in a Suit?: *Scandal's* Olivia Pope and the Post-Identity Regulation of Physical Agency

Jennifer McClearen

Introduction

The US television drama *Scandal* (2012–present) provides a rare feature in American television: an African American heroine wielding considerable political clout as the series' protagonist. Olivia Pope (Kerry Washington) is a clever, driven, and highly successful crisis manager whose clients include politicians, businesspeople, and others with deep pockets and powerful allies. A self-professed 'gladiator in a suit,' she fights political battles for her clients and friends with fierce determination. At the Pope and Associates crisis management firm, Olivia surrounds herself with a team of law and intelligence specialists who assist her in spinning public relations stories, covering up accidental deaths, and brokering clandestine negotiations. Each episode revolves around a crisis while introducing numerous other complications – all with the lead gladiator charging the way. The series is brimming with melodrama, intrigue, and, yes, numerous scandals encircling the first black female protagonist in a US television drama in nearly 40 years (Vega 2013).[1]

While the mere presence of a powerful black woman in a highly successful television series is certainly monumental, *Scandal* provides fodder for examining the state of feminism via its depiction of an empowered black heroine. Olivia Pope's ability to thrive in a world governed by the white male elite might suggest that she lives in a post-racial, postfeminist society – one free from institutional racism and gender discrimination that might inhibit her professional ascent. In each episode, *Scandal* depicts its protagonist as leading her gladiators with fortitude; her poise and posture reflect a physically assured heroine who is unfettered by dangerous situations or obstacles to her goals. Nevertheless, a peculiar change happens to Olivia's performance in intimate interactions with her white male lovers. In these scenes, Olivia often retreats, cowers, and unsuccessfully resists the advances of her lovers in a manner that contradicts the agency she radiates when managing employees, clients, and adversaries. While the show's depiction of an empowered heroine certainly gives pause to consider the progressive nature of this representation of a black woman on television, a close reading of Olivia's performance of physical agency – the ability to assert, protect, and defend one's body emotionally, mentally, and physically – reveals ingrained gendered and racial discourses of the body. In keeping with this, this chapter studies the representation of Olivia's empowerment via post-identity discourses and contrasts those with concurrent portrayals of her fragility. I perform close readings of Olivia's physical performance in seasons one and two of *Scandal* to highlight the show's treatment of her physical agency. In particular, I scrutinize the intersecting post-race and postfeminist discourses embedded in the text to illuminate scenarios where Olivia is a powerful agent, and others where she is not.

Post-identity ideologies celebrate the achievements of feminist and racial justice movements and cite that progress as evidence of the redundancy of further feminist or racial justice dialogues (Bonilla-Silva 2003; Forman & Lewis 2006; Gill 2007; McRobbie 2007; Tasker & Negra 2007) – effectively rendering feminism irrelevant for women of color in the twenty-first century. Yet, the assumption that black women have achieved equality overshadows protracted racial and gender inequalities. I argue that postfeminist and post-racial discourses valorize Olivia's professional clout as representative of a post-identity society. At the same time, characterizations of her as lacking physical agency in interactions with white male lovers reveals the cracks in the façade of universal empowerment.

Locating *Scandal* within post-identity literature

Reading *Scandal* through a lens of post-identity politics situates the television show within a perceived moment of unparalleled progress that is characterized by the belief that the histories of racism and sexism have been largely overcome and equality prevails in the twenty-first century. Scholars in the US and UK broadly argue that postfeminist discourse appropriates some of the successes of women's rights movements in the Western world and highlights greater opportunities for women at work and at school while celebrating the success of individual women in these arenas (Gill 2007; Joseph 2009; McRobbie 2007,

2008; Tasker & Negra 2007). Post-race discourse generally imagines Western culture as an equalized playing field in which a person of any race or gender can climb the career or political ladder (Bonilla-Silva 2003; Forman & Lewis 2006; Joseph 2009). Individual success narratives of women and people of color reign supreme while racial and gendered inequalities, such as the enduring legacy of violence against women (Gill 2007) or the disproportionate population of black men in US prisons (Lopez 2010), remain outside contemporary understandings of racism and sexism.[2]

Academic and popular debates surrounding the supposed achievements of a 'post' society are most prevalent in the US; however, various other scholars have discussed manifestations of post-race ideology throughout Britain and Europe (Aradau 2009; Gilroy 1998; Lentin 2012). Lentin (2012) links post-race discourse in the UK to contemporary multiculturalism debates surrounding immigration. Critics of multiculturalist policies assert that an increased focus on tolerance toward difference has led to segregation and unrest. In this logic, access to social, economic, and political power in the UK is no longer hindered by racial prejudice; thus, multiculturalism is redundant in a post-racial society. Although different exigencies and cultural and political contexts inform the postfeminist and post-race discussions on either side of the Atlantic, American and British post discourses favor viewing racial and gendered barriers as historical relics of a now 'civilized' West.

A popular media text such as *Scandal* affords the opportunity to examine how 'post' discourses intersect and interact with one another in framing a professionally successful black woman. Joseph (2009) and Banet-Weiser (1999) describe a media climate that allows narratives of a black woman's individual prosperity in her profession, yet regulates the boundaries of that success via post discourses. A continual focus on narratives of progress allows dominant understandings of other issues to remain unchallenged. This particular analysis of *Scandal* seeks to expand understandings of intersecting discourses of the body embedded in post-identity politics to consider how representations of physical agency can serve as an undermining force within a text that depicts an otherwise empowered black woman.

Performing physical agency

The terms 'physical,' 'embodied,' or 'bodily' agency collectively illustrate an attempt to expand feminist understandings of agency to also encompass the body and women's control over it (De Welde 2003; Roth & Basow 2004). The terms converse with a history of emphasizing cognitive agency in feminist literature (Bannerji cited in De Welde 2003) and highlight the under-theorization of the body within scholarly understandings of agency. Feminist literature on self-defense and sport seems to offer the most concerted efforts to include the body within discussions of agency (Dowling 2002; Lawler 2002; Roth & Basow 2004). Scholars who examine physical agency within self-defense contexts assert that the agency of the body, that is, the confidence in one's ability to assert or defend oneself physically, is a key element of empowerment (De Welde 2003; Dowling 2002; McCaughey 1997). These authors point to the embodied experiences of athletics and/or self-defense training as a performance that is dependent on the subject's social-psychological concept of bodily efficacy.

Scholars who examine gender, race, and sexuality as performative identities expand notions of physical agency to connect broader social and cultural structures to an individual's performance of agency (Butler 2004; Johnson 2003; Noland 2009). Butler (2004) reminds us that 'self-determination becomes a plausible concept only in the context of a social world that supports and enables that exercise of agency' (p. 7). In other words, social environments often promote physical agency for certain identity groups and deny it to others. In US culture, the identities granted physical agency and self-determination are most commonly able-bodied, white, heterosexual, middle- and upper-class men. In contrast, Johnson (2003) notes that black bodies have historically been sites of violence and trauma, and this history exacts a collective memory of that trauma that can negatively impact an individual's performance of agency. Butler and Johnson's work cautions us that even though an individual black woman might not have experienced racial and sexual violence on her personal body, the collective memory of violence against her race and gender can negatively impact her ability to perform physical agency.

As a result of these interventions in our understandings of physical agency and performance, Olivia Pope's agency (or lack thereof) can be framed as more than just the individual assessment of one character on one television show. Her physical agency is tempered by racialized and gendered perceptions of the black female body within a society that is believed to be beyond such regulating forces. Moreover, Olivia's vacillation between performing physical agency in some contexts to embodying passivity in others signals a slippage in the post discourses that are of central concern to this discussion.

The physical agency of Olivia Pope

Olivia Pope is a character who displays an exceptional ability to conquer the melodrama she faces each episode. She freely accesses power players and excels at convincing them to abide by her rules. Her clients include congressmen, businesspeople, governors, billionaires, a South American dictator, and the President of the United States. Olivia explains the depth of her connections to the Director of the CIA in *Snake in the Garden* (season two, episode 17): 'Half my clients have your pay grade or higher which means half my clients would happily intervene on my behalf and kick your ass in whatever special way their office allows.' As Olivia stands toe-to-toe with one of the most powerful intelligence officers in the country, she remains undaunted by his position and assures the man that her influence in Washington runs deep. Via the logic of post-identity discourses, Olivia Pope can succeed in each episode because there are few remaining racial or gendered barriers to restrict her.

Olivia's capacity to perform physical agency on the job is best illustrated through the show's introduction to the character in the series premiere, *Sweet Baby* (season one, episode one). We first meet Olivia as she and Steven, one of her employees, are riding a freight elevator to a clandestine meeting with the Ukrainian mafia. The dialogue begins with the characters having two conversations at once – Steven highlighting that they are entering a dangerous situation and Olivia inquiring into Steven's love life. As Steven's fear climaxes with an attempt to articulate the severity of the situation, Olivia remains untroubled and relaxed. A wide shot shows the full frames of the two characters as Steven emphasizes his distress. Steven faces Olivia squarely and stands less than a foot away from her as he leans further into her personal space. In contrast to Steven's tense and earnest posture, Olivia's body is turned slightly away from him. Her hands rest casually in her coat pockets and her shoulders are relaxed. After hearing Steven's fears, Olivia faces forward and grins a close-lipped smile, ambivalent to Steven's objections to the impending meeting. Steven responds to Olivia's serenity by assuring himself that Olivia will prevail. He tells her, 'We are in a situation here. Focus. Do what you do.'

Scandal's opening moments establish Olivia as a woman with unobstructed physical agency. The scene begins by showing her as cool under pressure. Her relaxed posture and unruffled demeanor present her as self-assured and able to manage life-threatening situations. In fact, conventional notions of gender and race might have the audience expecting Steven, a white man, to be the confident professional in control of his environment. However, Steven is visibly more concerned about the Ukrainians than Olivia, which speaks to *Scandal*'s commitment to a post-identity discourse that showcases a minoritized subject's ability to rise above previously institutionalized raced and gendered limits. In an interview with Oprah Winfrey, Kerry Washington describes her character as 'a fully realized woman' who 'is not just in this [professional] role because she is African American' (Washington & Winfrey 2012). Following this logic further, any remaining vestiges of racism or sexism become irrelevant as Olivia thrives within a new cultural moment.

Olivia's interactions with the armed Ukrainian mafia in the show's premiere further highlight her ability to radiate bravado in the dangerous situations her unique profession requires. Olivia approaches the international criminals first with Steven in tow. Her pace is brisk and determined and her shoulders display the same relaxed posturing as the elevator scene. Never registering fear or acknowledging the fact that the Ukrainian men are armed, Olivia manages the situation with assertive poise. As she negotiates with one of the men, she emphatically leans into his physical space and looks him squarely in the face. The arrangement and contrast among the characters' body positioning do not demarcate a difference in bodily size; Olivia negotiates with the man at eye level and stares unblinkingly as she frightens the men with her political connections. Once the men falter and agree to her terms, Olivia blithely says 'good boys' and exits the room in the same brisk and unwavering manner she entered it.

Scandal presents its heroine as able to control her environment with assurance – a characteristic required of a high stakes crisis manager and supported by post-identity understandings of the professional possibilities for women of color. Olivia's ability to dictate the terms of a hazardous negotiation is not hindered by her race or gender. The men's bodies never infringe into her personal space and the brief flash of a gun only hints at potential danger to her body. Throughout the scene, Steven is positioned in the background and never speaks or physically intervenes in the negotiations. The absence of Steven's orthodox authority as a white man forefronts Olivia as capable of intervening on behalf of her clients and herself. She does not need to be saved; she is a gladiator who embodies the authority of her job and rarely meets a true professional rival.

The 'flaws' of Olivia Pope

Even as the show portrays an empowered black heroine, *Scandal* refrains from depicting Olivia as a flawless or one-dimensional character; even the gladiator has cracks in her armor. Kerry Washington (2012) describes the characteristics of Olivia Pope that she finds most appealing in an interview with Oprah Winfrey:

> I love the dichotomy of how powerful she is – that Olivia Pope is empowered, powerful, in control, and in charge and strong in her professional life. And in her personal life, she is a mess, she's vulnerable, and she's torn. What a fully realized human being!

Washington finds the character refreshing; she is not a stereotypical black woman, she is not tokenized, nor is she flawless, which are characteristics Washington and Winfrey admonish in traditional representations of black women in mainstream media. They perceive Olivia as possessing a humanized depth; her flaws contribute to their ability to identify with her. Both women herald Olivia's complexity as a representational advancement for black women. Washington even suggests that her character in Quentin Tarantino's slavery-era action film, *Django Unchained* (2012), acts as a comparison to Olivia, which demonstrates 'a new moment for our culture.' She says, 'Olivia Pope is the answer to Broomhilda's prayers about what might be possible one day.' Washington's contrast between these two characters seeks to register the magnitude of political and cultural advancement post-slavery.

While *Scandal*'s significance in twenty-first-century television is evident, Washington and Winfrey favor the discourses of progress and overlook the problematic significance of Olivia's particular 'flaws.' Post-identity discourses present women like Olivia as examples of change: a black woman can now be successful because the American Dream is accessible to anyone. These same discourses determine that Olivia's faults – her vulnerability and confusion in her romantic relationships – are individualized and presented as her personal Achilles' heel, not a symptom of structural and perpetual inequalities imposed upon black women. These flaws become problematic when considering the structural inequalities surrounding black women's bodies. The depictions of her body and narratives of her susceptibility to her white male lovers affirm weaknesses in her gladiator attire. Olivia's power dissipates in physical interactions with two of her white male love interests on the show. Both of these men hold positions of power: Jake (Scott Foley) is a naval intelligence officer and Fitz (Tony Goldwyn) is the President of the United States. Olivia's performance with these two men marks a contrast to her physical agency in other non-sexual scenarios, and in her romantic relationship with a black US Senator.

Despite her confidence in dealing with the tangled webs of client dramas, Olivia becomes confused and physically overcome when engaging with Fitz. *Scandal* establishes the dynamics between Olivia and Fitz during the first episode of the series. Olivia confronts Fitz in the Oval Office for having an affair with an intern and the two begin to recount their own relationship. As Olivia cites the reasons she ended their relationship in the first place (that is, he is the married President of the United States), Fitz crosses the distance between his body and Olivia's. Olivia is standing near the darkened windows of the office. About half a foot taller than Olivia, Fitz looks down at her as she registers her complaints against him. He moves in closer and Olivia protests, 'Don't touch me,' as Fitz reaches for her waist. Hurt and reluctance are visible on her downcast face while Fitz remains stoic. 'Please don't,' she says and closes her eyes, grimaces, and shakes her head 'no.' Fitz pauses, poised to kiss her. She is breathing heavily and releases a sob. Olivia begins to revive herself and moves away from the window in an attempt to leave the Oval Office. The scene ends with Fitz following her and urgently grabbing Olivia's face to kiss her. He arches her back and lifts her face up forcefully to his. He leans in over her and his body envelops hers. She kisses him in return despite her previous protests.

Comparing this scene with Fitz to the earlier one with the Ukrainian mafia, it is evident that the physical agency Olivia is capable of performing fragments in the presence of Fitz. When negotiating with the international criminals, Olivia commands a room fearlessly; however, in Fitz's company, her body folds into his. Olivia intimidates the Ukrainian man by infringing on his personal space; yet her feeble attempts to thwart Fitz's advances demonstrate her as vulnerable. Olivia is able to look the Ukrainian man in the eye, but Fitz looms in over her registering the height difference between the two characters and highlighting his ability to physically dominate her. Olivia maintains a cool yet assertive demeanor throughout her negotiations with the Ukrainian men; however, her emotions envelop her in this scene with Fitz. Reading these two scenes in tandem, it is evident that Olivia's sovereignty over her own body is limited to professional spheres and that she is susceptible to white male domination in her personal life.

The physical inequalities between Olivia and Fitz become particularly apparent in *Defiance* (season two, episode 14) when Fitz violently forces himself upon a reluctant Olivia. Olivia attempts to leave a baby christening and Fitz chases after her. Olivia never turns around but her pace quickens with the awareness that Fitz is following her. Fitz grabs her arm and aggressively swings her around and pushes her through a closet doorway. They are facing each other as Fitz slams the door on the camera. As in the Oval Office scene, Olivia finds herself backed into a corner with Fitz advancing. Fitz closes the space between them and forcefully pulls her face toward his. Olivia pushes him away and slaps him; in that moment, there is a possibility that she will not allow him to dominate her. She stands there conflicted with furrowed brow and registered uneasiness. Olivia eventually gives in to Fitz's advances and a torrid sex scene between the two characters ensues.

While *The Huffington Post* described the closet scene as depicting 'angry, emotionally-complicated sex' (Hughes 2013), the scene also registers images of Fitz's violence against Olivia. At one point, Fitz forcefully holds Olivia's wrists against the wall. At another, he urgently grabs her face with his fingertips to twist her head to the side. Had Olivia not physically accepted his advances by moving to embrace him just previously, the audience might read the scene as sexual violence. Olivia's brief moment of consent allows the scene to proceed as a passionate love affair rather than one depicting rape. However, the physical interactions between the two characters walk a thin line between force and passion. Throughout the scene, Olivia continues to express concern, pain, and reluctance in her face as if she is unsure she wants to be there with him. She even disputes his forwardness by slapping him. Fitz, on the other hand, is very clear and direct with his intensions and he persistently advances despite her objections.

I am not suggesting that two consenting adults cannot have 'angry, emotionally-complicated sex'; rather, I assert that the scene's faithfulness to conventions of gendered and racialized physical relationships is problematic. Hill Collins (2005) and Donovan and Williams (2002) remind us of a historical legacy of the sexual victimization of black women since slavery. In contemporary society, black women are more likely than white women to be sexually assaulted and less likely to report violence or see a trial end in a conviction (Donovan & Williams 2002). By disregarding the legacy of white men's sexual violence against black women, *Scandal* ignores the implications of the characters' abusive, unequal relationship in favor of the dramatic storyline of a torrid love affair. Effectively, a post-identity focus on celebrating Olivia's power ignores the dubious aspects of her relationship with Fitz. If *Scandal*'s writers were to reverse this scene so that Olivia chases Fitz and forces him into a closet despite his repeated objections, then it would be read differently by an audience conditioned by ideologies of race and gender. If Fitz were to show emotional pain and continual reluctance while Olivia forcefully pulled his face toward hers, then the audience might negatively judge her as an angry, aggressive black woman and him as an emasculated white man. Instead, the show relies on conventions of race and gender to create Olivia's tragic flaw: her physical agency in the company of her white romantic partners. In this fashion, post-identity discourses permit the persistence of gendered and racialized assumptions of physical agency by sanctioning Olivia's tragic flaw as her body's vulnerability to Fitz.

Scandal introduces Jake Ballard in season two as an alternative love interest for Olivia; yet her relationship with him also presents problematic images of physical power and even violence. The relationship between Olivia and Jake climaxes in a scene in episode 18 where she discovers he has been secretly filming her apartment. After accidentally discovering the video footage, Olivia becomes distraught and confused by the discovery of Jake's deception. Rather than fleeing a potentially threatening situation, she stands transfixed by the images of her apartment on the monitors. Jake suddenly appears and approaches her slowly with his hand raised, gesturing her to be calm while Olivia begins to back away. She puts up her palm in the 'stop' gesture and yells, 'stop moving right now!' Jake does not heed her warning and replies, 'I can't let you leave, Olivia.' When Olivia finally attempts to run, Jake grabs her arm and forcefully swings her around toward him. After several failed attempts to break away from his grip, she finally pushes away and slides backwards to hit her head against a piece of furniture, falling to the floor. Jake immediately climbs on top to straddle her and pins her wrists against the floor. He yells, 'Stop, I'm not going to hurt you. Calm down.' As she struggles, Jake assures her that he is trying to protect her. He then plants his palm against her face and pushes it toward the monitors. The camera cuts to reveal what Jake wants her to see: there is an armed intruder on the monitor depicting Olivia's apartment. Jake assures Olivia that his intentions are to protect her from the threat. Olivia then loses consciousness from a head injury incurred during the struggle.

For a woman privy to national plots and conspiracies, Olivia's lack of physical agency in this scene marks a contrast against moments where she manages high-stakes crises and threats. As the lead gladiator of Pope and Associates, Olivia notoriously follows her 'gut' and makes decisions that sometimes conflict with her team's opinions. Nonetheless, Jake benevolently 'protects' her without her consent or knowledge and makes decisions concerning her safety without consulting her. In the scene described above, Jake physically positions himself as a white patriarchal figure who knows what is best for Olivia and feels justified in restraining her because of that omnipotent knowledge. A characteristically composed Olivia becomes paralyzed with fear when she realizes that Jake might be a threat. The contrast between Jake's benevolence and Olivia's paralysis allows him to assert himself as the person with Olivia's best interest at heart. This is further evidenced by Olivia's hospitalization for a concussion after fighting against Jake. In this logic of Jake's benevolent knowledge, Olivia causes her own injury because she resists Jake's authority as protector and her disobedience yields physical consequences. Following the logic further, Olivia's body is not sovereign nor can she make decisions to protect herself since her physical agency is no match for his. Her body remains relegated to a position of powerlessness via discourses of white male authority.

Olivia's relationship with US Senator Edison Davis (Norm Lewis) provides a compelling counterpoint to Jake and Fitz. In addition to being a US Senator, Edison is a member of the Senate Intelligence Committee. He is a black man who we learn was previously engaged to Olivia before she ended their relationship. Edison re-enters Olivia's life in season two and provides yet another alternative love interest to Fitz. Olivia's physical agency with Edison is a stark contrast to Jake and Fitz. For example, when Olivia ends her relationship with Edison in *Nobody Likes Babies* (season two, episode 13), she is calm and assured in her rejection of him. The two characters stand several feet from each other and Edison never makes advances toward her. Olivia stands firmly and speaks with him matter-of-factly; the emotion of the scene is controlled until Edison loses his composure and yells, 'What do you want, Olivia?' Olivia is startled by his outburst at first, but quickly regains herself. She says, 'I want painful, difficult, devastating, life-changing, extraordinary love.' She is clear that Edison cannot provide her the type of love she seeks and her resolve is evidenced in the firm stance she takes opposite him and her stoic face as Edison exits her apartment. Olivia's physical agency in this scene speaks to her power in the relationship. She is firm and resolute in her demeanor, her words, and her decisions; she does not show the same incertitude in her face nor does she physically shrink as in emotionally tense moments with Jake and Fitz. By depicting Olivia as having physical agency in the presence of Edison but not in similar intimate situations with Fitz and Jake, *Scandal* allows the power of the white male body to remain unchecked even while the show more broadly attempts to present Olivia as uninhibited by racial or gendered inequalities.

Conclusion: the gladiator's mimicry

Scandal's portrayal of Olivia Pope's physical agency provides a caveat to the post-identity celebration of her achievements. While postfeminist and post-racial discourses applaud the successes that evidence Olivia's equality within society, the depiction of her body demonstrates her as mimicking the power of the white masculinity. Bhabha (2004) asserts that the concept of mimicry allows a minoritized (in Bhabha's language, 'colonized') subject to demonstrate herself as resembling white masculine power, but as an imperfect semblance. In Olivia's case, she mimics the unbridled, individually driven professional power that post discourses permit gendered and racialized subjects. However, in the logic of mimicry, it is always necessary to find the subject lacking and unable to fully realize herself as equal to the subjectivity she is mimicking. Post-identity discourses fixate on rendering Olivia's body as lacking fully realized physical agency in order to show her as merely mimicking power, not fully possessing it. Olivia's 'messy' and 'flawed' personal life provides fodder that the post discourses need to find her lacking. In the process, postfeminist and post-race ideologies valorize her successes as evidence that a new day has dawned and ignore the problematic depictions of a black woman's physical agency.

Assessments of popular texts such as *Scandal* allow us to take the pulse of dominant ideologies and determine the ebbs and flows of power within the popular imagination. Thus, *Scandal*'s contemporary resonance suggests that the professional success of black women is imaginable and appealing and may be touted as evidence of the irrelevance of feminism for women of color in particular. Nevertheless, a critical examination of the discourses of black feminine power in popular television reveals persistent anxieties and contradictions surrounding the black female body – including the body of a 'gladiator in a suit,' such as Olivia Pope.

Notes

1. *Scandal* appears to be gaining popularity with US audiences and abroad: 10.5 million US viewers watched the season three premiere in October 2013 – a record high for the show. Fans tweeted 712,900 times during the premiere, which was the highest number of any television show during the same week (Levin 2013). *Scandal*'s US-based success has also led to circulation of the series in other television markets. The UK's Channel 4 and France's Canal Plus acquired the series for distribution in 2012 and 2013 respectively (Obenson 2012). All the while, *Scandal* stars an African American actress in the lead role, is based on the professional career of a black woman in Washington DC, and was created and written by a black woman – Shonda Rhimes of *Grey's Anatomy* fame (Vega 2013).
2. It is important to acknowledge the diverse dynamics that form postfeminist and post-race understandings of gender and race respectively. For example, Joseph (2009) asserts that postfeminism depends on 'what are often assumed

to be biologically based performances or hyper-signifiers of heterosexuality, femininity, and maternity' (p. 240) while discourse of post-race focuses on the assumed irrelevance of legal measures to equalize educational and career opportunities (Bonilla-Silva cited in Joseph 2009). Each of these discourses is born from established assumptions about the respective identity category. Additionally, scholars examine each of these discourses in a variety of ways that produce a vigorous debate on the precise meanings of terminology.

References

Aradau, C. (2009) 'The Roma in Italy: Racism as Usual?,' *Radical Philosophy*, 153, 2–6.

Banet-Weiser, S. (1999) *The Most Beautiful Girl in the World* (Berkeley: University of California Press).

Bhabha, H.K. (2004) *The Location of Culture* (New York: Routledge).

Bonilla-Silva, E. (2003) *Racism without Racists: Color-blind Racism and the Persistence of Racial Inequality in the United States* (Lanham, MD: Rowman & Littlefield).

Butler, J. (2004) *Undoing Gender* (New York: Routledge).

De Welde, K. (2003) 'Getting Physical: Subverting Gender through Self-defense,' *Journal of Contemporary Ethnography*, 32(3), 247–78.

Django Unchained (2012) (Film) (US: The Weinstein Company & Columbia Pictures).

Donovan, R. and Williams, M. (2002) 'Living at the Intersection: The Effects of Racism and Sexism on Black Rape Survivors,' in T.C. West (ed.) *Violence in the Lives of Black Women: Battered, Black, and Blue* (New York: The Haworth Press), 95–106.

Dowling, C. (2002) *The Frailty Myth* (New York: Random House International).

Forman, T. and Lewis, A. (2006) 'Racial Apathy and Hurricane Katrina: The Social Anatomy of Prejudice in the Post-Civil Rights Era,' *DuBois Review*, 3(172), 202.

Gill, R. (2007) 'Post-feminist Media Culture,' *European Journal of Cultural Studies*, 10(2), 147–66.

Gilroy, P. (1998) 'Race Ends Here,' *Ethnic and Racial Studies*, 21(5), 838–47.

Hill Collins, P. (2005) *Black Sexual Politics: African Americans, Gender, and the New Racism* (New York: Routledge).

Hughes, J. (2013) '"Scandal": Fitz and Olivia Have Angry Sex in a Closet,' *The Huffington Post*, 15 February, www.huffingtonpost.com/2013/02/15/scandal-ten-months-later-video_n_2691896.html (accessed 10 November 2013).

Johnson, E.P. (2003) *Appropriating Blackness: Performance and the Politics of Authenticity* (Durham, NC: Duke University Press).

Joseph, R. (2009) 'Tyra Banks is Fat: Reading (Post-)racism and (Post-)feminism in the New Millennium,' *Critical Studies in Media Communication*, 26(3), 237–54.

Lawler, J. (2002) *Punch!: Why Women Participate in Violent Sports* (Terre Haute, IN: Wish Publishing).

Lentin, A. (2012) 'Post-race, Post Politics: The Paradoxical Rise of Culture after Multiculturalism,' *Ethnic and Racial Studies*, 1, 1–19.

Levin, G. (2013) 'Nielsons: "Scandal" Has a Shockingly Huge Debut,' *USA Today*, 9 October, www.usatoday.com/story/life/tv/2013/10/08/nielsen-tv-ratings-highlights/2944827/ (accessed 10 November 2013).

Lopez, I.H. (2010) 'Post-racial Racism: Racial Stratification and Mass Incarceration in the Age of Obama,' *California Law Review*, 98(3), 1023.

McCaughey, M. (1997) *Real Knockouts: The Physical Feminism of Women's Self-defense* (New York University Press).

McRobbie, A. (2007) 'Postfeminism and Popular Culture: Bridget Jones and the New Gender Regime,' in Y. Tasker and D. Negra (eds) *Interrogating Postfeminism* (Durham, NC: Duke University Press), 27–39.

McRobbie, A. (2008) *The Aftermath of Feminism: Gender, Culture, and Social Change* (London: Sage).

Noland, C. (2009) *Agency and Embodiment: Performing Gestures/Producing Culture* (Cambridge, MA: Harvard University Press).

Obenson, T. (2012) 'UK's Channel 4 Acquires UK Premiere Broadcast Rights to Shonda Rhimes' "Scandal",' *Shadow and Act: On Cinema of the African Diaspora*, 12 October, http://blogs.indiewire.com/shadowandact/uks-channel-4-acquires-uk-premiere-broadcast-rights-to-shonda-rhimes-scandal (accessed 10 November 2013).

Roth, A. and Basow, S.A. (2004) 'Femininity, Sports, and Feminism: Developing a Theory of Physical Liberation,' *Journal of Sport & Social Issues*, 28(3), 245–65.

Scandal (2012–present) (Television series) (US: ABC).

Tasker, Y. and Negra, D. (2007) 'Introduction: Feminist Politics and Post-feminist Culture,' in Y. Tasker and D. Negra (eds) *Interrogating Postfeminism* (Durham, NC: Duke University Press), 1–25.

Vega, T. (2013) 'A Show Makes History and Friends: "Scandal" on ABC is Breaking Barriers,' *The New York Times*, 16 January, www.nytimes.com/2013/01/17/arts/television/scandal-on-abc-is-breaking-barriers.html?_r=0 (accessed 10 November 2013).

Washington, K. and Winfrey, O. (2012) 'Kerry Washington, Shonda Rhimes and Judy Smith on Oprah: Next Chapter,' *YouTube*, www.youtube.com/watch?v=ryYBP1WHWZs (accessed 1 October 2013.)

Part III
Becoming Mother

10
Got Milk?: Motherhood, Breastfeeding, and (Re)domesticating Feminism

Kumarini Silva

Introduction

In 1949, Simone de Beauvoir wrote in *The Second Sex* that 'Woman has ovaries, a uterus: these peculiarities imprison her in her subjectivity, circumscribe her within the limits of her own nature.' She went on to note that while women are often critiqued (and ridiculed) for thinking with their 'glands,' that 'Man superbly ignores the fact that his anatomy also includes glands, such as the testicles, and that they secrete hormones. He thinks of his body as a direct and normal connection with the world, which he believes he apprehends objectively, whereas he regards the body of woman as a hindrance, a prison, weighed down by everything peculiar to it' (p. 27). At that time, Beauvoir's reflections – that women's biological functions and reproductive practices were being translated into social conventions about femininity and the feminine – were met with considerable criticisms, and little support. More than 60 years later, the value of her observation is much clearer, especially as women *continue* to be the 'second sex' within patriarchal social, economic, and political structures that govern much of the globe. Cultural tropes that reinforce women as more emotional, more impulsive, and therefore in greater need of domestication, have long been critiqued by feminists, but continue to thrive in contemporary US culture. This is in spite of the great strides made by feminist activisms, especially in the last 40 years.

A similar critique of reproductive essentialism is offered in Mahasweta Devi's short story 'The Breast Giver' (1997). From a different time and culture, Devi too speaks to the larger conditions of biology and its cultural translation that prescribe particular locations for the essentialized feminine. Much like my early introduction to Beauvoir as a student,

Mahasweta Devi's short stories influenced me while still in my early twenties. Over the years, 'The Breast Giver' has stayed with me as a text that is wonderfully illustrative of the social, economic, and political aspects of mothering and breastfeeding that are often glossed over in the general celebration of the practice, as both effortless and 'natural.' In Devi's poignant short story, Jashoda, high-caste but extremely poor, uses the one tool she has in abundance, her breast and its milk, to become a professional milk mother:

> Jashoda does not remember at all when there was no child in her womb, when she didn't feel faint in the morning, when Kangali's body didn't drill her body like a geologist in a darkness lit only by an oil-lamp. She never had the time to calculate if she could or could not bear motherhood. Motherhood was always her way of living and keeping alive her world of countless beings. Jashoda was a mother by profession, professional mother. Jashoda was not an amateur mama like the daughters and wives of the master's house. The world belongs to the professional. (Devi 1997, p. 39)

In Devi's critique of economic and caste exploitation and the burden of womanhood, Jashoda literally sells her blood (via breast milk) to feed the wealthy (but lower caste) children of the Halder family, thereby professionalizing her reproductive abilities. Through this, Jashoda's breasts are literally a commodity, and her eventual neglect, illness, and subsequent demise speak to the ways in which various aspects of breastfeeding, whether they be in the global north or south, ignore the larger systemic inequalities that are inherently tied to women's labor, especially outside the formal economy (though it is severely impacted by such).

Beauvoir's and Devi's divergent approaches to women's bodies through different genres undergird the continuing fractures between women's progress, the discourses around mothering, and the systemic raced, classed, and gendered inequalities that persist in the US. Contextualized within these larger systems, this chapter is an attempt to map connections between these contradictions of women's progress and the ways we use mothering – an essential (and essentialized) biological practice – as a means of regulating and policing women's behaviors. Here, I look at multiple discourses – from breastfeeding, to women's work, to popular representations of both – in order to illustrate the ways in which women's mothering labor becomes subsumed and co-opted within and by postfeminist, backlash culture.

Setting a context: locating motherhood within postfeminism and backlash culture

I begin with Beauvoir and Devi in the spirit of 'articulation' that, borrowing from Stuart Hall, Angela McRobbie describes as 'a process where various progressive social movements (trade unions, feminism, anti-racism, gay and lesbian rights) might forge connections and alliances with each other, and in so doing would be constantly modifying their own political identities' (2009, p. 25). Juxtaposed against this definition of articulation, McRobbie speaks of contemporary *disarticulation*, where women are discouraged from making connections with and to other women – across cultures, identities, and/or intergenerationally – to foster and maintain movements (like the feminist movement) that will make a systemic shift for the equitable distribution of recourses and rights. Instead, young women and men, especially in the global north, are encouraged to disarticulate from the systems that question or make visible their own oppressions. In place of the very real work of making these connections and building on them, we are increasingly asked to celebrate various 'faux feminist' symbols that permeate (popular) culture. McRobbie writes that there is an 'over-supply of post-feminist substitutes from within the new hyper-visible feminine consumer culture' (p. 26). This is especially evinced in classrooms where gender and culture are the focused subject matter.

For example, every year I ask the university students I teach how many identify as feminists. Out of 25–30 students each year, for almost a decade, maybe one or two will raise their hands. Sometimes no hands go up at all. I then ask how many of them believe in equal pay, a living wage, parental leave, and job security. Every hand in the classroom goes up. When I ask them how they hope to achieve these goals within the current sociopolitical context in which, for the last four decades, recessions have become somewhat of a norm in the US, I am routinely told through 'opportunities' and 'hard work,' especially now that women have 'the same opportunities as men.' This (neo)-liberal notion of the value of hard work, and of taking advantage of every opportunity that presents itself, has become the mantra of a generation of women (and men) who see little-to-no connection between the feminisms and feminist politics of the past and their own lives (McRobbie 2009).

In a mediated society where women are incessantly reminded of the 'opportunities' that are available to them, that they have 'come a long way,' and that it was the social movements and activisms of earlier generations that brought them those rights, the continued need to fight to achieve equality is now said to be irrelevant and of little consequence. The Virginia Slims cigarette slogan of the 1970s 'you've come a long way, baby' now resonates more than ever because it *does* seem like we have come a long way. A new generation of postfeminists are told that they are leaning in (Sandberg 2013), that women are CEOs of Fortune 500 companies,[1] that they are getting paid *almost* as much as men, and that, reflecting women's progress in society and the workplace, more women are getting college degrees than are men of the same age.[2] Popular shows such as *Girls* (2012–present) educate a new generation of 'feminists' about sexual power (or the struggle for such) as actual power, just as *Sex and the City* (1998–2004) did in the 1990s. For all intents and purposes, women seem on track, and it seems that the women's movements – as formalized, politicized entities – are done. But here is the reality: fewer women are actually leaning in,[3] only 4.6 percent of CEOs of Fortune 1000 companies are women (Catalyst 2014), and women are still only earning $0.81 to every $1.00 their male counterparts earn (Perez 2014). The reality indicates that we haven't arrived at all.

By saying we haven't 'arrived,' I do not mean to disregard the very real progress that has been made in contemporary culture through the untiring efforts of those in feminist and women's advocacy movements regarding women's rights. Instead, my desire is to ask how these contradictory realities of rights and rights discourses become interpellated by the social expectations of the 'essential feminine.' More simply, following Beauvoir, I am interested in looking at the ways in which this broader context of 'faux feminism' accommodates and talks about the most essential biological functions of femininity: reproduction. And in turn, how this reproductive labor becomes a way to (re)domesticate women within contemporary backlash culture.

Against the broader context of hyper-consumerist and hyper-mediated realities of contemporary US culture (and the global north, in general), motherhood sits incongruously as a practice of – and discourse about – womanhood and femininity. When motherhood is discussed within this broader celebratory context of women's progress and 'arrival,' it tends to ignore larger, deeply historical, systemic inequalities associated with race, class, gender, and sexuality that sustain narratives of idealized motherhood. This disarticulation, between the past and present, speaks to the ways in which feminism and feminist discourses become co-opted in the neo-valorizing of motherhood as a domesticated practice.

Breast is best: for whom?

Breastfeeding, and its social and health benefits, has been extensively studied in recent times, both locally and globally, including in the natural sciences, psychology, and public health (Labbok 2013; Xu et al. 2009): studies that show the value of and need for breast milk in an infant's life. These academic studies have been supported by a movement of breast-is-best advocates, who in turn are supported by a publishing industry around breastfeeding that sell 'must have' guides to learning 'the womanly art of breast feeding' – the title of the eponymous tome on breastfeeding and motherhood published by the La Leche league. New mothers are encouraged to breastfeed by following instructions in books that have titles like *Breastfeeding Made Simple: Seven Natural Laws for Nursing Mothers* (Mohrbacher 2010) and *The Breastfeeding Mother's Guide to More Milk* (West & Marasco 2008), which are sold in bookstores around the US and Europe, and are enormously popular. These books, along with others in that genre, advocate breastfeeding by presenting it as both natural (for the mother) and necessary (for the baby). For example, in *The Womanly Art of Breastfeeding* (Weissinger et al. 2010), under a section titled 'How Important is Breastfeeding, Really?,' the authors respond to the title question with a resounding 'Extremely!' Furthermore, they argue that, 'There is almost nothing you can do for your child in his whole life that will affect him both emotionally and physically more profoundly than breastfeeding' (p. 5). This notion that there is 'nothing you can do' that is better is echoed in both popular and medical cultures, where, as Cindy Stearns notes, in line with 'public health messages about the value of breast milk for babies, breastfeeding is increasingly a symbol and a measure of good mothering in the West' (2009, p. 63).

Especially in the last decade, advertising campaigns and public service announcements targeting young mothers about the value of breastfeeding have been on the rise, and much has been written about their success. Some triumphantly note that with:

> [T]he energy of an epidemic and the passion of a crusade, breastfeeding has become the norm. It has not been the norm since the turn of the last century. With the collaboration of many organizations, hundreds of health professionals, and thousands of women around the world, breastfeeding is moving forward. (Lawrence 2012, p. 311)

Such glowing reviews of the breastfeeding campaigns acknowledge that, 'Going back to work has been offered as the key reason why women stop breastfeeding,' but that in modeling policies long in place in Europe, 'significant efforts have been initiated in the past decade to improve conditions for working women, including legislation to require employers to provide time and space for mothers to pump their milk ... employers in the US are getting the message' (Lawrence 2012, p. 313).

While it is hard to disagree that breastfeeding has become more popular in the US, it is worth challenging assumptions that Americans have changed their views toward *women in general* in such a way as to accommodate the ever increasing call for women to breastfeed by both the State and by the wider culture. The continued objectification of women in other areas of American society, including popular and consumer culture, as well as the restriction of labor and pay, do not allow for breastfeeding to thrive without considerable personal, economic, and professional costs to women. As Paige Hall Smith (2013) notes, 'The view that breastfeeding itself is the location of the constraint glosses over the mediating role that gender inequality plays in the relationship between breastfeeding and its constraining effects' (p. 374). But such broader considerations are often lacking from popular conversations and representations around breastfeeding, where, as Hall Smith notes, the act itself becomes the focus that obfuscates larger issues of inequality.

A perfect example of this was the cover story for the May 2012 issue of *Time* Magazine. Titled 'Are you Mom Enough?' with a tagline that read 'why attachment parenting drives some mothers to extremes – and how Dr. Bill Sears became their guru,' the story looked at mothering from the perspective of those who follow Dr Bill Sears's attachment parenting guidelines. Sears, a long-time pediatrician, is the author of several popular parenting books in the US, including *The Baby Book: Everything you Need to Know about Your Baby from Birth to Age Two* (2013) and *The Baby Sleep Book: The Complete Guide to a Good Night's Rest for the Whole Family* (2005). He (and his family) enjoy an almost cult-like following amongst parents who embrace 'alternate' methods of childrearing. While the story in *Time* magazine was about Sears and parents who follow his parenting and care techniques (including co-sleeping and breastfeeding into toddlerhood), the accompanying image was not the doctor himself. Instead, it featured 26-year-old Jamie Lynn Grumet, who stands with her right hand at her hip, wearing a tank top and skinny jeans, staring directly at the reader, her left arm circled around her four-year-old son, Aram. Aram stands on a stool, also staring directly at the reader, while he breastfeeds from Grumet's left breast. The accompanying story also carries a photo spread of three mothers breastfeeding their toddlers and newborn infants. While the article itself raised controversy for focusing on attachment parenting as 'extreme,' what caught public attention and animated public discussions was the cover image itself. As one person wrote, 'It's not his age that bugs my friends and me *at all*. It's that this image debases something beautiful. The fact that they're not looking at one another, but millions of us, makes what they're doing seem illicit. And we become voyeurs' (Scanlon Stefanakos 2012).

This nuanced observation speaks to the ways in which the cover image which managed to *imply* sexuality (to draw in the readership), while seeming to be speaking of mothering and parenting, was present in a range of other responses as well. For example, in a story about the controversial magazine cover titled 'Jamie Lynne Grumet, Breastfeeding Mom on *Time* Magazine Cover, Illustrates Attachment Parenting' (Miller 2012), *The Huffington Post* chose to lead with a cropped image of only Grumet's breast and Aram's face. This tight framing emphasizes the voyeuristic nature that Scanlon Stefanakos refers to above. In addition, online discussions around the cover image frequently featured commentary about its sexual nature, and questioned the mental state of mothers who pursue breastfeeding beyond infancy. For example, in response to the *Huffington Post* story, one reader noted that 'These mothers are more than likely insecure, shallow and do not have much of a life outside of child rearing,' while another noted that 'Whenever I hear a story of a 4 or 5 year old breast feeding I hear dueling banjos in my head.'[4] Yet another 'jokingly' stated that he would like to have what Aram was having (the breast) (response to Miller 2012). These responses to the image of Grumet breastfeeding (and interpretations that code a four-year-old as a sexual 'accessory') indicate the myriad ways that the breast, and by extension women (as metonymically the breast), becomes a focus for negotiating cultural norms around the feminine. Where the exposed breast provokes disgust for some readers, for others it provides an opportunity to discuss breastfeeding in sexualized terms. Both responses are remarkably representative of the contradictory attitudes we have toward women's bodies in our culture. On the one hand, displaying and consuming the breast for pleasure is sanctioned by society, as seen by its ubiquitous deployment as a signifier of beauty and sexual agency in advertising imagery, entertainment products, and other mediated contexts. On the other hand, the basic biological function of the breast – to produce milk – renders it abject and unsightly. In addition, the comment about banjo playing speaks to the classed aspects of breastfeeding that are also contradictory, where gender intersects with issues of race and class privilege that are rarely probed outside academic contexts. For example, throughout the article itself, attachment parenting is presented as time consuming, labor intensive, and a form of manic commitment that requires inordinate amounts of time. Here, while not explicitly stated, economic stability undergirds the discussion about being 'mom enough.' Framing breast-feeding as 'good mothering' and then outlining the extreme versions of such – with visuals of Caucasian breastfeeding mothers – without an interrogation of the economic and social systems that provide such opportunities, regurgitates and valorizes a framing of biological repro-duction that has been extensively critiqued by feminists since the 1970s (for example see Ortner 1974). This notion of the breast as abject/object is further complicated in the US by the intolerance shown to women who choose to breastfeed in public. It is especially important to situate these often times scathing and virulent attacks on breastfeeding moth-ers within the larger cultural norms, where breast augmentations, larger breasts, and the overexposure of women's bodies is coded as 'empower-ing' and 'progressive.' For example, in 2010 reality star Kim Kardashian tweeted 'EWW Im at lunch, the woman at the table next 2 me is breast-feeding her baby w no coverup' (quoted in Sattar 2010). When she was accused of being 'anti-breastfeeding,' she followed up with 'My sister breast feeds! I natural beautiful thing, there's nothing wrong w it, but she covers herself, not w her boobs exposed' (quoted in Sattar 2010). Kardashian's carelessly tweeted thoughts about public breastfeeding speak to a cultural reality where gratuitous exposure of the breast is embraced as empowerment – for example, the repeated nudity in shows like *Girls* – while an act of nourishment is considered unacceptable for public display.[5] This hierarchical 'value' (mediated pleasure vs. nourish-ment) placed on breasts is especially problematic because it implies that conversations about pleasure and nourishment are disconnected. This supposed disconnect allows breastfeeding (as well as women's bodies in general) to be separated from larger systemic inequalities like wages, labor, and resource distribution.

In/formal economies: putting breasts to work

Breastfeeding – as the ultimate signifier of good mothering – is not just a social or academic conversation. Especially in the past two decades, governmental and non-governmental entities have actively worked to encourage women to breastfeed, touting numerous health and cogni-tive benefits for both the infant and the mother (see Clark et al. 2011; Schmidt 2013). Their efforts have largely centered around advertising campaigns to raise public awareness, and their work has been supported by medical professionals who both publish research on, and advertise in their work spaces, the benefits of 'the breast.' One such example from 2003 is from a brief introduction to the journal *Obstetric and Gynecology* by Dr John T. Queenan. Writing in support of a breastfeeding campaign that was about to take off in the US, he noted that breastfeeding was an 'important gift' and asked, 'How did we get to a situation in which we need to promote breastfeeding?' Answering the question, Queenan noted that during 'World War II, while men were off to war, women entered the workforce in droves. During the war and in the good times that followed, fewer and fewer American women practiced breastfeeding. Formula feeding was on the rise as breastfeeding fell to an all-time low of 25 percent in 1971' (2003, pp. 3–4). While there is no doubt that Queenan's intention here is to promote a healthy feeding habit, what is of note is the way he blithely refers to the *conditions* under which women moved *away* from breastfeeding. In his description and summary, Queenan seems to imply that women's transition from private spaces to public spaces, in the form of professional work (and war efforts), jeopardized the 'important gift' of mothering vis-à-vis breastfeeding. In addition, the time period he notes as an 'all-time low' is also during the second wave of feminism in the US, when feminist organizations were actively demanding more considerations for women and women's rights in the public sphere. Against this larger context, such implicit connections, made often and carelessly, between women's (re)domestication and the value of being a good mother are enormously misleading, and resonate ideologically with the *Times* headline 'Are You Mom Enough?' In presenting women's organized transition to the labor force during the war as the reason for declining numbers in breastfeeding, Queenan ignores larger socioeconomic and cultural conditions that contributed to those numbers. Conditions, for example, such as the introduction and commoditization of formula as a 'healthy' substitute for breast milk, which had a significant impact on breastfeeding statistics, perhaps more than women entering the workforce. In addition, even more importantly, it glosses over raced and classed realities and perpetuates mythologies that have long surrounded women's labor in the US – including the fact that women, especially women of color, worked in factories and as domestic labor long before World War II. And finally, building on those two previous assumptions, it propagates a notion that breastfeeding and good mothering can, and should, happen in the domestic/private space. In essence, what is assumed here is a common connection made between women's transition to the workforce (and the 'good times'), and the decline in 'good mothering,' including breastfeeding. While not explicit, it speaks to the myriad of ways that women's work outside the home continues to be positioned as 'bad' for the welfare of the infant, the family, and, consequently, even the nation state. In the latter case, breastfeeding is positioned as an economic boon that resonates with and within a capitalist society.

Speaking directly to this, the US Department of Health and Human Services' Office on Women's Health notes that 'the nation benefits overall when mothers breastfeed ... The US would also save $13 billion per year – medical care costs are lower for fully breastfed infants than never-breastfed infants. Breastfed infants typically need fewer sick care visits, prescriptions, and hospitalizations' (Office on Women's Health 2011). So, here breastfeeding becomes – much like the war efforts during the 1930s and 1940s – a way of helping the country, and doing one's part, as a woman. But unlike the past, instead of joining the workforce and earning a living wage, women's participation in the economy, in this instance, is reduced to her breasts. While breastfeeding is touted as a boon for the nation's economy, and the family, there is little-to-no conversation about the connections between these macro-economics and the micro economy of women's lives. The impact of this disconnect was made clear in a recent conversation I had with a doctor of family medicine.

During our conversation about breastfeeding and breastfeeding economics, Dr R. shared with me her experience of treating a young African American[6] woman who brought in her four-month-old infant who seemed to be unable to process breast milk. According to Dr R, as the conversation proceeded, and she attempted to ask the young mother about her diet in the hopes of identifying what could be causing the child's health issues, it became increasingly clear that the young mother was uncomfortable sharing information about what foods may have been digested through breast milk. Eventually, as their conversation proceeded, and the mother became more comfortable with Dr R, she shared the fact that she worked in the fast-food industry, which paid minimum wage, and provided no maternity leave, and that in order to maintain her income and ensure her child's wellbeing, the baby was being nursed on and off by the mother's friend who also had recently given birth. Because of their schedules and because they could not take time off in between working hours to breastfeed their own babies, the two young mothers shared breastfeeding duties. In order to be able to work in a formal economy and in environments that did not provide support or resources for young mothers – in more ways than one – they traded childcare and the feedings. As a result, the young mother was unable to answer questions about food and diet because she wasn't sure what her friend had eaten during the day – a diet that may have impacted her own child's health.

While Dr R's experience is shared here anecdotally, it speaks to the often-overlooked issues of labor and time that are faced by women who are financially unable to stay home after childbirth to follow the daily, sometimes hourly, and often times grueling, practice of establishing breastfeeding patterns with a newborn infant. In addition, the general assumption that all mothers *can* breastfeed, and therefore *should* because of its economic viability, ignores the emotional and physical disruptions experienced by women after childbirth that may force them to rely on alternate methods of feeding and care.

In January 2011, National Public Radio (NPR) aired a story, titled 'Moms Who Can't Nurse Find Donors Online' (Shute 2011). In it, they shared the experience of Lindsey Ward from Woodbridge, Virginia, who, determined to breastfeed her second child (her first was exclusively formula fed), was 'heartbroken' to find that her newborn was rapidly losing weight in spite of her efforts at nursing him. Seeking solutions, she went online and discovered 'Eats-on-Feets,' a group started by 'Shell Walker, a midwife in Phoenix, who had helped clients find breast-milk donors when they had a health crisis or other problem that kept them from nursing' (Shute 2011).

Eats-on-Feets is not the only breast milk exchange group in the US, but it is one of the largest and most formally organized movements to provide breast milk to new mothers. While Eats-on-Feets outlines a rigorous screening process for potential families as they donate and accept milk, the Food and Drug Administration (FDA), as well as the American Academy of Pediatricians, warn against such organized but informal exchanges, noting 'When human milk is obtained directly from individuals or through the internet, the donor is unlikely to have been adequately screened for infectious disease or contamination risk. In addition, it is not likely that the human milk has been collected, processed, tested or stored in a way that reduces possible safety risks to the baby' (FDA 2010). Instead they advise that potential recipients use one of the 17 milk banks located across North America, where the milk is accepted 'from nursing mothers who have been tested to make sure they don't have infectious diseases' and 'the donated milk is pasteurized to further ensure its safety.' But such vigilantly tested products come at a cost, as Ward found out: she was told that she not only needed a prescription, but also that an ounce of milk could cost $3.50 (Shute 2011).

When breast-is-best proponents blithely advocate for breast milk as a 'must' or a 'gift' or an 'absolute,' they ignore the very real costs, both emotional (especially when one cannot produce enough) and economic (both in terms of time off, and the cost of buying) associated with breast milk. The desire to breastfeed one's child for many mothers (not all) is seemingly natural, but the larger societal obligations and economic realities do not often support the realities of breastfeeding.

Such contradictory messages create anxieties for mothers who are forced to make choices between economic labor and mothering labor. Even when popular media talk about breastfeeding and mothering as a 'challenge,' they rarely engage with these economic and classed considerations.

Conclusion

Recently in class I was asked by a student what I thought of the connection between Yahoo CEO Marissa Mayer's decision in 2013 to end telecommuting for employees at the same time that she built a nursery for her own child, adjacent to her office at work (see Carlson 2013). The student was outraged that 'a mother would do such a despicable thing!' When I asked her what she considered was despicable on Mayer's part, the student seemed momentarily taken aback, but responded that it was the connection between the two things: first, not allowing her employees to work from home, and then building a nursery on-site for her own child. For me, the framing of the question (the seamless folding in of motherhood into patriarchally institutionalized business practices) encapsulates the inherent contradictions in women's progress that has been touted in recent times. Because Mayer is female, her essentialized identity is framed through the 'feminine' even as she is applauded for achieving success in a male-dominated industry.

The broader context of patriarchy, and its singular role in ordering and organizing everyday lives (including the world of business and economics), is largely overlooked in discussions about women's rights and access to power. This is further complicated by the fact that feminism – as a practice and a word – is rejected in its entirety by both men *and* women.

Because of this disconnect, contradictory attitudes toward feminism's value, and its values, abound. For example, in addition to the controversy of telecommuting and nurseries, Mayer herself is an exemplar of this contradiction. Even as she benefits from the labor of feminist and women's rights advocates, who have worked, and continue to work, tirelessly to ensure women's place in public life, she refuses to acknowledge that her success is possible in large part due to the efforts of this advocacy. In a recent interview in the documentary *Makers: Women Who Make America* (2013), Mayer notes that she wouldn't consider herself a feminist, though she believes 'in equal rights. I believe that women are just as capable, if not more so, in a lot of different dimensions. But I don't, I think, have sort of the militant drive and sort of the chip on the shoulder that sometimes comes with that.' This notion that feminism is a 'chip on the shoulder' has become a mantra for many (especially younger) women, who see their success as part of a 'natural' progression toward greater equality, and as outside a more formal movement on behalf of women.

As a response to the student's question about Mayer's telecommuting/ nursery controversy, we – the entire class and I – collectively mapped broader issues that connected these two facts. The list included the fact that shortly after Yahoo made the no-telecommuting policy public, the male CEO of Best Buy, a technology sales-based corporation, implemented a similar policy, but that it was not seen as an 'anti-mothering' or as an 'anti-child' policy. Instead it was recognized as a sound strategy for revitalizing the company. We also talked about parental leave policies in the US, compared to the rest of the industrialized world, and the ways in which the very limited legal requirements of family leave in the US are often exploited by large corporations. Furthermore, unlike many other industrialized countries, there are no laws requiring employers to provide nursery facilities or breastfeeding facilities for women. By using the conversations around Mayer's two decisions (which are only connected by larger, systemic inequalities rather than the basic 'she's a mother, so she should allow telecommuting' logic), we talked about various rights discourses in contemporary culture. We looked at how the outcry against Mayer, *as a woman*, rather than a CEO, reflected the ways in which sociopolitical conversations around women's bodies, and their biological functions, are an integral part of those rights discourses. As one of the students said in response to the mapping, 'these things are so much more complicated!' He's right. They are.

And it is because it is complicated that I conclude the chapter with Mayer. Her rejection of feminist rights movements as instrumental to her own success, at the same time as she is forced to respond to public outcries against her business policies, highlight the ways in which backlash culture becomes internalized as 'normal' and 'natural.' And this is the foundation of backlash culture: it actively encourages women to reject the very movements and processes that have brought them rights, with false notions of 'arrival,' at the same time that it produces women as the essential feminine, especially tied to reproductive practices and discourses. These reproductive discourses of essentialized femininity, in turn, become ways to subtly demarcate gendered spaces, while ignoring and disconnecting from larger systems of oppression that continue to reproduce the second-class status of women.

Notes

1. Much has been made of the appointment of Marissa Mayer who became the CEO of internet giant Yahoo in 2012, at the age of 37.
2. According to data provided by the US Department of Education, 56.7 percent of the total number of graduates with a bachelor degree were women (Institute of Education Sciences 2012).
3. In January 2014 Mary Barra took over as first female CEO of General Motors. While this was hailed as a massive victory for women's rights, and a sign of changing times, the reality is that while Barra has the title, her pay will be less than half of her male predecessor, Dan Akerson. In fact, in his capacity as 'senior adviser' to the company, Akerson will make more money than Barra as CEO (Picci 2014).
4. The reader is referencing the film *Deliverance* (1972), and the common stereotype of using banjo playing to refer to inbreeding and backwardness in the US.
5. It is also ironic considering that, on a recent episode of her reality show, Kardashian, as a new mother, was offended at her brother's disgust when her breasts leaked milk.
6. I note her ethnic identity because it is important to recognize that the well-known history of African slavery in the United States, and the sociopolitical structures it created, continue to significantly and adversely impact a large proportion of African Americans even today, especially in terms of economics, education, and access to resources. Such systemic inequalities manifest in social conditions which result in a lesser proportion of young African American mothers breastfeeding their newborns, compared to their Caucasian and Hispanic counterparts (Currie 2013).

References

Beauvoir, Simone de ([1949] 1989) *The Second Sex*, trans. H.M. Parshley. New York: Vintage.

Carlson, N. (2013) 'The Truth about Marissa Mayer: An Unauthorized Biography,' *Business Insider*, www.businessinsider.com/marissa-mayer-biography-2013-8#ixzz3Aqpw60m7.

Catalyst (2014) 'Women CEO's of the Fortune 1000s,' *Catalyst*, 15 January, www.catalyst.org/knowledge/women-ceos-fortune-1000 (accessed 11 April 2014).

Clark, D.L., Mangasaryan, N. and Rudert, C. (2011) 'Breastfeeding: A Priority for UNICEF,' *Breastfeeding Medicine*, 6(5), 349.

Currie, D. (2013) 'Breastfeeding Rates for Black US Women Increase, But Lag Overall: Continuing Disparity Raises Concerns,' *The Nation's Health*, 23 April, 43(3), 1–20.

Deliverance (1972) (Film) (US: Warner Bros).

Devi, M. (1997) 'The Breast-Giver,' in *Breast Stories*, trans. G.C. Spivak (New York, London and Kolkota: Seagull Books).

Food and Drug Administration (FDA) (2010) 'Use of Donor Human Milk,' *Food and Drug Administration*, 30 November, www.fda.gov/scienceresearch/special-topics/pediatrictherapeuticsresearch/ucm235203.htm (accessed 11 April 2014).

Girls (2012–present) (Television series) (US: HBO).

Hall Smith, P. (2013) 'Breastfeeding and Gender Inequality,' *Journal of Women, Politics & Policy*, 34(4), 371–83.

Institute of Education Sciences (2012) 'Digest of Education Statistics,' *Institute of Education Sciences*, http://nces.ed.gov/programs/digest/d12/tables/dt12_310.asp (accessed 2 February 2014).

Labbok, M.H. (2013) 'Effects of Breastfeeding on the Mother,' *Pediatric Clinics of North America* (60)1, 11–30.

Lawrence, R.A. (2012) 'Breastfeeding Triumphs,' *Birth: Issues in Perinatal Care*, 39(4), 311–14.

Makers: Women Who Make America (2013) (Television mini-series) (US: PBS).

McRobbie, A. (2009) *The Aftermath of Feminism* (Thousand Oaks, CA: Sage).

Miller, F.L. (2012) 'Jamie Lynne Grumet, Breastfeeding Mom on *Time* Magazine Cover, Illustrates Attachment Parenting,' *Huffington Post (US)*, 10 May, online.

Mohrbacher, N. (2010) *Breastfeeding Made Simple: Seven Natural Laws for Nursing Mothers* (Oakley, CA: New Harbinger Publications).

Office on Women's Health (2011) 'Breastfeeding,' *Office on Women's Health*, 4 August, www.womenshealth.gov/breastfeeding/why-breastfeeding-is-important/index.html (accessed 11 April 2014).

Ortner, S. (1974) 'Is Female to Male as Nature is to Culture?,' in M.Z. Rosaldo and L. Lamphere (eds) *Woman, Culture and Society* (Stanford University Press), 68–87.

Perez, T.E. (2014) 'Equal Pay,' *Department of Labor*, www.dol.gov/equalpay/ (accessed 11 April 2014).

Picci, A. (2014) 'GM's First Female CEO is Paid Half of Male Predecessor,' *CBS News*, www.cbsnews.com/news/gms-first-female-ceo-is-paid-half-of-male-predecessor/ (accessed 11 April 2014).

Pickert, K. (2012) 'Are You Mom Enough? Why Attachment Parenting Drives Some Mothers to Extremes – and How Dr. Bill Sears Became their Guru,' *Time*, 21 May.

Queenan, J.T. (2003) 'Breastfeeding: It's an Important Gift,' [Editorial] *Obstetrics & Gynecology*, 102(1), 3–4.

Sandberg, S. (2013) *Women, Work, and the Will to Lead* (New York: Knopf).

Sattar, M. (2010) 'Kim Kardashian Gets Slammed after Twitter Breast-Feeding Rant,' *Time*, 21 June, http://newsfeed.time.com/2010/06/21/kim-kardashian-breastfeeding-tweets/ (accessed 11 April 2014).

Scanlon Stefanakos, V. (2012) 'Time Cover Milks Breastfeeding for All its Worth,' *Time*, 11 May, www.forbes.com/sites/forbeswomanfiles/2012/05/11/time-cover-milks-breastfeeding-for-all-its-worth/ (accessed 2 April 2014).

Schmidt, M. (2013) 'Social Marketing and Breastfeeding: A Literature Review,' *Global Journal of Health Science*, 5(3), 82–94.

Sears, W., Sears, M., Sears, W. and Sears, J. (2005) *The Baby Sleep Book: The Complete Guide to a Good Night's Rest for the Whole Family* (Boston and New York: Little, Brown).

Sears, W., Sears, M., Sears, W. and Sears, J. (2013) *The Baby Book: Everything you Need to Know about Your Baby from Birth to Age Two* (Boston and New York: Little, Brown).

Sex and the City (1998–2004) (Television series) (US: HBO).

Shute, N. (2011) 'Moms Who Can't Nurse Find Milk Donors Online,' NPR, online.

Stearns, C.A. (2009) 'The Work of Breastfeeding,' *WSQ: Women's Studies Quarterly*, 37(3&4), Fall/Winter, 63–80.

Weissinger, D., West, D. and Pitman, T. (2010) *The Womanly Art of Breastfeeding* (New York: Ballantine Press).

West, D. and Marasco, L. (2008) *The Breastfeeding Mother's Guide to More Milk* (New York: McGraw-Hill).

Xu, F., Qiu, L., Binns, C.W. and Liu, X. (2009) 'Breastfeeding in China: A Review,' *International Breastfeed Journal*, 16 June, 4(6), 1–7.

11
Running Mother Ragged: Women and Labor in the Age of Telework

Eric Lohman

Introduction

In February 2013, the CEO of Yahoo!, Marissa Mayer, declared an end to telework – or the ability to work from home – for her employees. Mayer, who left Google for Yahoo! while five months pregnant, famously announced that she only required two weeks of maternity leave before returning to work. Mayer also built a nursery in her office for her new-born son, and has a nanny on site to help with childcare; the irony was not lost on her employees. In a *Daily Mail* article from 26 February, an employee asked what would happen if his wife brought their son to work at Yahoo! and set the baby up in the adjacent cubicle (Larson & Peterson 2013, p. 1). Mayer can afford to work from home because she simply built her house into the Yahoo! offices. Lisa Belkin, a columnist for *The Huffington Post*, accused Mayer of being out of touch with the needs of working mothers, and of being stuck in the past when she ended telework (Belkin 2013). In another article called 'The New Mommy Wars' (2013) Joanne Bamberger of *USA Today* alleged that Mayer had launched 'the latest salvo in the war on moms. The amount of household help they (wealthy female executives) can afford to manage their family lives isn't a reality for the vast majority of women and never will be.'

It is easy to sympathize with the outrage at Mayer's decision to rescind flexible work arrangements, especially when Mayer herself enjoys the finances to create whatever childcare model is most convenient for her, a luxury that most other working mothers could never imagine. While many families rely on telework to balance careers and family, it is not without its own set of problems, as Mayer discovered. A growing number of authors that study telework find it is problematic for a variety of reasons. Many scholars have found that it has the potential to be exploitative, despite its family friendly appearance. For example, Hill et al. (1996) argue that 'one of the major benefits of mobile telework might be a greater flexibility to manage household chores and child care' (p. 298). However, the authors conclude that telework is likely to blur the boundaries between work and home, leading to increased frequency of 'work/family transition periods,' which are moments when a parent is leaving for work, or coming from work (p. 298). These can often be very stressful periods of time, and so to increase the amount of work/family transition periods per day can lead to a subsequent intensification in feelings of anxiety, or the perception of being 'out of control.' According to surveys done by Ursula Huws et al. (1990), women with children find that telework does not represent a substitute for going out to work in an office, but is an alternative to not working at all (p. 43). Without the option of working from home, where women are able to perform their 'primary' tasks as domestic laborers, many women might remain unemployed.

Telework therefore appears to offer working mothers freedom from one of the most sinister trappings of patriarchal culture: they're given more freedom to pursue fulfilling careers without having to sacrifice time with their children. Employers can see the advantages in telework in that they can retain, or even increase, the work output of their employees, while at the same time offsetting certain costs like office space, heating and electricity expenses, or the costs associated with parents missing work to care for sick children.[1] In this chapter, I will examine discourses around telework and gender in the popular press so that I may expose the inherently counterproductive nature of capital-determined solutions to the problems of working mothers. I contend that telework is a market-driven response to problems in the work/life balance of employed mothers that unevenly privileges the interests of employers over that of women with children, primarily because it fails to account for the gendered division of domestic labor. But more importantly, the limited scope of the argument on telework and gender is toxic because it fails to denounce labor itself as an institution of patriarchal subjugation. Therefore, any feminist analysis that does not criticize work under capitalism as an inherently exploitative institution is condemning feminism to obscurity.

Autonomist Marxism and telework

I intend to situate telework within a historical and theoretical framework that argues that worker resistance is the engine of social change.

According to Kathi Weeks, this is sometimes called the 'autonomist hypothesis.' Weeks contends that the hypothesis is the 'autonomist tradition's methodological center of gravity,' in that most of the scholars in this tradition argue that 'working-class resistance precedes and prefigures developments in capitalist production' (Weeks 2011, p. 94). Another autonomist scholar, Nick Dyer-Witheford, suggests that capital (which we generally think of as a mode of producing goods and organizing labor in such a way that workers are paid a wage, and the owners of the means of production realize a profit at the end of the working day) attempts to maximize exploitation either 'absolutely' (by extending the working day) or 'relatively' (by raising the intensity or productivity of labor) (Dyer-Witheford 1994, p. 7).

Telework fits uniquely between these two horizons. On one hand, we can think of telework as an attempt by employers to lengthen the working day. Indeed, as Mary Noonan and Jennifer Glass reported, teleworkers average five to seven hours of overtime work per week more than their non-teleworking counterparts (2012, p. 45). I suspect that this is likely a low estimate, since many workers might not include checking or responding to emails on a smartphone as work, especially if they are engaged in some leisure activity when they respond. On the other hand, telework can be thought of as part of the feminist and worker struggles against capital to realize more family or leisure time. However, this latter argument is only valid, I posit, if we think of domestic labor (or even most leisure time) as not 'real' work. When domestic labor is categorized as necessary to capital's ability to extract profit from employee labor power, as many of the scholars in the autonomist tradition believe it does, then it becomes clear that telework holds little benefit for those already responsible for domestic labor. From the autonomist perspective, telework merely allows employers to maximize absolute exploitation, by increasing the length of the working day, and also maximizing relative exploitation, by raising worker productivity and allowing them to weave both waged and domestic labor together throughout the day.

The autonomists believe that capitalism reorganizes work in the 'social factory,' which includes the home, as this type of work is essential to capitalism because it reproduces rested, clean, content, well-fed workers (Weeks 2011, p. 120). Therefore, it benefits capitalism to make feminist discourses invisible, or at least render them unpopular, because feminism has historically challenged the gendered divisions that relegate women to second-class statuses. As an organizing theoretical perspective of this project, I contend that contemporary discussions over telework represent an important moment in the cycles of both feminist and working-class struggles, as it signifies drastic changes to the organization of both domestic and waged labor. As such, in an effort to maintain control over workers, capitalism must also seek to maintain control over the gendered divisions that keep us all from realizing a common enemy in patriarchal capitalism.

Working hard or hardly working?

In an article published on CBS's *MoneyWatch* website entitled '5 Ways to Make Telecommuting Work for You' (2012), Kathy Kristof offers some advice for would-be teleworkers. At the top of the article is an image of a young woman smiling at the camera while working on a laptop computer. Between the computer and the woman is a child, presumably her daughter, sitting quietly and attentively in her lap while her mother works from home. The article addresses a number of the hurdles a typical teleworker may encounter while working, but the author does so without speaking to the gendered division of domestic labor that makes many of these problems persistent. Four of the tips the author explores deal directly with how to eliminate family interferences from the workday when one is at home. What it essentially boils down to is the creation of strict boundaries between work and family. The smiling mother–daughter duo in the photograph implies that there can be a happy balance between a job and family so long as firm restrictions are established and rigidly observed by everyone involved.

To put it another way, telework makes it possible for women to spend more quality time raising their young children, while simultaneously enjoying a fulfilling career, if they are willing to put their children aside for the entire workday. The suggestions are, perhaps not surprisingly, from the perspective that work must come before family obligations, which is illustrative of the fact that telework is often seen as an ideal compromise from the perspective of employers, as a solution to the work/life balance problem. The author suggests that 'one of the big benefits of working from home is being able to spend more time with your family, put them on your schedule for lunch.' This creates a discourse where working mothers are being told that it is their responsibility to care for children and the home while working full-time, and that it's just a matter of striking the right timing between all that work to achieve perfect harmony. It is very likely that men would be free to heed the author's advice and arrange for someone to watch the kids while working from home, or set up a private home office that is kept free from interruptions. According to a study by Mirchandani (1999), the difference between male and female teleworkers and their ability to work from home is a matter of self-control. For men, interacting with family is a 'temptation,' but for women it is a responsibility. Men view the family as an impediment to getting work done, an enticement that must be carefully mitigated if they are to be productive. Women see the family as an essential part of their daily labor responsibilities, meaning the boundary between paid work and domestic work has to remain permeable if either is to be completed (Mirchandani 1999, p. 98). Therefore, in order for women to experience the benefits of telework, they would have to work on the same terms as men, essentially limiting their role as domestic caretakers. While one option is for male partners to take on an equal role in domestic labor, this option is usually sacrificed in favor of paid domestic help in the form of babysitters, day cares, nannies, and maids (Mirchandani 2009, p. 98). In this way, telework seeks to increase the absolute exploitation, by lengthening the waged workday as long as possible. It also indicates that the only way to enjoy a successful career like men is to prioritize work over family as men often do.

Telework takes for granted the fact that domestic labor exists and that women are under a different set of pressures to attend to that work than men are. A study by Arlie Russell Hochschild (1990) concluded that when both men and women in a domestic partnership are employed full-time, there exists roughly a month's worth of extra labor per year that must be done around the home; this labor disproportionately falls onto the shoulders of women. Whether it's cleaning the house, cooking meals, or caring for sick children in the middle of the night, it is likely that the working mother will be responsible for ensuring this work is completed. What makes telework different from traditional work is that employers are able to benefit financially from the seamless transition women experience between this domestic work and their waged labor. For example, if a working mother needs to take her child to the doctor, under a traditional work arrangement she would have to take time off, which ends up costing the company a lot of money in missed work, paid vacation time, sick time, or the like. Under a telework arrangement, the employee never actually has time 'off,' but instead she would likely just finish her work later on in the day. This is how telework is able to maximize the relative exploitation of labor, by mitigating the cost of those occurrences that usually draw workers away from the job, and thus result in lost productivity. On 17 November 2012, in a *Baltimore Sun* article entitled 'Hurricane Sandy Boosts Federal Telework,' author John Fritze reported that during the hurricane, around a third of the employees at federal agencies continued to work from home while

Washington DC and New York were essentially shut down. On one hand, this is an improvement, since distributing vital services during a natural disaster is a great benefit of telework. However, this has the potential to be problematic, as knowing that employees will work from home can result in an increased expectation for employees to preclude any outside circumstances from interfering with their workday. Work must get done as a matter of course, and everything else must fit in between the breaks in waged labor.

The autonomist tradition has made a very convincing case for the reconceptualization of domestic labor as being vital to the production of surplus value under capitalism. The month of extra labor Hochschild theorized is not only done by women, but is also indispensable if workers are to be reproduced from day to day. To put it another way, when workers spend their day toiling, they need to go home and rest if they are to be ready to come back the next day. It is not in the interest of employers to work employees to death. As Maria Rosa Dalla Costa and Selma James argue, it is the homeworker then who is responsible for producing, from day to day, that which is most integral to capitalism's ability to function: the 'living human being' (1972). Leopoldina Fortunati argued that the wage for this reproductive work used to be concealed in the male breadwinner's earnings; however, that is not exactly relevant at a time when women have paid employment of their own (1989, p. 42).[2] In any case, if domestic labor is not completed, capitalism suffers the consequences because the labor pool is not willing or able, both physically and emotionally, to submit to the stress of the workday. Therefore, not only does telework allow for the extraction of value by allowing women to integrate waged and domestic labor into the day, but since that unwaged work done in the home also benefits capitalism, telework ensures the cheap and efficient reproduction of capitalism's workforce.

We can start to see the boundaries of the problem with telework from a feminist and autonomist Marxist perspective. The telework discourses fail to account for the 'relative' exploitation, in that telework increases the productivity of working women by allowing for seamless transitions between domestic and waged work, both of which help employers realize profits, but also the 'absolute' exploitation of telework, which maximizes the hours put into waged work. To that end, I want to turn now to the problems that arise while trying to conceptualize telework as a means of emancipation from patriarchy. In the disputes between socialist feminists and more mainstream liberal feminists, I think it is safe to say that the latter's platform has been more popularly accepted.

As Wendy McKeen argues, radical feminists such as those from the Wages for Housework campaign of the 1970s – of which autonomist Marxist feminists Selma James and Mariarosa Dalla Costa were founders – were met with fierce resistance by groups such as the National Action Committee on the Status of Women in Canada, whose platform of equal opportunity, equal pay, and the elimination of gender-based stereotypes was threatened by discussions of class domination (1994, p. 33).[3] The concept of 'women's liberation' is objectively simple in that members seek to identify the best way to liberate women from patriarchal oppression. One of the main strategies that have been employed since the women's liberation movement began has been emancipation from patriarchy through economic self-sufficiency. But I argue that what this has amounted to, as Mariarosa Dalla Costa and Selma James might articulate, is that women have traded slavery to the kitchen sink for slavery to the assembly line *and* the kitchen sink.

The liberal-feminist rhetoric of liberation and empowerment through work has led to the obfuscation of perhaps the most important goal of early feminist struggles: self-actualization, which under capital is at best a disappointing compromise. As Anne-Marie Slaughter wrote in her article 'Why Women Still Can't Have It All' (2012), the problem is that women are forced to accept male behaviors and male choices – which includes spending long hours working rather than spending time with children, putting in 'face time' with bosses and co-workers, overtime and weekend work, and extensive work travel – as the default for professional success. Slaughter learned that her ability to 'have it all,' that is, to have professional success while raising a family, was dependent upon the type of job she had. Once she was no longer given the freedom to make her own schedule (which had been the norm when she was an academic, but not the case after she accepted a government job), she found that she could no longer balance her family and career without one of them suffering. Her analysis is important because it helps illuminate the anxieties that underpin the ways in which post-second-wave liberal feminist work discourses have failed to challenge patriarchal assumptions about what constitutes success. One's ability to scale the work ladder *while* being a parent is the only acceptable definition of success for a woman in postfeminist parlance. And yet, it is well documented that this combination of waged and unwaged labor spreads women incredibly thin. Even if women have a partner that equally shares domestic responsibilities, professional success requires so much more effort and sacrifice from women than it does from men.[4]

Slaughter's solution to the problem is a reconstitution of society so that it more clearly favors women's choices about how to work, which in large part is another way of arguing for more flexible labor opportunities. While I agree that a macro-level change is needed, one that ceases to blame women who choose family over work for being insufficiently committed, I again question the assumption that telework is the solution. For example, research has shown that when telework or flexible arrangements are offered to women, they are reluctant to take advantage of it because the culture of work punishes these approaches to labor. As Arlie Russell Hochschild argues in *The Time Bind* (1997), flexible work arrangements that appear to serve women with families are not sufficient if the structure of face time and glad-handing is left in place; it will disadvantage women who choose family over work, and leads many to reject flexibility altogether. 'Women have entered the workforce on male terms,' says Hochschild. And it is not a level playing field; it is slanted noticeably in favor of men and employers (1997, p. 247). Slaughter recounts how in years passed she would shake her head in condescending disappointment as her younger colleagues left the professional track to raise a family, only realizing decades later that she was reproducing the same type of patriarchal dedication to work that feminists have argued keeps fathers separated from their children, and reproduces the gender hierarchy generation after generation. She came to realize that she had helped make millions of young women feel like it was their fault if they couldn't 'have it all' (2012, p. 2). Slaughter's article makes a convincing argument that the masculine culture of work is firmly in place, which means that telework has the potential to be an inferior and disadvantageous model for women with children.

For some scholars such as Slaughter, increasing flexibility, which would include telework among other things, solves the problems inherent with working on male terms. While others argue that flexibility is exploitative of women because it normalizes an arrangement whereby they are expected to devote all of their time to labor that valorizes capital in one way or another. These work arrangements appear to produce a very problematic understanding of work/life balance, in that there remains a conflict over which method of organizing work most accurately reflects the contemporary desires of working women. The choice is as follows: you can 'have it all' by sacrificing time with family in order to climb the ladder. Or you can 'have it all' by rejecting the trappings of 'feminism' and embracing choice and tradition, which will allow you to stay home with your family but still create value for capitalism. And there is a third choice: you could 'have it all' by toiling assiduously at home with family whenever you are not working relentlessly to advance your career. The discourses on telework pretend to solve this problem by arguing that technology can provide workers with the ability to perform tasks from anywhere at anytime, which would benefit women since they are also homeworkers as well as wage laborers and need flexibility to make all the tasks fit. Under the same circumstances though, technology could afford women and men the opportunity to be productive while doing considerably less paid work overall.

Therefore, if telework isn't reducing the total amount of work that is required of women – and research shows it is more likely to increase the amount of work – then its value to women as it currently stands must be challenged. A radical feminist project can only truly reemerge if women are able to determine their own livelihoods and define success for themselves, free from the structures of capitalism and patriarchy, which are both in a constant battle with one another over whose definition of 'female success' will rue the day. The debate has often been limited to the extremes. On one end you have 'new traditionalism,' Susan Faludi's (1991) term for the 'resurgence of the traditional family' (pp. 18–19) that followed the second wave, and on the other end you have the liberal feminist preoccupation with success defined alongside male workaholic standards, which Anne-Marie Slaughter has come to lament. This, I argue, is what has led to the marginalization of feminist discourses. Feminism has become defined by work, and so the decisions about whether or not to work or raise a family is a Hobson's choice, where any decision will likely lead to further subjugation to patriarchy.

Marilyn Frye (1983) has a better name for this phenomenon: oppression. 'One of the most characteristic and ubiquitous features of the world as experienced by oppressed people is the double bind – situations in which options are reduced to a very few and all of them expose one to penalty, censure or deprivation' (p. 11). The erasure of feminist discourses is a result of the double bind that women are presented with when it comes to work and family life under modern capitalism. Selecting a career puts women into a situation where they are forced to curtail family responsibilities in order to rise to the top of their profession. Opting for family life leads to isolation from sociality, suspension of personal goals and ambitions, and reliance upon a partner for economic survival. Part-time work can lead to disappointing wages, reduced benefits, and deferment of one's chances at a promotion. And telework is likely to lead to mutually exploitative overwork, as the full-time responsibilities of family and professional labor converge in the home, stripping women of any semblance of personal time. Telework is but one wire in the infamous birdcage that Frye (1983) theorized. When taken on its own, it's difficult to see telework's potential for restriction, but when you step back and see how it combines with other wires to form a cage, a network of systematically related barriers (p. 13), the oppressive nature then becomes impossible to ignore.

The core of what defines feminist struggles, to varying degrees, has always revolved around impediments women face as they try to determine their own paths, identities, and goals. This struggle has often been co-opted by neoliberal pundits who cheerlead the abundance of 'choice' as the great equalizer, in spite of rampant and persistent structural gender inequality. Therefore, whether working from home or working in an office, whether in a lecture hall as a professor or sweeping the floors after the class as the janitor, unless the conditions under which women take on paid work is determined by them and them alone, never will the exploitation of women cease. Their paths, identities, and goals will always be determined and influenced by powers beyond their control.

An alternative solution: zero work and self-determination

In this section, I would like to explore some potential solutions that I feel would serve working mothers, or potential mothers, better than telework. Freeing women from the need to decide what type of work will allow them to fulfill conflicting and contradictory obligations is in turn freeing them from the double bind that snares them. Therefore, I argue that separating labor from wages leads to work occupying an ever-dwindling importance in how we organize our society, opening the door to more creative and self-organized methods for spending time, caring for one another, and performing other socially necessary and fulfilling work on terms set out by us. As it stands, telework focuses intently on the results that employees are able to accomplish rather than the amount of labor time they put in to a project. This method of arranging labor is hopelessly instrumental. In the long run, telework will require increased results and growth, and without safeguards in place to monitor how work is being done and what toll that labor is taking on workers, employers will be free to exempt themselves from the costs – financially, socially, and morally – associated with overworking their employees. This is already the case with teleworking women.

One potential method to address the double bind that is wage and domestic labor exploitation is a guaranteed annual income. Although this approach isn't new, it has renewed importance in the contemporary context of deficient work/life balance for women. According to Nick

Dyer-Witheford, a guaranteed annual income 'perhaps tied to a requirement for men and women alike to participate in activities such as child
raising, caring for the sick and elderly – would effectively annihilate
the hierarchical division of waged and non-waged labor that has so
closely entwined capitalism and patriarchy' (1999, p. 200). I share the
belief that a guaranteed annual income for every man and woman is an
important goal that may one day play a role in severing the inhumane
relation between our need to work for wages and our desire to survive. A
significant first step in reaching this goal could be a guaranteed annual
income for women, regardless of marital status or employment. This
would have a myriad of positive effects, not least of which would be the
separation of women from any financial dependence on male partners,
or dependence on their ability to sell their labor power to capital, which
would create a situation whereby women's work, childcare, educational,
volunteer, and leisure options could be true choices: determined with
minimal influence from external factors.

In a *Sydney Morning Herald* article entitled 'Get a Life? Sorry, No Time,'
Rachel Browne (2012) said that researchers are increasingly concluding
that 'flexible hours, part-time work, telecommuting and technology
have not lived up to their promise of liberating workers from the daily
grind ... instead, they have allowed work to encroach on home life,
leaving many workers at breaking point.' The technology that makes
telework possible is actually just extending the workday into the home.
To be sure, this is a result of the fact that patriarchal and capitalistic
interests structure these programs to serve their ends. This need not
be the case. Much feminist attention has been devoted to the role of
technology in the struggle against patriarchy. Generally speaking the
debates have focused on whether technology is problematic because
men have a monopoly over its use and development, or if technology
itself is inherently patriarchal (Wajcman 2004, p. 12). Some argue that
because technology is produced under the sociopolitical order of patriarchal capitalism, technology tends to serve that ideology (Rothschild
1983, p. 84). I prefer Donna Haraway's Cyborg project, which insists
on the possibility of using the technological products of militarism and
patriarchal capitalism against itself. Haraway argues for a politics rooted
in the transition from 'an organic, industrial society to a polymor-
phous, information system' (1991, p. 161). Technology, regardless of its
politics, can be put to social ends if we so desire. Haraway encourages
us to embrace our various political positions, as well as the noise and
miscommunications inherent in modern society, in order to subvert
the reproduction of patriarchy and capitalism. Flexible hours, part-time

work, telework, and technology could potentially liberate laborers from overwork provided that workers are the ones that determine the conditions under which these technological tools are to be employed. If left unchallenged, employers will use all of these apparatuses to create value, and workers will suffer. Fortunati (2007) argues that 'people possess at a mass level a whole series of communication and information technologies and have become better at using them' (p. 153). She continues, 'The alternative use of new media is crucial for the new political subjects' (p. 153).

In addition to a guaranteed annual income, reappropriating technology so that it empowers women to self-determine their time and self-valorize their labor is another critical step in the transition toward a new feminist project. This project would encourage women to use communications technology in a way that frees them from the demands of compulsory waged and domestic labor. For example, using the internet to set up and coordinate childcare cooperatives, with the goal of allowing women the ability to pursue personal leisure interests. The same could be done with other facets of domestic labor, including food preparation. Essentially women have two options to address domestic labor like childcare or food service: either pay for a service (fast food, day care, babysitter, etc.), or do the work on their own. A cooperative could greatly diminish the amount of labor involved in completing these tasks (especially if male partners are enlisted), but would also eliminate the need to rely on commercial enterprises to reduce this labor. By harvesting the potential inherent in emerging communication technologies, women could reallocate their labor power in a manner that allows them to reduce the amount of work overall, while allowing them more time to devote to the alleviation of collective problems.

Conclusion

From a socialist feminist perspective, the erasure of feminist discourses begins and ends with work. The once counter-hegemonic potential of feminism has, for at least the mainstream populations of the West, been co-opted and neutralized by neoliberal capitalism. Much feminist literature views work as liberating, while patriarchal capitalism continues to use work as a means of control, domination, and exploitation. This is a hegemonic contradiction, as work cannot be both liberating and exploitative. This contradiction is used, however, to mask the double bind and thus place the onus of making work workable for women squarely on the shoulders of those subjected to its oppressive logics and rhythms. According to Raymond Williams, 'A lived hegemony is always a process.' It cannot exist as a stable form of domination, but must be 'continually renewed, recreated, defended, and modified' (1977, p. 112). Feminist resistance to patriarchy in the 1960s and 1970s forced the latter to adopt a new method of domination. Rather than cede domestic labor as value producing to capital or socially valuable in general, paid work (and hence overwork) for women became the symbol of feminist success. And the radical energy of feminism has been usurped, so that it now is the engine that pushes capitalist exploitation even deeper into our homes.

Notes

1. A trade report commissioned by the Telework Research Network in Canada argues that telework can reduce all manner of employee costs, including sick time, office space, vacation, or employee inefficiency (see Lister & Harnish 2011).
2. George Caffentzis (1992) calls this wage the 'Oedipal Wage,' as it functions to give the male control over his wife and children, since it is he who 'earns' it.
3. Many radical feminist groups were not at all interested in assimilating women into the mainstream, and advocated instead for female separation from men and/or masculinity completely. Radical feminist groups such as Redstockings and Cell 16 frequently derided mainstream feminists for their willingness to work with patriarchal institutions, such as advertising. For more on the tension between mainstream and radical feminism see Echols (1989).
4. As Slaughter (2012) points out, women who make it to the top of their profession are not extremely committed to success, 'they are genuine superwomen.' The great many top women must reject the idea of raising a family in order to achieve the type of success that men with families easily obtain.

References

Bamberger, J. (2013) 'The New Mommy Wars: Column,' *USA Today*, 25 February, www.usatoday.com/story/opinion/2013/02/25/thenew-mommy-wars-column/1947589/ (accessed 18 March 2013).

Belkin, L. (2013) 'Marissa Mayer's Work-From-Home Ban is the Exact Opposite of What CEOs Should Be Doing,' *Huffington Post*, 23 February, www.huffington post.com/lisa-belkin/marissa-mayer-work-from-home-yahoo-rule_b_2750256. html (accessed 16 August 2014).

Browne, R. (2012) 'Get a Life? Sorry, No Time,' *Sydney Morning Herald*, 12 February, www.smh.com.au/executive-style/management/get-a-life-sorry-no-time-20120211-1sy9b.html (accessed 18 March 2013).

Caffentzis, G. (1992) 'The Work/Energy Crisis and the Apocalypse,' in Midnight Notes Collective (eds) *Midnight Oil: Work, Energy, War 1973–1992* (New York: Autonomedia).

Dalla Costa, M. and James, S. (1972) *The Power of Women and the Subversion of the Community* (Bristol: Falling Wall Press).

Dyer-Witheford, N. (1994) 'Autonomist Marxism and the Information Society,' *Capital and Class*, 1(52), 1–33.

Dyer-Witheford, N. (1999) *Cyber-Marx: Cycles and Circuits of Struggle in High Technology Capitalism* (Chicago: University of Illinois Press).

Echols, A. (1989) *Daring to Be Bad: Radical Feminism in America 1967–1975* (Minneapolis: University of Minnesota Press).

Faludi, S. (1991) *Backlash: The Undeclared War Against American Women* (New York: Doubleday Books).

Fortunati, L. (1989) *Arcane of Reproduction: Housework, Prostitution, Labor and Capital* (New York: Autonomedia).

Fortunati, L. (2007) 'Immaterial Labour and its Mechanization,' *Ephemera Journal of Theory and Politics in Organization*, 7(1), 139–57.

Fritze, J. (2012) 'Hurricane Sandy Boosts Federal Telework: Agencies Expanding Work-From-Home Policies,' *The Baltimore Sun*, 17 November, http://articles. baltimoresun.com/2012-11-17/news/bs-md-sandy-telework-20121116_1_hur ricane-sandy-telework-exchange-federal-employees (accessed 16 August 2014).

Frye, M. (1983) 'Oppression and the Use of Definition,' in M. Frye, *The Politics of Reality* (Trumansburg, NY: The Crossing Press).

Haraway, D. (1991) *Simians, Cyborgs and Women: The Reinvention of Nature* (London and New York: Routledge).

Hill, J.E., Hawkins, A.J. and Miller, B.C. (1996) 'Work and Family in the Virtual Office: Perceived Influences of Mobile Telework,' *Family Relations*, 45(3), 293–301.

Hochschild, A.R. (1990) *The Second Shift: Working Families and the Revolution at Home* (New York: Penguin Books).

Hochschild, A.R. (1997) *The Time Bind: When Work Becomes Home and Home Becomes Work* (New York: Macmillan).

Huws, U., Korte, W.B. and Robinson, S. (1990) *Telework: Towards the Elusive Office* (New York: Empirica Press).

Kristof, K. (2012) '5 Ways to Make Telecommuting Work for You,' *CBS MoneyWatch*.

Larson, L. and Peterson, H. (2013) 'Yahoo! Boss Marissa Mayer Under Fire for Building Personal Nursery Next to Her Office Before Telling Employees they Can NOT Work From Home,' *The Daily Mail Online*, 26 February, www.dailymail.co.uk/news/article-2284828/Yahoo-boss-Marissa-Mayer-angers-employees-building-nursery-baby-office.html (accessed 16 August 2014).

Lister, K. and Harnish, T. (2011) 'WORKshift Canada: The Bottom Line on Telework,' Telework Research Network.

McKeen, W. (1994) 'The Wages for Housework Campaign: Its Contribution to Feminist Politics in the Area of Social Welfare in Canada,' *Canadian Review of Social Policy*, 33 (Spring/Summer), 21–43.

Mirchandani, K. (1999) 'Legitimizing Work: Telework and the Gendered Reification of the Work–Nonwork Dichotomy,' *Review of Sociology*, 36(1), 87–107.

Noonan, M.C. and Glass, J.L. (2012) 'The Hard Truth about Telecommuting,' *Bureau of Labor Statistics Monthly Labor Review*, 135(6), 38–45.

Rothschild, J. (1983) *Machina Ex Dea: Feminist Perspectives on Technology* (New York: Pergamon Press).

Slaughter, A.-M. (2012) 'Why Women Still Can't Have It All,' *The Atlantic*, July/August, www.theatlantic.com/magazine/archive/2012/07/why-women-stillcanthave-it-all/309020/ (accessed 15 March 2013).

Wajcman, J. (2004) *Technofeminism* (Cambridge: Polity Press).

Weeks, K. (2011) *The Problem with Work: Feminism, Marxism, Antiwork Politics, and Postwork Imaginaries* (Durham, NC: Duke University Press).

Williams, R. (1977) *Marxism and Literature* (Oxford University Press).

12
Infertility Blogging, Body, and the Avatar

Rosemary Hepworth

Introduction

Blogging is now considered to be a widespread and lasting phenomenon and yet, with some notable exceptions, critical reception has been limited by several factors. Geert Lovink (2008) notes the tendency of scholars to presume that 'blogs have a symbiotic relationship with the news industry,' and he argues that in order to provide a more comprehensive assessment of blogging this must be countered. For example, he suggests that 'it would be important to dig into the rich history of literary criticism and see how blogging relates to diary keeping' (p. 6).

In addition to being excluded from academic literary studies by its automatic inclusion within 'popular culture,' perhaps the reluctance or reticence of many literary critics to adequately explore the blog can be explained by the growing perception that (diary) blogging is a feminine activity. In 2009, roughly a decade since the diary blog's transformation of the blogosphere, a report by 'BlogHer,' a widely recognized network for women bloggers, asserted that the proportion of women blogging was increasing (Wright & Camahort 2009). However the increase in women bloggers coincides with the proliferation of diary blogs, which, as Lena Karlsson notes, are generally ignored or derided. She asks: '[i]s what we find here a new take on the very old story about gendered forms of popular culture enjoyed and in this case produced by women and scholarly neglect and embarrassment?' (2007, p. 138). This assessment of scholarly reception echoes that of Lidia Curti, who laments the 'double standard' inherent in the ways literary and media critics discuss other kinds of 'feminine narratives,' television soaps for example (1998, pp. 57–8). What this suggests to me is that there are still, despite all the promises of the digital age, narrative forms that are (critically, at least) irrelevant by virtue of their women authors and association with feminine narrative forms. Consequently, the women producing these narratives, and using and shaping blogging technologies, remain invisible. So too are the infertile (or sub-fertile, to use the medically accurate term) women upon whose bodies new reproductive technologies are developed and measured.

This chapter begins with a comparison of the narratives promoted by science, the media, and feminist theorists, and demonstrates how each of these narratives has failed to fully acknowledge the voices of infertile women. It then examines the diary blogs of two women bloggers in the online infertility community and demonstrates how blogging about their experiences enables them to renegotiate the subject positions ascribed to them by these traditional infertility and IVF (in-vitro fertilization) narratives. I draw upon the conceptual figure of the avatar – related to but distinct from the avatar of social media – to demonstrate how the diary blog allows a powerful rewriting, both of self (in the context of infertility) and of the story of modern fertility treatment. These avatar-selves constitute a challenge to the persistent erasure of the infertile woman from narratives arising from infertility and its treatment by reproductive technologies, particularly in-vitro fertilization (IVF).

Infertility, IVF, and the 'hero-narrative'

In the information 'brochure' that prospective patients receive from The London Women's Clinic (LWC), 2008 success rates for IVF/ICSI (intracytoplasmic sperm injection) embryo transfer were given as 55 percent for the under 35 age group and 22 percent for the 40–42 age group. 'Success' is defined here as pregnancies that have been confirmed by ultrasound. There is no indication of the number that result in live births. The LWC success rates are presented on a single, non-illustrated sheet of paper, along with a list of treatment costs, in the back of a pack that includes the Clinic's information material: a promotional brochure, and a colorful, glossy issue of *Ova* magazine, which is edited by the Clinic's managing director. This clinic, as an example of UK fertility clinics, contributes to what Michael Mulkay calls the 'rhetoric of hope,' which is carefully cultivated by embryologists and fertility specialists (Mulkay 1997, p. 75). The promotion of a selective narrative by the media is one of the ways that women and their bodies are effectively erased from the story of infertility and its treatments.

The welcome page of The London Women's Clinic's brochure states that:

> The desire to have a child is an exciting and natural part of most people's lives. Unfortunately some people experience difficulty in fulfilling this wish. The London Women's Clinic (LWC) has centres across the UK and provides a range of fertility treatments to assist couples and individuals in overcoming these difficulties. (LWC 2009)

Even in this introductory paragraph the rhetoric subtly manipulates the reader's perception of the clinic. The words used to describe the impact of treatment as 'assist[ing],' 'overcoming,' and 'fulfilling' have clear connotations of triumph. By contrast, the euphemistic and repetitive use of words like 'difficulty' and 'difficulties' reduces the experience of infertility to something vague, as though it is merely a setback or glitch rather than the full-stop the patient may have feared. For most infertile people, the only sense in which they would consider themselves as having 'overcome' their infertility would be by becoming parents as a direct result of the treatment. The 'success' rates (in whatever form they are presented) cannot disguise the fact that many of these people will not become parents by these means. This narrative of hope is heavily promoted in the brochure, and the inside of its front and back covers features photographs of their 'baby wall,' attended by a note that reads: '[w]e are pleased that many of our families stay in touch, regularly sending photos of their children as they grow up.' Photographic evidence employs a visual grammar in the service of its printed narrative in order to validate further the message that the LWC is able to transform infertility into a temporary difficulty, whilst translating hope into a take-home baby.

The media have also privileged these success stories over the failures of IVF treatments. This has had a significant impact on cultural perceptions of IVF treatments, and has shaped the dominant narrative of infertility. As part of his 1997 study, Mulkay examines British newspaper articles about IVF and infertility treatment. These articles were printed during the debate surrounding the legislative activity around IVF and embryology research in the 1980s. Mulkay observes that, during this time, the IVF success stories presented by the British media far outnumbered those in which fertility treatments such as IVF failed to result in a live birth. The stories of the 'much greater number of women for whom the technology had failed, and for whom there may have been more suffering than joy, were almost completely ignored' (Mulkay 1997, p. 73). Furthermore,

Mulkay points out that there was another agenda at work in the selection of these stories. The women featured were not representational of infertile women seeking reproductive assistance but were selected in order to negate anxieties surrounding technological intervention by subtly endorsing conventional images of femininity and motherhood. In her analysis of public pregnancies and the reverence directed toward pregnant women in the context of technological reproduction, Anne Balsamo remarks upon the subtitle of reproductive medicine expert E. Peter Volpe's book, *Test-Tube Conception: A Blend of Love and Science* (1987). Balsamo highlights how medical discourse adopts this kind of cultural reverence toward conception and pregnancy (Balsamo 1997, p. 81). This title is revealing in several ways. The word 'conception' itself suggests fertilization, whilst the subtitle replaces the sexual coupling of two human beings with a coupling between two motivations: 'love' and 'science.' Science is elevated to the status of a parent in the process of conception, and framed as a requisite without which conception cannot take place. Rather than a man's sperm fertilizing a woman's ovum, as in the traditional narrative of biological reproduction, here the masculine business of science fertilizes love, an altogether more feminine occupation. Volpe reinscribes the traditional alignment of masculinity with the logical, rational, and productive discourse of the public domain, and femininity with the caring, nurturing, domestic discourse of the private domain. This appeal to traditional gender relations invokes the natural order of things, thereby playing down anxieties about technological intervention whilst naturalizing test-tube conception.

In her 1988 study on the cultural stigma of infertility, Naomi Pfeffer includes the following quotation, taken from the UK's House of Commons debate on Enoch Powell's Unborn Child Protection Bill:

> The object of our interest in medical research into embryology and human fertilization is to help humanity. It is to help those who are infertile and to help control infertility ... The researchers are not monsters, but scientists. They are medical scientists working in response to a great human need. We should be proud of them. The infertile parents who have been helped are grateful to them. (House of Commons Debates 1984–85, p. 73, column 654 cited in Pfeffer 1988, p. 81)

Here we see a reiteration of the hero-scientist of Volpe's subtitle, and the narrative of hope promoted by the LWC. The grand claims to altruism are evident here. The agenda as it is presented here is not about profits or reputation, but about selfless people working hard to help humanity.

Like Volpe's subtitle, this narrative suggests that science and love are not only compatible, but co-dependent in their common pursuit of a shared goal: a healthy baby.

In his analysis of press clippings from November 1989 to July 1990, Mulkay notes that:

> [W]omen were visually outnumbered in the newspapers by their off-spring ... For women were present only as potential or actual bearers of children ... Without the baby, there is no role for the woman to perform. (Mulkay 1997, pp. 73–5)

Mulkay points out that most of these stories originated with scientists and fertility clinics who would release heart-warming success stories to the press in order to promote the hope narrative, thus serving their pro-research agenda (Mulkay 1997, pp. 73–5). This generation and regulation of the British media's coverage of reproductive technology signals a patriarchal construction of the infertility and IVF narrative, and a systematic suppression of alternative narratives, especially ones created by women. Not only have IVF failures been underrepresented to the point of erasure, so too have women's experiences of the *processes* involved in assisted reproduction been erased. Instead, the focus has been placed on the triumphant end result: the baby.

It is important to note, however, not just *how* this rhetorical and visual erasure has taken place, but *where*. Like the promotional material of the LWC, the press functions as an interface between the public and private spheres of society. As such, it can be seen as an inherently political interface that significantly influences power relations between the two. It is significant that there is an observable erasure of women's voices from the public sphere. The political implications of this systematic silencing of women's voices from the dominant IVF narrative are that women will continue to be characterized as silent and passive objects in the performance of it, subjugated and controlled by its authors and heroes.

Feminist responses to reproductive technologies

It could be argued that this second narrative, which primarily focuses its attention on the question of New Reproductive Technologies (NRT) rather than that of infertility, does little to alleviate the marginalization of infertile women. The debate surrounding IVF and NRT has polarized feminists. For some, these technologies represent a greater number of reproductive choices, particularly for single women and lesbian couples, whilst others, responding to the political implications of the medical narrative discussed above, see such new technologies as a potentially dangerous extension of patriarchal dominion over the bodies of women. Elizabeth Grosz explains this ambivalence: 'Their difference resides in the fact that for such feminists of equality, maternity is what must be overcome, while for the advocates of in vitro programs, maternity is the or an ultimate goal of femininity' (Grosz 1994, p. 16).

What I notice in Grosz's articulation of these conflicting positions is an echo of the same rhetorical formulation employed by the LWC's promotional brochure. The Clinic's acknowledgment that 'the desire to have a child is an exciting and natural part of most people's lives' finds an answering sentiment here in the idea that maternity might be the 'ultimate goal' of femininity. Similarly the idea that maternity 'must be overcome' also recalls the LWC's promise to help infertile couples 'overcome' their infertility difficulties. The dichotomy is extended further when one considers that, for many 'feminists of equality,' other kinds of reproductive technologies, such as the contraceptive pill, or those technologies associated with abortion, *do* represent women's choice to 'overcome' maternity. This creates a double standard by which only fertile women are acknowledged as having reproductive choices. As a result, infertile women (whose reproductive choices have already been severely limited) are disenfranchised by this kind of feminist discourse.

Even where infertility is acknowledged in these discussions, infertile women are not represented as possessing agency. Rather, their decisions to pursue fertility treatments are often presented as a passive acceptance of their status as maternal objects. Rebecca Albury suggests that, '[a]lthough the social practices surrounding IVF and other technologies of reproduction do not formally articulate assumptions about female sexuality and women's place in society, they certainly reproduce them' (Albury 1984, p. 58), and that, consequently, '[t]he unquestioned availability of technological conception could provide increased pressure on women to conform to the definition of femininity that requires motherhood' (p. 63). Adrienne Rich, too, points out that, '[w]oman's status as childbearer has been made into a major fact of her life. Terms like "barren" or "childless" have been used to negate any further identity' (1984, p. 11). Whilst it is probably true that childbearing is a major contributory factor of feminine identity, Rich's expression declares that it *has been made* so.

I would not challenge the validity of this position *per se*, but what makes me uncomfortable here is the intimation, compounded by Rich's second sentence, that an infertile woman's identity is predominantly formed by society's judgment of her (in)ability to have children rather than her own conscious, active, response to that (in)ability. Societal expectations may indeed contribute to a woman's perception and understanding of herself, but this perspective risks ignoring the possibility that, for the infertile woman who desperately wants a child (irrespective of how much this desire is conditioned by society), it might not be the terms *barren*, *childless*, or *infertile* that negate any further identity, but rather the bodily state and psychological experience of *being* infertile. By marginalizing, even trivializing, women's experiences of infertility, these feminist responses to maternity in the context of NRT may not (to invert Albury's own words) formally articulate masculine assumptions about women's place in society. However, they do reproduce the terms under which infertile women are threatened with erasure from the NRT narrative, thereby eliminating them from public discourse and reinforcing their passive place in the private spheres of society.

Feminist arguments against NRT assign infertile women passive identities through two key representational strategies. Firstly, they are consistently characterized as being 'desperate,' and secondly, their bodies are represented only as a site of technological intervention. Pfeffer's study, one of the few that deals primarily with the experience of infertility and the infertile body, addresses this insistence on desperation as the primary characteristic of infertile women. She warns that '[f]ocusing on desperation to the exclusion of all other emotions serves not to explain but to make a caricature of infertile men and women' (Pfeffer 1988, p. 83). Perhaps it is time that feminist academic discourse took a closer look at the (bio)politics of infertility itself, not just those of reproductive technologies. As long as the voices of infertile women are excluded from these spaces of discussion, and their bodies only represented in relation to a 'masculinist' medical treatment, they will continue to be carelessly represented as desperate, hysterical, and weak.

The 'IF' narrative: telling their own stories

Julie is in her late thirties and lives in New England, US. Having started her blog as a 'personal journal' during her first IVF cycle, Julie describes why she began to embrace the blog's capacity to attract a public readership:

> I spent a lot of time scouring the Internet to learn more about what was happening to me. But I wasn't always able to find the kind of information that would have helped me ... This led me to continue

my journal in a more public way. I don't know that anyone who stumbles across my highly opinionated account of my personal experiences will find it exactly *useful*, but I suppose it's theoretically possible. (Julie, 'About Me')

In spite of her disclaimer, the comments left by readers of Julie's blog indicate that people who stumble across it do indeed find it useful, and that a huge number of them become regular readers.

Tertia Albertyn is a woman in her forties living in Cape Town, South Africa. After nine IVF cycles, two miscarriages, and the death of her ten-day-old son, Ben, she became pregnant with her twins, Adam and Kate, who, at the time of writing, are six years old. In 2008, she gave birth to another son, Max, thus bringing that 'horrible, soul destroying infertility part' of her life to a close. Tertia began her blog in April 2004 as 'a chronicle of [her] journey through infertility' and 'as a way to connect with people who were living in a similar world' to her (Albertyn, 'About').

In her 2005 article, Erin Striff writes about the public performance of infertility in blogs. She considers the public performances of these private experiences, concluding that: 'Authors of infertility weblogs defy the privacy of infertility treatment, performing it blatantly and irreverently, resisting their own role as the compliant patient' and that in doing so, 'bloggers assert control over the infertility narrative through which they might affirm their own subjectivity' (Striff 2005, p. 190). For Striff, then, performing private experiences in the public space of the blog is a way of regaining control of one's personal story, of narrating the self rather than being a self who is only narrated by others. To illustrate this point she explores how the private functioning of the infertile body is publicly represented in a performance of the grotesque; whilst 'the performance of infertility is ... perceived as personifying lack,' '[f]ertility treatment ... is often perceived as the performance of technological excess' (p. 193). By performing this excess publicly through their blogs, Striff argues that infertile women are confronting the public's perception of their lack, and can counter the characterization of being passive, desperate, and powerless objects.[1] A key trope in this 'attitude of excess' is the public performance of explicit or graphic details of their treatment (p. 196).

This attitude of excess can be identified in the blogs of Julie and Tertia. Responding to the perception of passivity I identified in the public space of feminist discourse, and in the popular media, Tertia writes:

[Infertile women] pay thousands of dollars, they mortgage their lives, they take on extra jobs, they move states to try and find insurance cover ... They inject themselves in the belly, thigh, wherever. I remember injecting myself in the toilet at a party; I hit a vein and blood came shooting out my belly. There I stood, stabbing a needle into my belly, trying to stop the flow of blood shooting out. While other people laughed, and danced and drank. I once heated up my PIO [progesterone in oil] injection a bit too much and injected too hot oil into my butt, which burnt me from the inside out, leaving a massive welt of a scar. (Albertyn, 'Infertility Reflections')

By performing this attitude of excess, Tertia is bringing the private rituals of infertility out of the privacy of the toilet cubicle and into the intermediate space of the blog, which echoes the shared community spirit of the party – a more typical arena for the performance of excess. In doing so, she is also using this intermediate space to frame a discourse that exemplifies the fine line between lack and excess in relation to infertility and its treatments. Tertia responds to public perception by laying bare the magnitude of her sacrifices, the indignity, the grief, and the anguish she has experienced. Injecting herself with fertility drugs in the toilet might seem desperate and even shameful when done in private at a party, but performed in public in this way the attitude of excess is underpinned by a sense of pride in her own determination and, like her scarred body which reminds her of all that she suffered in pursuit of parenthood, her blog, too, is marked by this defiant excess.

When Julie's IVF pregnancy failed and she had to undergo an induced abortion, she reported the story afterwards in a blog post entitled 'Note to Self: Clean Floor Before Dying':

After I passed the big clump of tissue last night, it seemed that the worst was over. I limped into the den and arranged myself very carefully on the sofa, aching and enervated but feeling rather triumphant. I couldn't stop talking, making poor Paul [her husband] listen to Blood-soaked Tales of Horror from the Master Bathroom, rendered in glorious verbal Technicolor. I guess I was giddy. I know I was proud of myself for making it through ... Not two hours later, though, I was back on the bathroom floor, planning my many bequests. I didn't know whether there was still more tissue that my tube was trying to jettison, or whether it was just trying to shrink back to its normal size, or whether it was spraying a hot jet of blood through my abdominal cavity like a garden sprinkler. Maybe it was all of the above. (Julie, 'Note to Self')

The blog represents an intermediate space where the privacy of the bathroom is opened up to the intimate community of public reader-ship. Despite the physical and emotional pain of losing a pregnancy in this way, despite the indignity of lying 'naked on a towel' on the floor of her bathroom, Julie writes that she was 'triumphant,' 'proud of myself.' By performing this publicly, she shows that even when every-thing goes horribly wrong, she is telling a story of determination rather than desperation. Like Tertia, she adopts an attitude of excess in order to situate herself, as narrator, in an intermediate public/private space from which she can make herself, an infertile woman, the subject of her own story. For Striff, this constitutes an assertion of 'control over the infertility narrative through which the bloggers might affirm their own subjectivity' (2005, p. 190). Whilst I agree with this reading of the blogs, I would argue that an attitude of excess is only one of the ways in which this form of self-representational writing enables women to challenge their prescribed position of passivity in relation to dominant infertility narratives.

Striff's article tends to assume a distinction between the public and private that I am not sure can be applied to the space of the blog. For Striff, infertility takes place in the private space of an individual's life and can be made public by the blogger in the space of the blog. Striff also maintains a distinction between the real-world self and body and its virtual representation – a distinction that largely corresponds to the difference she sees between the private and the public. However, the relationship of the public to the private in these online spaces is complex and unstable, refusing to be so easily classified. If our under-standing of this space is flawed, then so too is our reading of the subject within it. In Striff's reading, the body of the text is always divorced from the real-world blogger: 'By blogging her experiences, the blogger creates a technological, textual body related to, but separate from, her lived experiences' (2005, p. 199).

There are two central problems with these assumed divisions between private and public, real body and textual body. Firstly, the implication that women are only reclaiming narrative agency in a virtual sense, and that this public affirmation of subjectivity remains distinct from the private individual. Secondly, that this empowerment can only be obtained by undergoing a writing process that divorces the online self from its body. This reinscribes the terms by which dominant infertility narratives present the perception of infertility at a remove from the real, lived experience of it and the many ways in which the processes of undergoing reproductive technologies can be said to alienate a woman from her body. Striff's argument fails to recognize fully the blog as a space of discourse in which public and private constantly interrupt each other and have become irretrievably intertwined. Consequently the Self that occupies this space cannot be seen merely as a public/virtual representation of a private/real individual. The blogged-self is an iteration of the blog*ging* self and is therefore simultaneously real *and* virtual. Clearly, it relies to a great degree on the woman who writes and yet it is not accurate to argue that it has no existence in its own right. It lives online, growing in relation to the fabric of networked relations from which it cannot be considered independently. This is the avatar.

In his study of digital avatars in online environments such as 'Second Life,' Mark Meadows emphasizes the point that avatars are intrinsically social and interactive creatures: 'Usually avatars are a mix of the real and the imagined ... Avatars are what allow users to interact in social spaces' (2008, p. 13). We must put this space of interaction at the center of our understanding of a blogger's online presence in order to fully appreciate that the blogged-self is not a one-way construction whereby the real self creates a virtual representation of herself. In other words, just as the real enters the virtual, the interactive nature of the avatar means that the virtual feeds back into the real, the public feeds back into the private self. 'Psychologically,' Meadows writes, 'you are your avatar' (2008, p. 50). Tom Boellstorff, too, reports this reciprocity in the relationships between 'Second Life' residents and their avatars:

> One resident noted how 'experimenting with appearance or behavior in Second Life potentially opens up new ways to think of things in real life' ... a third observed that 'my offline self is becoming more like my avatar, personality-wise. It's like S[econd] L[ife] has grown on me and looped back.' (Boellstorff 2008, p. 148)

I would argue that avatars constitute a feedback loop between offline and online space, real and virtual identity, private individual and public network.

Let us now determine how this feedback loop might operate, and examine how the construction of, and interaction through, the online avatar-self affords Julie and Tertia an empowered subjectivity. The focus here is the relationship between the infertile body and self-identity, and I aim to show that blogging does not create a public textual body merely as an escape from the private physical body as Striff has argued.

True agency in relation to dominant perceptions of infertility cannot be attained unless subjectivity is embodied. Rather than divorcing the infertile body from the blogger, the avatar is a vehicle through which Julie and Tertia reconnect with their bodies and reconcile the alienation experienced as a result of their infertility.

Identifying the avatar in infertility blogs

Women undergoing the processes of IVF and other reproductive technologies experience a sense of alienation from their body. This alienation begins when the body fails to operate 'naturally,' and is compounded by the 'unnatural' processes of assisted reproduction. Freud's notion of the uncanny – or *Unheimlich*, which translates as 'unhomely' and is closely bound with its opposite, *Heimlich*, or 'homely' – is useful here because it links the alienation from the body with the idea of alienation from a space, a homely place. In the context of the infertility blog, bodily alienation is expressed through the familiar, reassuring space of the online fertility community:

> A genuine sanity saver for me has been getting online support through bulletin boards etc ... *Find one where you feel at home.* (Albertyn, 'Surviving Infertility,' my emphasis)

This home-from-home, where one can be oneself, is accessed via the internet from the private, domestic space which has often, along with the body, become a place of estrangement, a constant reminder of the absence of a long-desired family. Tertia describes her body as a place in which she no longer feels 'at home':

> [M]y body had let me down, had fooled me into believing it was to be trusted, and then betrayed me yet again. I hated it. I felt so trapped by it ... I feel so ugly, so fat. Fat and barren. (Albertyn, 'The Good, the Bad')

The body is described as a prison that Tertia longs to escape from. Her embodied experience becomes uncanny in the sense that the experiences of infertility have revealed something 'unnatural' and unfamiliar in Tertia's relationship to her body – in Nicholas Royle's words, 'something unhomely at the heart of hearth and home' (2003, p. 1). Julie also writes her alienation from the *Unheimlich* space of the body into the *Heimlich* space of the blog, reinforcing what Josh Cohen calls 'Freud's philological unearthing of the word *Unheimlich* as originally an extension, rather than a simple negation, of the *Heimlich*' (2005, p. 68).

As she begins her second cycle of IVF, Julie imagines her body becoming monstrous as a result of the fertility drugs she must inject into her bloodstream:

> I am imagining myself as the Incredible Hulk, with my clothing hanging around me in fashionable tatters as the bloat and the emotional upheaval turn me into a raging green-skinned beast. (Julie, 'Stuck in the Middle')

This self-description shows the extent to which the infertile body is experienced as *Unheimlich* as a result of infertility treatment. It is her body, and yet it is experienced as being unfamiliar, having been 'made strange' through the ritualistic cycling of IVF. It is the ritualistic nature of fertility treatment that increases this sense of the imagined body as being something 'Other' to the writing self, something that both *is* the body and yet is separate from it; something which should belong to the self and yet imprisons it.

The infertile body undergoing IVF treatment is ritualistically disciplined and regulated in similar ways to the disciplining that Sandra Lee Bartky describes in her account of women's embodied relationship to what she calls 'the fashion-beauty-complex' (1990, p. 39). Although the purpose of the self-discipline might be very different for the woman pursuing pregnancy and the woman pursuing beauty ideals, the execution of it shares certain characteristics. Bartky argues that women internalize and pursue deep-rooted masculinist definitions of ideal femininity (p. 72). It is this influence, according to Bartky, that causes most women to engage in the rituals of beauty regimes. Her analysis centers on three categories of regulation of the feminine body: body size and configuration; a body with a specific repertoire of gestures; and the body as an ornamented surface (pp. 63–82). These categories are, in many ways, totally incomparable to the regimes adopted by couples trying to conceive. However, given the general critical consensus on the prominence of institutionalized motherhood in our society, a fourth category of regulation, that of the reproductive body, could be usefully added. Consider the way that Julie describes the ritualized monitoring of her body after she did not immediately become pregnant:

> Never was a woman more engrossed by mucus than I! ... I was trying hard to keep the more intricate plotting and scheming to myself: Pee on a stick in the morning; frolic gaily in bed at night while seeming

not to have a care in the world; keep hips elevated for half an hour while clenching teeth grimly; mark the calendar the next day and count the days until my period inevitably arrived again. Lather, rinse, repeat. (Julie, 'The Story So Far')

The self-monitoring of the feminine body, as Bartky describes it, is surprisingly applicable to Julie's subjection of her body to the rituals of predicting ovulation and trying to aid conception by adopting uncomfortable post-coital postures. This self-manipulation of the body recalls the ritualistic regulatory practices – exercise, diet, and beauty regimes – that many women adopt. When Julie turned to IVF, there were yet more monitoring and regulating activities:

I started on birth control pills to regulate my cycle, then began a course of Lupron to prevent me from ovulating prematurely. Once my hormones had been beaten into submission, I started twice-daily injections of Follistim and Repronex, along with the Lupron I'd already been taking. Twelve days later, I was given an injection of hCG to mature the eggs that were studding my ovaries, and on February 23, 7 mature eggs were retrieved from 11 large follicles. (Julie, 'The Story So Far')

Monitored and 'beaten into submission' in this way, the infertile body is disciplined to such an extent that, like the beautified body, it becomes objectified and begins to exist solely as an external point of focus, an 'Other' for this panoptical self to cultivate. Bartky explains this fascination and alienation as a kind of narcissism:

The fashion-beauty complex produces in woman an estrangement from her bodily being: On the one hand, she *is* it and is scarcely allowed to be anything else; on the other hand, she must exist perpetually at a distance from her physical self, fixed at this distance in a permanent posture of disapproval. (Bartky 1990, p. 40)

This description of the fashion-beauty complex could also describe the feelings of a woman trapped in what we might call the infertile-maternal complex, a woman who feels, as Tertia does, that her body has 'betrayed her' in a cruel and 'unnatural' way. In a blog post entitled 'Trying to Love the Skin I'm In,' Tertia writes about her uneasy relationship with her body:

My body was poked, prodded, injected, operated on, cut, scarred. I put on weight, I lost weight. I got pregnant, I miscarried. My body fatally failed my one son, failed to provide him with whatever he needed to live, and he died within. My other son was cut out of my body, ripped out too early, and then died. I was left with leaking breasts and a raw wound. And no son. Needless to say, infertility did little to improve my relationship with my body. (Albertyn, 'Trying to Love the Skin I'm In')

In light of this it seems absurd to suggest that infertile women derive any sort of narcissistic pleasure from the disciplining of their bodies. Bartky asks, 'how is it possible for sexual objectification, which is profoundly alienating, to produce narcissistic states of consciousness, which are profoundly satisfying?' (1990, p. 37). Although there is no enjoyment, 'profound' or otherwise, to be had from infertility or invasive fertility treatments, the blogs of these women show that compulsive disciplining does give rise to a sort of narcissistic fascination with their bodies. After one of her hard-won pregnancies proved to be ectopic and took several days to miscarry, Julie wrote a long and detailed post about the experience of miscarriage, pausing to explain her complicated reaction to it:

Now, I should make some excuse for my deep fascination with this. All along I've *felt like a human science experiment.* My body's reaction ... my weird pregnancy symptoms, my apparent inability to miscarry when told to – I've found all of these things mysterious and interesting. Since my *narcissism is apparently infinite,* maybe it's no surprise that I wanted to inspect the yield this time, too. (Julie, 'This Too Shall Pass,' my emphases)

In the discipline and regulation involved in infertility, the pursuit of medical treatments, pregnancy, and even in miscarriage (which, for both women, had to be induced), the way these women relate to their bodies demonstrates exactly the objectification of the body, and alienation from it, that Bartky observes in cosmetic disciplining. Here, Julie's alienation from her body seems to be complete, and yet we see that this estrangement is paradoxically entwined with compulsive self-surveillance.

If the body, which is experienced as being uncanny, is subjected to this kind of narcissistic surveillance in 'real' life, then blogging this uncanny, monstrous body constitutes an insertion of this 'Other' body into the blog. One of the charges most commonly leveled at bloggers is that blogging is fundamentally narcissistic (Karlsson 2007, p. 38). Certainly the almost compulsive repetition of the act of updating the blogged account of those rituals extends this narcissistic fascination with the body to the uncanny space of the blog. This compulsive cultivation of the text mimics the compulsive disciplining of the body, and gradually the blogged-self also becomes an object of narcissistic pleasure. This shift of the site of narcissistic surveillance arises from what we might call a mis-recognition: the blogger sees the textual Self she has created through the blog and this becomes the object of self-conscious surveillance. For all intents and purposes, the blogger becomes her avatar. Meadows's account of the effort he put into cultivating his avatar in 'Second Life' illustrates this reciprocity:

> When I saw my avatar again, I realized I had work to do ... I really needed to put some energy into the design. *It would, after all, become 'me.'* (Meadows 2008, p. 48, my emphasis)

Through this mis-recognition the blogger is able to interact with her avatar in such a way that the *Unheimlich* experience of the corporeal body is partially resolved.

In Ovid's version of the Narcissus myth, a blind seer, Tiresias, prophesies that Narcissus will only live to old age if he never 'knows himself' (Spaas 2000, p. 1). Consequently Narcissus is prevented from seeing his own reflection until one day he catches sight of it in a pool of water. Enchanted with its beauty, he mistakes it for the face of another person and eventually he pines away, adoring it. Significant here is the issue of 'knowing' oneself. Narcissus mis-recognizes himself in the pool; he sees himself without knowing it to be his own reflection. So, in fact, he does not truly 'know himself' at all. If we subscribe to Striff's idea that in attempting to transgress the limits of materiality bloggers experience a fundamental disconnect with their body, then, like Narcissus, they are merely gazing at an uncanny 'Other' who they do not recognize as themselves. The result of this would be a continuing experience of disconnect, not only with their bodies but with their own identity – raising the question of how they can affirm their subjectivity in the infertility narrative.

However, in my model, after this initial mis-recognition, the daily cultivation of the avatar-Self promotes a relationship in which the narcissistic gaze ceases to be one-way. Unlike Narcissus's reflection, the avatar gazes back. Meadows emphasizes this reciprocity when he describes the avatar as a machine connected to the psychology of its user, claiming that: 'the driver can also look into himself, as if gazing into his navel, and find a new landscape inside as well' (2008, p. 48). This description encapsulates the transformative power of the avatar. It does not exist merely as the object of the narcissistic gaze but as the owner of a gaze that it directs back upon its user thereby informing her subjectivity in relationship to herself and the world around her. In this way the blogger's avatar can be read as a Foucauldian 'technology of the self' that enables the initial mis-recognition of the self as Other to be replaced by a process of interaction whereby the subject truly begins to 'know' herself.

Foucault's notion of technologies of the self investigates the Delphic precept of 'knowing oneself' and the related concept of 'taking care of oneself' to describe the ways in which individuals comply with or resist the social discourses and institutions that produce their subjectivity. For Foucault individuals are disciplined and regulated by these social discourses in such a way that their bodies become a resource of society and their subjectivities become defined by it. Crucially, however, Foucault's technologies of the self are not just methods through which we comply with this biopolitical regulation of subjectivity. They also constitute a technique of resistance as Geoff Danaher et al. (2000) explain:

> As he writes in *The History of Sexuality*, technologies of the self are ways of attempting to love the truth, tell the truth, and be changed by the truth. One of the important technologies of the self is self-knowledge: 'knowing the self' involves determining the truth about the self, because only in knowing this truth can we work on ourselves to achieve perfectibility. (p. 128)

For Foucault, then, knowing the self is not just about narcissistic preoccupation but about a *modification* of the self through these techniques of knowing.

I have argued here that the avatar, itself a complex interface between the realms of public and private, is an appropriate vehicle for the representation of the infertile self which has been obscured from feminist approaches to the body, from twentieth- and twenty-first-century discussions of selfhood, and from the dominant hero-narrative currently promoted by the medical industry. In writing these blogs, these women have written an avatar-self that has the potential to break silence that the dominant narratives of feminism and medical authorities have imposed on these experiences.

Note

1. Striff follows Cixous, Irigaray, and Kristeva in her appropriation of 'excess' in place of a perception of 'lack' in women.

References

Albertyn, T. (n.d.) (Blog) *So Close*, www.tertia.org/ (accessed 3 April 2013).

Albury, R. (1984) 'Who Owns the Embryo?,' in R. Arditti, R. Duelli-Klein and S. Minden (eds) *Test-Tube Women: What Future for Motherhood?* (London: Pandora Press), 54–67.

Balsamo, A. (1997) *Technologies of the Gendered Body: Reading Cyborg Women* (London: Duke University Press).

Bartky, S.L. (1990) *Femininity and Domination: Studies in the Phenomenology of Oppression* (London: Routledge).

Boellstorff, T. (2008) *Coming of Age in Second Life: An Anthropologist Explores the Virtual Human* (Princeton University Press).

Cohen, J. (2005) *How to Read Freud* (London: W.W. Norton).

Curti, L. (1998) *Female Stories, Female Bodies: Narrative, Identity and Representation* (London: Macmillan Press).

Danaher, G., Shirato, T. and Webb, J. (eds) (2000) *Understanding Foucault* (London: Sage).

Grosz, E. (1994) *Volatile Bodies: Toward a Corporeal Feminism* (Indianapolis: Indiana University Press).

Julie (n.d.) (Blog) *A Little Pregnant*, www.alittlepregnant.com (accessed 3 April 2013).

Karlsson, L. (2007) 'Desperately Seeking Sameness: The Processes and Pleasures of Identification in Women's Diary Blog Reading,' *Feminist Media Studies*, 7(2), 137–53.

London Women's Clinic, The (LWC) (2009) (Brochure).

Lovink, G. (2008) *Zero Comments* (New York: Routledge).

Meadows, M. (2008) *I, Avatar: The Culture and Consequences of Having a Second Life* (Berkeley: New Riders).

Mulkay, M. (1997) *The Embryo Research Debate: Science and the Politics of Reproduction* (Cambridge University Press).

Ovid, *Metamorphoses*, trans. Sir Samuel Garth et al., http://classics.mit.edu/Ovid/metam.3.third.html (accessed 27 March 2013).

Pfeffer, N. (1988) 'Artificial Insemination, In-vitro Fertilization and the Stigma of Infertility,' in M. Stanworth (ed.) *Reproductive Technologies* (Oxford: Polity Press), 81–97.

Rich, A. (1984) *Of Woman Born: Motherhood as Experience and Institution* (London: Virago).

Royle, N. (2003) *The Uncanny* (Manchester University Press).

Spaas, L. (2000) 'Introduction,' in L. Spaas (ed.) *Echoes of Narcissus* (Oxford: Berghahn Books), 1–10.

Striff, E. (2005) 'Infertile Me: The Public Performance of Fertility Treatments in Internet Weblogs,' *Women & Performance: A Journal of Feminist Theory*, 15(2), 189–206.

Volpe, E.P. (1987) *Test-Tube Conception: A Blend of Love and Science* (Macon, GA: Mercer University Press).

Wright, S. and Camahort, E.P. (2009) 'Women and Social Media Study,' *BlogHer, iVillage and Compass Partners* (Nashville: Compass Partners), www.compassconsultingpartners.com/2009CompassBlogHerSocialMedia%20Study.pdf (accessed 18 August 2014).

Part IV
Feminism/Activism

13

SlutWalk, Feminism, and News

Kaitlynn Mendes

Introduction

In January 2011, Toronto Police Constable Michael Sanguinetti addressed a small group of York University students on campus safety. Prefaced by the statement, 'I'm told I'm not supposed to say this,' he went on to advise that 'women should avoid dressing like sluts in order not to be victimized' (Kwan 2011). While his intentions might have been to protect women, his comments that 'slutty' women attract sexual assault perpetuated the long-standing myth that victims are responsible for the violence used against them. In response to PC Sanguinetti's comments, a group of local women translated their concern into political activism. Three months later, the first SlutWalk took place in Toronto, attended by thousands. By the end of the year, SlutWalks were organized in over 100 cities in 40 nations, mobilizing tens of thousands of women, men, and children.

Because there has been an erasure of (Western) news coverage of feminist activism and protest since the second wave (Mendes 2012), with feminism frequently being labeled 'dead' or 'redundant' (see Gill 2007; McRobbie 2009; Mendes 2011; Smith 2003), SlutWalk's global reach and its ability to generate international headlines provide an opportunity to assess how women's collective activism has been represented cross-nationally. Although I would argue SlutWalk is clearly part of the broader feminist (anti-rape) movement, is it fair to assume that all those organizing and participating in SlutWalk feel the same? Such questions are particularly pertinent in this 'postfeminist' era when feminism is frequently repudiated, particularly by a younger generation who separate themselves from what they see as the concerns of an older, 'second-wave' generation (see Jowett 2004; Scharff 2010; Zaslow 2009). Because of its grassroots nature, and the different ways it has been adapted to fit various cultural climates (see for example Gwynne 2013), this chapter does not seek to 'prove' SlutWalk is part of a wider feminist movement. Instead, it raises questions about how the relationship between SlutWalk and feminism has been represented, asking to what extent feminism has been erased or made invisible in global mainstream news coverage.

Methodology

This chapter attempts to answer questions around the mediated aspects of SlutWalks through a content and critical discourse analysis of mainstream news from eight nations which have organized SlutWalks (Australia, Canada, India, New Zealand, South Africa, Singapore, UK, and US). The textual analysis was supplemented through interviews with SlutWalk organizers.[1] I specifically focused on mainstream news media because of its crucial role in maintaining and (re)producing hegemonic ideologies (Dow 1996; Meyers 2006). In total, I collected 284 news articles between 1 January 2011 and 31 December 2012 using the search terms 'SlutWalk' and 'Slut walk.'[2] I make no claims that my study provides a definitive picture of how the relationship between SlutWalk and feminism has been represented. Instead, I argue that this study provides a snapshot into results from one global case study.

Is SlutWalk a feminist movement?

One of the more interesting debates surrounding SlutWalk is if it in fact can be constituted as part of a wider 'feminist' movement. Although I initially assumed it would be, given feminism's long-standing involvement in anti-rape activism and consciousness-raising surrounding sexual violence, I was surprised to notice the absence of any serious discussion of feminism in the mainstream news. This absence was also noted by feminists writing about the movement in alternative online spaces (for an excellent overview see Sarkeesian 2011). The relationship between SlutWalk and feminism was at times taken up by the broadcast media which organized a number of debates, pitting SlutWalker supporters/organizers against feminists who opposed the movement (see for example BBC 2011; Q 2011; The Agenda 2011). Consequently, because of feminism's absence in many news texts, and feminists' rejection of SlutWalk in others, I felt it was worth asking: What is SlutWalk's mediated relationship with feminism? To what extent has SlutWalk been represented as a feminist event?

Perhaps unsurprisingly, my research presents the relationship between SlutWalk and feminism as ambiguous and complex. For example, when asked about this relationship, SlutWalk Toronto co-founder Heather Jarvis indicated that she has identified as a feminist for 'many years – at least 10' (2012, personal interview). She added that when creating their biographies for the SlutWalk Toronto website, her feminist identification was always clearly visible, as it was for many others involved in the movement. Similarly, SlutWalk Perth organizer Beth Castieau has long identified as a feminist, and is someone who is 'passionate about feminist issues' (2012, personal interview). Although Castieau says she has 'always seen it [SlutWalk] as part of the feminist movement' she recalled the 'aha' moment when a fellow organizer came to embrace this identity after organizing a local event. Jarvis recounted a similar experience with her co-founder Sonya Barnett:

> Sonya didn't have the same experience as I had with women's studies, and she said she had a lot of misconceptions about feminists – as being angry, or living a life of a certain aesthetic. When we talked about it initially, she said she wasn't sure about if she identified as a feminist. I remember saying that was ok, and that I'm not going to tell you how to identify. However, in later conversations, she talked about how she did come to identify with feminism. (Jarvis 2012, personal interview)

Both Jarvis and Castieau, as well as other SlutWalk organizers interviewed, explained that aside from these few individuals, all of the other organizers for their events, past and present, joined the movement with a pre-existing feminist identification (see also Diondra 2013; Haugen & MacDonald 2014; Wraith 2013).

To embrace feminism or not, that is the question?

While many SlutWalk organizers were happy to identify as feminists, others such as SlutWalk Singapore organizer Vanessa Ho expressed a different relationship with feminism:

> I personally have a very complicated relationship with the label 'feminist'; however, many of my team members do identify with the label. That said, we never once labeled the movement a feminist movement, but we always agreed that there are strong feminist aspects to it. We work closely with local feminist groups and NGOs, but we are not part of them. We are made of independent individuals

with varying beliefs and ideologies. That said, the feminist 'movement' in Singapore is very second wave, and has a tendency to be co-opted by the government. This is one of the reasons why we do not always call SlutWalk feminist. (Ho 2012, personal interview)

Ho went on to explain that the term feminism is 'completely misunderstood' in Singapore – a nation in which some of its most public feminists are a mixture of 'right-winged fundamentalists, women who oppress men,' and others who are anti-gay and anti-human rights. In this context, because of the wide variety of (oppressive) ideological positions associated with feminism, Ho asserts that it is more beneficial that SlutWalk Singapore not be labeled 'feminist' (2012, personal interview).

Cognizant of issues surrounding class in South Africa, SlutWalk Cape Town organizer Umeshree Govender argued that while she considered herself to be a (non-radical) feminist, she doubted many South African SlutWalk supporters would embrace this label, noting that:

> I think that feminism is largely a luxury of educated, middle-class women in South Africa, and there may be a lot of uneducated women from poorer areas who are feminists but don't know that's the term that describes it. I think the march did attract some feminists, but for the most part it was a lot of ordinary people who turned up. I don't think it was a feminist thing. (2014, personal interview)

SlutWalk Singapore and Cape Town were not the only cities which consciously chose *not* to embrace the feminist label as part of its marketing strategy. SlutWalk Johannesburg organizer Karmilla Pillay-Siokos argued that a disassociation between SlutWalk and feminism was 'a good thing for our publicity' as 'people tend to have formed a stereotype about feminists and feminism that could alienate people who would otherwise have supported the cause' (2013). Similarly, despite identifying as a feminist, SlutWalk St Louis organizer David Wraith acknowledged a conscious decision not to brand their walk as 'feminist' for risk of alienating it, noting that the word 'feminist has as much baggage as the word slut' (2013). Wraith went on to state, 'I know there are a lot of people who won't support us because the word slut is in the title and I think a lot of people wouldn't support us if the word feminist was in the title.' Such sentiments were also expressed by SlutWalk Vancouver organizers Margaret Haugen and Caitlin MacDonald (2014, personal interview). Their responses indicate that although feminist activism is certainly not dead (for a recent example, see McVeigh 2013), there is still a long way to go, particularly amongst the younger generation who attend SlutWalk, before the 'f-word' is reclaimed as a positive label.

SlutWalk, feminism, and the news

Given that the relationship between SlutWalk and feminism was ambiguous and complex amongst SlutWalk organizers, it is of little surprise that the same was the case in mainstream news. In my quest to explore the relationship between SlutWalk and feminism, I conducted a content and critical discourse analysis of 284 mainstream news articles from eight nations in which SlutWalks took place. One of the questions asked in the content analysis was how many references were made to feminism or the women's movement. I should point out that these results do not measure how often SlutWalk was *labeled* a feminist movement, but merely indicate how many times feminism or the women's movement were discussed. In total, only 88 out of 284 news articles (or 31 percent of total) mentioned feminism or the women's movement. Such absence raises questions such as, why was feminism so rarely mentioned in news accounts of SlutWalk? Can this be constituted as part of a general erasure of feminism in popular culture? Is there a perception that the two are not connected? Or alternatively, is it *assumed* SlutWalk is part of feminism, and therefore this connection does not need to be made explicit? Without speaking with each individual author, these questions are difficult to answer. However, I can attempt to provide insights through more qualitative reading of the texts. Broadly speaking, articles can be broken down into three categories: articles which discuss feminism; articles which make no reference to feminism; and articles in which feminist rhetoric or analysis was used but which fail to make any mention of feminism itself.

A relationship exists

Out of 284 articles, only 88 (31 percent of total) made any reference to feminism or the wider women's movement. Of these, several explicitly discussed SlutWalk in the context of feminism. This is evident in headlines such as: 'New Feminism or Just a Parade?' (*Toronto Star* 2011a, p. A26), 'SlutWalk: Is a Woman's Body the Best Way to Get a Feminist Point Across?' (Rogers 2011), 'The New Feminists: As Slutty as We Want to Be' (Valenti 2011), and 'Toronto SlutWalk Sparks Blogosphere Feminism Debate' (Barmak 2011, p. IN2). In addition to being linked, it also became clear that some articles constructed SlutWalk and feminism as being mutually beneficial. For example, one article optimistically identified SlutWalk as a potential route into feminism: 'SlutWalks Bring in Different People Who May Not Be as Exposed to Feminist Issues' (Chen 2012). Because it was seen as 'fun' and 'fresh' (Midgley 2011, p. 33), SlutWalk was also constructed as more accessible to the supposedly disengaged youth (see Barnhurst 2003), being labelled 'feminism for the Facebook generation' (Bannerman 2011, p. 32). SlutWalk was also used as evidence of a resurgence of feminism and a model for 'what the future [of feminism] could look like' (Valenti 2011, p. B01; see also Barton 2011; Craig 2011; Gold 2011; Laucius 2011; Purves 2011; Watson 2012).

Although a handful of articles clearly connected SlutWalk and feminism, a number of others highlighted ambivalence between the two. Canada's *Globe and Mail* described how a 'trio of 20-something women' attended the march, despite 'not considering themselves political' (and therefore presumably not feminist) and in fact had never before attended a demonstration; nonetheless it was a 'quasi-feminist uprising' (McArthur 2011). Similarly, the BBC quoted a Slutwalk London organizer who acknowledged that: 'A lot of people are taking part [in SlutWalks] who would not describe themselves as feminists, but they are doing it' (Bell 2011). This last quote is particularly interesting and can be interpreted in two ways: either that participants are *unaware* that SlutWalk is part of a larger feminist movement, or that they have decided to participate *despite* its feminist orientation. Neither option is particularly appealing, as the former highlights young people's ignorance of feminist history (see Baumgardner & Richards 2000), while the latter indicates their rejection of feminism (see Jowett 2004; Scharff 2012; Zaslow 2009). The latter explanation was unfortunately evident in other articles, including one commenting that SlutWalk was evidence that women were 'bending over backwards – in high heels – not to look like feminists' (Petri 2011).

SlutWalk, fashion, feminism, empowerment, and choice

Because previous research has highlighted the news media's tendency to link feminism to such 'lifestyle' issues (Genz & Brabon 2009; Mendes 2012), it was no surprise to find a range of articles focusing on feminism, fashion, empowerment and choice. This was evident in headlines such as: 'Feminism and Fashion: The (Other) Two Solitudes' (Onstad 2011, p. L14), 'Frocks are Not a Feminist Issue: The Fight for Women's Rights is Being Waylaid by Needless Talk about what Women Wear' (Coren 2011, p. 34), 'Feminists should Promote the Right to be Openly Sexy' (McCartney 2011), and 'The New Feminists: As Slutty as We Want to Be' (Valenti 2011, p. B01). Interestingly, however, while a handful of the 88 articles mentioning feminism solely constructed SlutWalk as a means to demonstrate women's empowerment – for example, 'no one has the right to tell me how to dress' – most approached this relationship from a more critical point of view. For example, several articles critiqued the neoliberal logic which constructs *all* free choice as empowering. One *Globe and Mail* columnist rejected the notion outright that women could be empowered merely through the act of *choosing*, claiming that such logic was 'false consciousness gone mad' (Dhillon 2011, p. A13). Another columnist used fashion as a means to reflect upon the challenge of raising a daughter in a patriarchal society. While rejecting the common myth that 'slutty' clothing 'provokes' rape, she admitted to perpetuating rape culture by advising her daughter to 'cover up' and not to 'leave the house looking like a hooker' (Timson 2011, p. L3). Such confessions demonstrate the difficulty even feminists have in challenging rape myths in their everyday lives.

Through these brief examples, it is fair to say that fashion was not necessarily a *frivolous* topic, and was often used as an entry point into more serious discussions about feminism, feminist issues, or feminist critiques. For example, in the column 'Feminism and Fashion: The (Other) Two Solitudes,' author Katrina Onstad (2011) spends nearly 1000 words discussing the historically tense relationship between women's appearance and women's liberation. She relays how suffragettes and second-wave feminists discouraged women's interest in fashion as a distraction from their fight for equality. She also explains how a focus on 'natural beauty' (for example, a rejection of makeup and body-contorting clothing) has long been a radical way of giving the 'middle finger to conventional notions of femininity' (p. L14), and presumably patriarchy. Onstad rounds up the article by asking how clothes might continue to be used as a political tool for protest, or if fashion will always be another means of upholding patriarchy. Cognizant that SlutWalk raised questions about women's dress, another columnist lamented the fact that 'feminism is suddenly all about clothing' and worried that SlutWalk is being co-opted as 'just another way to chat about fashion' (Coren 2011, p. 34). Conversely, others complained that 'fighting for the right to decide what to wear is not on the feminist agenda' (*Times of India* 2011). Writing about the Indian context, one author recalls a story about a local woman who was branded a 'witch' when her husband died because she refused to wear white, as is the custom for a widow. With regards to SlutWalk, the author insists that the focus on fashion is justified because by 'never questioning that unwritten law of dress codes, we actually endorsed the "I'm asking for it" line of thought' (*Times of India* 2011).

Given the importance of consumption and the reign of neoliberal ideologies in contemporary culture, it is unsurprising that SlutWalk was used as an entry point to discuss fashion, empowerment, and choice. Although most of these articles within the overall sample failed to discuss feminism (many were simply focused on the advantages and disadvantages of dressing like a 'slut'), my analysis reveals that others used SlutWalk as an opportunity to introduce feminist critiques to these issues. While this section focused on articles in which feminism is clearly visible, I will now explore articles in which feminism has been ignored, erased and actively repudiated.

Erasing feminism

Evidence from the content analysis indicates that most articles (196 or 69 percent) in this sample made no reference to feminism or the women's movement. If drawing only data from the content analysis, the easy conclusion would be to assert that feminism has indeed been erased from representations of SlutWalk. However, a more qualitative analysis of the texts reveals that the relationship is far more complex. For example, as the next two sections will show, the absence of the term 'feminism' does not necessarily mean feminist critiques or ideologies are absent. Similarly, I argue that erasure does not happen merely by the absences of the term 'feminism,' but occurs when the news media actively attempt to construct it as dead, redundant, or frivolous. Because the active undoing of feminism is particularly problematic (see McRobbie 2009), I will address these articles first.

Backlash

Although it is worrying that two-thirds of all articles failed to mention feminism, thus assisting in its general erasure, I was particularly concerned by the presence of backlash discourses throughout the sample. Backlash discourses are a particular type of anti-feminist discourse which suggests that feminism is redundant, unnecessary, and often harmful either because its goals have been achieved, or because it has gone too far (see Faludi 1991; Mendes 2011). In this particular study, SlutWalk was often used as evidence of feminism's frivolity and redundancy. Although such discourses tended to be found in my more conservative publications, they were scattered throughout the sample. For example, the religious and conservative *Washington Times* had one article titled 'SlutWalking our Way to Gomorrah' (Shaw Crouse 2011, p. B1), making reference to the biblical city which God burnt to the ground because its inhabitants were consumed with vice and sin. This article not only suggests that SlutWalk is headed down a dangerous path, but insists that SlutWalkers are merely 'publicity starved feminists' who persistently used 'in your face' tactics to harp on and on about 'women's rights' – which, presumably, have already been won. The author also wrote SlutWalk off as evidence of how 'outrageous and passé the [feminist] movement has become' (p. B1). In a similar vein, Britain's conservative *The Daily Mail* had one headline reading: 'These "SlutWalks" now Prove Feminism is Irrelevant to Most Women's Lives' (Phillips 2011), noting that feminism is now well past its 'sell-by date' and that 'The great causes which animated it [feminism] have been won.' Such discourses are part of the long-standing backlash to feminism which insists on feminism's illegitimacy by claiming either feminism's goals have gone 'too far' (and therefore must be rejected), that they are 'out of touch,' or that the public was better off before feminism (see Faludi 1991; Mendes 2011). I argue that such articles are part of a general erasure of feminism, not because they ignore it, but because they actively contribute to its dismantling. Ironically, previous research has also indicated that backlash discourses tend to emerge at times of renewed feminist activism (see Mendes 2011), suggesting that as long as SlutWalks continue, so too will discourses which attempt to erase their potential.

While the above section presents a few examples of how feminism has actively been erased or discredited, the next section will discuss instances when feminist theory and rhetoric, if not the label itself, have been used, and raise questions about the extent to which feminist thought has been slowly appropriated into public consciousness.

A more ambiguous relationship

Although not quantified in the content analysis, I noticed through qualitative reading of the texts that, although ignoring the feminist label, a series of articles did indeed employ feminist language and concepts. For example, a few articles discussed how SlutWalk brought issues of sexual violence into the public arena or sphere (Chemaly 2011; Hichens 2011). Since at least the 1960s, feminists have played an influential role in calling for personal, private issues such as sexual assault to be renamed as public political questions (see Jaggar 1983; Petchesky 1981). In doing so, feminists have encouraged society to question the supposedly 'natural' and inherently gendered division between these spheres. Although neither of the news texts above discuss feminism or the women's movement, both use a range of other feminist terminology and rhetoric. For example, in the article 'SlutWalk Brings Sexual Violence Squarely in the Public Arena,' author Joanne Hichens (2011) draws from feminist theory which dismisses claims that rape is a crime of passion or sex, and instead argues it is about power, domination, and control (see Brownmiller 1975; hooks 1982, 2000; Jaggar 1983; Rozee 1999). This reconceptualization of the nature of rape has been a key feminist argument since at least the 1960s, and is one of SlutWalk's key goals (Jarvis 2012). Other familiar feminist arguments were found in Soraya Chemaly's column titled 'Why You Should Bring Your Teenager on SlutWalk' (2011):

> This [SlutWalk] is not about teaching people about the insidious damage that pervasive gender bias, often internalized, causes every day. It isn't about the right to wear revealing clothes or have frequent orgiastic sex. SlutWalkers march for safe and equal access to the public sphere even if, god forbid, you're born with a vagina.

Although there is no mention of feminism or the wider women's movement here, Chemaly's insistence that women should have safe and equal access to the public sphere has long been a feminist goal, dating back to the first wave (Bryson 2003). Although Chemaly is well known for writing about feminist issues, it is reasonable to assume that such views have largely been appropriated by the general public, at least in the Western world.

Other feminist discourses can also be found throughout the sample. For example, a handful of articles discussed the concept of patriarchy, noting for example how the word 'slut' is deeply rooted in a patriarchal 'madonna/whore view of women's sexuality' (Dines & Murphy 2011, p. 25). Others relay how SlutWalk demonstrates women's collective resistance to 'sexual assault, rape and the patriarchal controlling attitudes towards them' (Schutte 2011, p. 9). Consciousness-raising (CR) and education about rape culture and prevention were also highlighted as key SlutWalk goals (see Clarke 2011). For example, one article constructed SlutWalk as a movement which refocuses the 'spotlight on a culture that makes acts of sexual violence against women not only commonplace but actually accepted' (Moodie 2011). Making people aware that supposedly 'individual' or 'personal' problems such as sexual violence are in fact collective, public issues, and having safe spaces to share personal experiences, have long been a first step in paving the way for political activism and women's potential liberation (Jaggar 1983; Sarachild 1973). Despite the absence of the word 'feminism' or references to the women's movement, articles such as these provide a clear indication that feminist ideology has slowly become appropriated into public consciousness and discourse (see also Durham 2013). Consequently, while the feminist label might be missing, the foundation and message are clearly liberatory, and challenge patriarchal power.

While a number of articles used explicitly feminist language or concepts (even if there was no mention of feminism itself), the link between feminism and SlutWalk was more ambiguous in a number of other articles. For example, some headlines constructed SlutWalk as part of a 'fight for women's rights,' but made no further connection to the women's movement or other feminist ideology. Surprisingly, only a handful of articles made any direct connection between SlutWalk and the larger anti-rape movement or demonstrations (such as Reclaim the Night/Take Back the Night) which have existed since the 1960s and 1970s in places such as the US, Canada, Australia, India, Belgium, Italy, Germany and the UK (see Cuervo 2011; Hope 2011; Horin 2011; Szego 2011; Tanenbaum 2011). As scholars have argued, having a historic understanding of women's quest for equal rights and liberation is important and might prevent feminists from having to 'reinvent the wheel every fifty years or so' (Baumgardner & Richards 2000, p. 68). It would also help situate movements such as SlutWalk into a broader feminist context and build upon the successes feminists have already made in challenging rape culture.

Although SlutWalk was not recognized as part of a long-standing anti-rape movement, it was regularly constructed as a contemporary global movement. Such articles therefore do help create a sense of collective activism – and represent a shift away from the (neo)liberal feminist rhetoric of individual freedom and choices which have dominated much of the (Western) news media of feminism in recent years (see Gill & Scharff 2011; Mendes 2012; Thornham & Weissmann 2013). Typical examples include: 'SLUTWALK, an international movement rapidly gaining momentum worldwide after being started earlier this year to object to a suggestion that women could avoid sexual assault by not "dressing like a slut," is coming to South Africa' (Mposo 2011, p. 5), and 'WOMEN protesting for the right to wear what they like and behave how they choose without facing sexual harassment are set to hold "SlutWalks" across Australia as the movement goes global' (*Daily Dispatch* 2011). The global nature of the march was also evident in headlines such as: 'SlutWalk Goes Global' (*Toronto Star* 2011b, p. A2), 'SlutWalk Sparks Worldwide Movement' (Church 2011, p. A6), and 'New Delhi "SlutWalk" Brings Global Sexual Violence Protest Phenomenon to

India' (*Huffington Post* 2011). That SlutWalk was seen as a global phenomenon once again provided it with credibility and a certain amount of newsworthiness, important for burgeoning social movements, but historically rare for feminist activism. And while I argue that this global frame was useful in providing the movement with credibility, and challenging the idea that women cannot get along (Douglas 1994), it is necessary to ask why it is not contextualized as part of a global or historic *feminist* movement. Has feminism simply been forgotten, or, worse yet, does this suggest it has deliberately been ignored?

Conclusion

It is clear from this analysis that SlutWalk's relationship – and its mediated associations – with feminism is complex, particularly in regards to its (in)visibility in the mainstream news. Although most of the (Western) SlutWalk organizers interviewed identified as a feminist, and acknowledged the movement's feminist roots, feminism or the wider women's movement was only mentioned in one-third of all mainstream news articles in this sample. As a result, I argue that there has indeed been a general erasure of feminism from the mainstream news media not only in terms of its sheer absence and lack of feminist critiques, but also through the ways many articles actively erased feminism's utility through the continual insistence that it is dead, redundant, and passé. These articles contribute to an overall backlash toward feminism which has been ongoing for decades (see Faludi 1991; Mendes 2011). At the same time, however, there is evidence that feminist rhetoric has at times seeped into public consciousness, even if not identified as such. Several articles used explicitly feminist analysis of patriarchy, the public sphere, and the nature of rape without being linked to a wider feminist movement. Whether the omission of feminism was deliberate or not is hard to tell without interviewing each journalist; however, such articles indicate that while feminism may perhaps be 'invisible,' its aims and theoretical understanding of women's oppression are certainly not irrelevant.

Notes

1. To date, I have conducted interviews with organizers from SlutWalk Cape Town, Toronto, Vancouver, Singapore, St Louis, Perth, Victoria (Canada), New York City, LA, Johannesburg, and Winnipeg.
2. News Providers include: *Calgary Herald* (Canada); *Canberra Times* (Australia); *Cape Times* (South Africa); *Daily Dispatch* (South Africa); *Daily Mail* and *Mail*

on Sunday and *Mail Online* (UK); *Daily News* (US); *Globe and Mail* (Canada); *Hobart Mercury* and *Sunday Tasmanian* (Australia); *Indian Express* (India); *New Indian Express* (India); *New York Times* (US); *New Zealand Herald* (New Zealand); *Ottawa Citizen* (Canada); *Sowetan* (South Africa); *Sunday Star-Times* (New Zealand); *The Australian/Weekend Australian* (Australia); *The Straits Times* (Singapore); *The Guardian* (UK); *The Observer* (UK); *The Sun* (UK); *The Telegraph* (India); *The Times* (UK); *Times of India* (India); *Toronto Star* (Canada); *Washington Post* (US); *Washington Times* (US); *Sydney Morning Herald* (Australia); *Herald Sun* and *Sunday Herald Sun* (Australia); Australian Broadcasting Company (Australia); BBC (UK); CBC (Canada); *Huffington Post* (Canada, UK, and US); South African Broadcasting Company (South Africa); New Zealand TV (New Zealand); *The New Paper* (Singapore).

References

The Agenda (2011) (Television show) 6 May, http://theagenda.tvo.org/episode/140631/friday-may-6-2011 (accessed 14 March 2013).

Bannerman, L. (2011) 'I'm Strong and Proud, Says 17 Year Old Who Led the Way for "Sluts",' *The Times*, 11 June, 32–3.

Barmak, S. (2011) 'Toronto Slutwalk Sparks Blogosphere Feminism Debate,' *Toronto Star*, 9 April, p. IN2.

Barnhurst, K.G. (2003) 'Subjective States: Narratives of Citizenship among Young Europeans,' *Multilingua* 22, 133–68.

Barton, L. (2011) 'The View from a Broad,' *The Guardian Online*, 13 June, online.

Baumgardner, J. and Richards, A. (2000) *Manifesta: Young Women, Feminism and the Future* (New York: Farrar, Straus, and Giroux).

BBC (2011) 'Have Your Say,' *BBC World Service*, 10 May, www.bbc.co.uk/programmes/p00ggb5t (accessed 14 March 2013).

Bell, S. (2011) 'SlutWalk London: "Yes Means Yes and No Means No",' *BBC Online*, 11 June, online

Brownmiller, S. (1975) *Against Our Will: Men, Women and Rape* (London: Secker & Warburg).

Bryson, V. (2003) *Feminist Political Theory: An Introduction*, 2nd edn (New York: Palgrave Macmillan).

Castieau, B. (2012) Personal Interview, 5 September.

Chemaly, S. (2011) 'Why You Should Bring Your Teenager on Slutwalk,' *Huffington Post (US)*, 1 October, online.

Chen, K. (2012) '150 Join Ottawa's SlutWalk to Protest "Victim-Blaming" Attitudes,' *Ottawa Citizen*, 19 August, online.

Church, E. (2011) 'SlutWalk Sparks Worldwide Movement,' *Globe and Mail*, 11 May, A6.

Clarke, J. (2011) 'Perth "Sluts" Prepare to Walk Despite Lack of Support,' *Canberra Times Online*, 2 December, online.

Coren, V. (2011) 'Frocks are Not a Feminist Issue: The Fight for Women's Rights is Being Waylaid by Needless Talk about what Women Wear,' *The Observer*, 19 June, 34.

Craig, N. (2011) 'A Rally to Find the Slut in Everyone,' *Canberra Times Online*, 29 May, online.

Cuervo, I. (2011) 'Toronto "SlutWalk" Spreads to US,' *CBC*, 6 May, online.

Daily Dispatch (2011) 'Slutwalk Sweeps Australia,' *Daily Dispatch*, 12 May, online.

Dhillon, A. (2011) 'It Mocks India's Real Issues,' *The Globe and Mail*, 29 July, A13.

Dines, G. and Murphy, W.J. (2011) 'This is not Liberation,' *Guardian*, 9 May, 25.

Diondra (2013) Personal Interview, 17 April.

Douglas, S. (1994) *Where the Girls Are: Growing up Female with the Mass Media* (New York: Three Rivers Press).

Dow, B.J. (1996) *Prime-Time Feminism: Television, Media Culture, and the Women's Movement Since 1970* (Philadelphia: University of Pennsylvania Press).

Durham, M.G. (2013) '"Vicious Assault Shakes Texas Town": The Politics of Gender Violence in *The New York Times*' Coverage of a Schoolgirl's Gang Rape,' *Journalism Studies*, 14(1), 1–12.

Faludi, S. (1991) *Backlash: The Undeclared War against Women* (New York: Crown).

Genz. S. and Brabon, B.A. (2009) *Postfeminism: Cultural Texts and Theories* (Edinburgh University Press).

Gill, R. (2007) *Gender and the Media* (Cambridge: Polity Press).

Gill, R. and Scharff, C. (2011) *New Femininities: Postfeminism, Neoliberalism and Subjectivity* (Basingstoke: Palgrave Macmillan).

Gold, T. (2011) 'Marching with the SlutWalkers,' *The Guardian Online*, 7 June, online.

Govender, U. (2014) Personal Interview, 24 April.

Gwynne, J. (2013) 'SlutWalk, Feminist Activism and the Foreign Body in Singapore,' *Journal of Contemporary Asia*, 43(1), 173–85.

Haugen, M. and MacDonald, C. (2014) Personal Interview, 11 April.

Hichens, J. (2011) 'SlutWalk Brings Issues of Sexual Violence Squarely into the Public Arena,' *Cape Times*, 29 August, 9.

Ho, V. (2012) Personal Interview, 6 December.

hooks, b. (1982) *Ain't I a Woman: Black Women and Feminism* (London: Pluto).

hooks, b. (2000) *Feminist Theory: From Margin to Center* (Cambridge, MA: South End Press).

Hope, E. (2011) 'Rally to Counter Sexual Assault,' *Hobart Mercury*, 11 November, 15.

Horin, A. (2011) 'SlutWalk Turns Apathy into Action on Sex Attacks,' *Sydney Morning Herald*, 13 June, online.

Huffington Post (2011) 'New Delhi "Slutwalk" Brings Global Sexual Violence Protest Phenomenon to India,' *Huffington Post*, 10 June, online.

Jaggar, A.M. (1983) *Feminist Politics and Human Nature* (Totowa, NJ: Rowman & Allanheld).

Jarvis, H. (2012) Personal Interview, 7 December.

Jowett, M. (2004) '"I Don't See Feminists as You See Feminists": Young Women Negotiating Feminism in Contemporary Britain,' in A. Harris (ed.) *All about the Girl: Culture, Power and Identity* (New York: Routledge), 91–102.

Kwan, R. (2011) 'Don't Dress Like a Slut: Toronto cop,' *The Excalibur*, 16 February, www.excal.on.ca/news/dont-dress-like-a-slut-toronto-cop/ (accessed 21 June 2014).

Laucius, J. (2011) 'Sensible Shoes and a Grey Cardigan at SlutWalk,' *Ottawa Citizen*, 9 April, J1.

McArthur, G. (2011) 'Women Walk the Talk after Officer's Offending "Slut" Remarks,' *Globe and Mail Online*, 4 April, online.

McCartney, R. (2011) 'Feminists should Promote the Right to be Openly Sexy,' *Sydney Morning Herald*, 23 August, online.

McRobbie, A. (2009) *The Aftermath of Feminism: Gender, Culture and Social Change* (London: Sage).

McVeigh, T. (2013) 'Meet the New Wave of Activists Making Feminism Thrive in the Digital Age,' *The Guardian*, 3 June, www.guardian.co.uk/world/2013/jun/01/activists-feminism-digital?CMP=twt_gu (accessed 3 June 2013).

Mendes, K. (2011) *Feminism in the News: Representations of the Women's Movement Since the 1960s* (Basingstoke: Palgrave Macmillan).

Mendes, K. (2012) '"Feminism Rules! Now, Where's my Swimsuit?" Re-evaluating Feminist Discourse in Print Media 1968–2008,' *Media, Culture & Society*, 34(5), 554–70.

Meyers, M. (2006) 'News of Battering,' *Journal of Communication*, 44(2), 47–63.

Midgley, C. (2011) 'Clothes Don't Cause Rape. Rapists Cause Rape: They Aren't Fussy about what their Victims Wear,' *The Times*, 11 June, 33.

Moodie, D. (2011) 'Getting Past the Word "slut",' *Huffington Post (US)*, 7 October, online.

Mposo, N. (2011) 'SlutWalk is Coming to SA,' *Daily News*, 6 June, 5.

Onstad, K. (2011) 'Feminism and Fashion: The (Other) Two Solitudes,' *Globe and Mail*, 16 April, L14.

Petchesky, R.P. (1981) 'Anti-Abortion, Anti-Feminism, and the Rise of the New Right,' *Feminist Studies*, 7(2), 206–46.

Petri, A. (2011) 'Submissive Bachman Versus the Sluts,' *The Washington Post*, 12 August, online

Phillips, M. (2011) 'These "SlutWalks" Prove Feminism is Now Irrelevant to Most Women's Lives,' *Daily Mail*, 13 June, n.p.

Pillay-Siokos, K. (2013) Personal Interview, 25 May.

Purves, L. (2011) 'Lay Off the Bitching, Sisters! Just be Nice,' *The Times*, 13 June, 19.

Q (2011) 'SlutWalk Debate on Q,' *CBC*, 10 May, www.cbc.ca/player/Radio/Q/Excerpts/ID/1917407497/?page=9&sort=MostPopular (accessed 14 March 2013).

Rogers, K. (2011) 'SlutWalk: Is a Woman's Body the Best Way to Get a Feminist Point Across?,' *The Washington Post*, 6 June, online

Rozee, P. (1999) 'Stranger Rape,' in M.A. Paludi (ed.) *The Psychology of Sexual Victimization: A Handbook* (Westport, CT: Greenwood Press), 97–115.

Sarachild, K. (1973) 'Consciousness Raising: A Radical Weapon,' *Women's Rights in New York City Conference*, 12 March, New York City, http://library.duke.edu/rubenstein/scriptorium/wlm/fem/sarachild.html (accessed 14 March 2013).

Sarkeesian, A. (2011) 'Feminist Critiques of SlutWalk,' *Feminist Frequency*, 16 May, www.feministfrequency.com/2011/05/link-round-up-feminist-critiques-of-slutwalk/ (accessed 14 March 2013).

Scharff, C. (2012) *Repudiating Feminism: Young Women in a Neoliberal World* (Farnham: Ashgate),

Schutte, G. (2011) 'Stop Telling Women what to Wear,' *Cape Times*, 29 August, 9.

Shaw Crouse, J. (2011) 'SlutWalking our Way to Gomorrah,' *Washington Times*, 8 June, B1.

Smith, J. (2003) 'I'm a Feminist So I Must Be Dead,' *The Independent*, 6 July, www.independent.co.uk/opinion/commentators/joan-smith/im-a-feminist-so-i-suppose-i-must-be-dead-585886.html (accessed 5 July 2010).

Szego, J. (2011) 'Hold off the Hate Mail, Sisters, but Slutwalk Fails to Light my Fire,' *Sydney Morning Herald*, 28 May, online.

Tanenbaum, L. (2011) 'Topless Women at SlutWalk Demand Respect: Is This the Right Tactic?,' *Huffington Post (US)*, 5 October, online.

Thornham, H. and Weissmann, E. (2013) *Renewing Feminism: Narratives, Fantasies and Futures in Media Studies* (London: I.B. Tauris).

Times of India (2011) 'From Bra-burning to Bra-branding,' *Times of India*, 12 August, online.

Timson, J. (2011) 'Why SlutWalk Raises Hackles – and Hopes,' *The Globe and Mail*, 13 May, L3.

Toronto Star (2011a) Editorial: 'New Feminism or Just a Parade?,' *Toronto Star*, 12 May, A26.

Toronto Star (2011b) 'Slutwalk Goes Global,' *Toronto Star*, 27 April, A2.

Valenti, J. (2011) 'The New Feminists: As Slutty as We Want to be,' *Washington Post*, 5 June, B01.

Watson, A. (2012) 'The SlutWalk Paradox,' *The Ottawa Citizen*, 17 August, online

Wraith, D. (2013) Personal Interview, 28 April.

Zaslow, E. (2009) *Feminism, Inc.: Coming of Age in a Girl Power Media Culture* (New York: Palgrave).

14
A Critical Reading of SlutWalk in the News: Reproducing Postfeminism and Whiteness

Lauren McNicol

Introduction

Since its inception in April 2011, SlutWalk has exploded from a Toronto-based protest into a global grassroots movement against victim-blaming through virtual activism and traditional media coverage. Because of the unprecedented mainstream visibility of SlutWalk, I argue it is a key site of analysis for understanding the place of feminist politics and protest in Canadian culture. Drawing on the theoretical and methodological tools of feminism and cultural studies, this chapter presents some key findings from a contextualized reading and discourse analysis of the representations of SlutWalk across Canadian print, radio, and televisual media during its first nine months of press. I begin this chapter by describing my experience at SlutWalk in Kingston, Ontario on 9 March 2012; this narrative serves as an entry point into a discussion about my rationale and research methodology. Then, with reference to key excerpts and trends, I demonstrate how the media oversimplified both the problem of slut-shaming and the politics of SlutWalk primarily through a visual whitewashing of solidarity, victimhood, and resistance. I argue that the media spectacle surrounding SlutWalk is premised on an unmarked white positionality that renders invisible the experiences of people of color and essentializes gender differences. Ultimately, I argue that the spectacle overshadows and undermines the movement's political messages about victim solidarity and violence prevention.

Background

SlutWalk Kingston, Ontario

After an hour of preparation, backed by my months of research, my feminist friend and I were satisfied that our signs for Kingston's first SlutWalk showed action items for rape prevention:

HOW CAN YOU END SEXUAL VIOLENCE?
1) Don't rape. Duh.
2) Always get consent.
3) Speak out against sexism.
4) Celebrate non-violent masculinity.
5) Condemn rape jokes.
6) Teach your sons 1–5.

We need to stop teaching
our daughters to be afraid,
and start teaching our sons
to respect women
and feminist values.

FEMINISTS don't
think all men are rapists.
RAPISTS DO ...
SLUT-SHAMING & RAPE JOKES
VALIDATE RAPISTS!

Our signs obscured our fully clothed bodies, except when we hoisted them momentarily above our heads. We had expressly avoided the 'I'm a proud slut' messages that seemed omnipresent in media coverage of SlutWalks in other cities, and around which a swirl of critique and controversy had emerged. We worried that people wouldn't connect the 'proud slut' messages to sexual violence prevention, viewing it instead as some newfangled version of depoliticized 'girl power.' I felt satisfied that our signs worked more obviously toward challenging, rather than reifying, the patriarchal fantasy of a palatable feminist revolution. As my friend and I set out to join the crowd of protesters, I said, 'I'm determined that we get our awesome signs in the newspaper!' She quickly replied, 'Yeah, I don't think we're dressed slutty enough for that.' It remained to be seen if our clothes determined whether our messages about rape culture and violence prevention reached mass audiences.

Whenever someone I didn't know well, like a cab driver or distant relative, asked me about my research, I ironically avoided mentioning 'SlutWalk' in my description. But my canned response about studying media representations of feminist social movements was rarely sufficient. Upon explaining the connection to SlutWalk, I was met with awkward silence, a rape-myth rant about safety and responsibility, or a question about whether SlutWalk 'was about women wanting to dress slutty, right?' My constant struggle to explain the subversive and political elements of SlutWalk made me seriously question the purpose of my project. If I couldn't find a way to converse with people who had different experiences, viewpoints, and social positions, then how could I envision the popularization of feminism?

These moments of tension reveal the difficulties of inserting feminist politics into everyday conversation. Worse yet, these conversations told me that the SlutWalk vision of empowered female sexuality might fit too easily in the patriarchal status quo. It brought to mind feminist scholar Angela McRobbie's recent work on 'the taboo-breaking phallic girl' (2009, p. 84). She writes:

> Consumer culture, the tabloid press, the girl's and women's magazine sector, the lads' magazines and also downmarket, trashy television all encourage young women, as though in the name of sexual equality, to overturn the old double standard and emulate the assertive and hedonistic styles of sexuality associated with young men ... This [female] phallicism also provides new dimensions of moral panic, titillation, and voyeuristic excitement as news spectacle and entertainment. (p. 84)

If the images of SlutWalk protesters were easy fodder for a mainstream media spectacle of female phallacism – which, by the way, offers the 'pretence of equality' (p. 85) – then could I really blame anyone for 'missing the point'? For that matter, could I blame them for assessing the situation in *exactly the way* dominant discursive forces prime them to do? These questions can perhaps be better answered once we identify the contradictory forces that make up the visibility of SlutWalks in mediated culture and that make the work of SlutWalks invisible. In essence, SlutWalk has gained traction in the same sphere (mainstream news media) that is implicated in not only the discursive undoing of feminism, but also the (re)production of the phenomenon that SlutWalk is protesting (rape culture and victim-blaming).

Rationale

> By failing to create a mass-based educational movement to teach everyone about feminism we allow mainstream patriarchal mass media to remain the primary place where folks learn about feminism, and most of what they learn is negative. (hooks 2000a, p. 23)

This passage written by bell hooks over a decade ago still resonates in the contemporary context. I feel a mix of despair – *are we still here?* – and gratitude for hooks's reminder that, at some point, I must grapple with mainstream patriarchal mass media in order to promote feminist principles. The media comprise 'public arenas where images of domestic violence are constructed, debated, and reproduced' (Berns 2001, p. 263), and where meanings are constructed about the factors and actors that are accountable for the cause, prevention, and treatment of sexual violence. The media are thus a powerful vehicle for shaping public consciousness about sexual violence as a problem and about feminism as a political movement.

In contemporary North America, it is difficult to identify a feminist demonstration or event that has been as widely replicated, publicized, and critiqued as SlutWalk. As a highly visible media event, SlutWalk is part of the everyday cultural terrain; it is open for consumption and discussion by people regardless of their prior engagement with feminist politics or with movements against sexual violence. For most people with access to daily news media, SlutWalk is a Sunday headline to skim over rather than a Saturday event to participate in; it is a fleeting lunch-time discussion rather than an ongoing debate in the feminist blogosphere. In other words, SlutWalks are 'out there,' rather than something requiring a personal investment. Because of this, SlutWalk's media presence has implications beyond the event itself, in terms of how feminist politics are taken up, challenged, and embraced by the general public, and mainstream coverage is a compelling object of study.

Methodology

My most consistent and in-depth engagement with feminist thought has been through the work of black feminist cultural critic and scholar bell hooks (1990, 2000a, 2000b). I follow hooks's (2000b) definition of feminism:

> [It] is a struggle to end sexist oppression ... it is necessarily a struggle to eradicate the ideology of domination that permeates Western

culture on various levels, as well as a commitment to reorganizing society so that the self-development of people can take precedence over imperialism, economic expansion, and material desires ... A commitment to feminism so defined would demand that each individual participant acquire a critical political consciousness based on ideas and beliefs. (p. 26)

I subscribe to this definition of feminism because it emphasizes the cultural basis of domination and the 'interrelatedness of sex, race, and class oppression' (p. 33). This intersectional definition of feminism moves beyond a simple analysis based on gender, and thus lends itself to a nuanced, politicized, and culturally contextualized analysis of media representations of SlutWalk.

Foregrounded by this definition of feminism, I locate my project within the field of cultural studies, which Richard Johnson and colleagues (2004) describe as an ever-evolving bricolage of methods that tends to transcend disciplinary boundaries. There is no single method in cultural studies, but rather a theoretical sensibility known as 'contextualized reading' that makes researchers confront and engage with the current epistemological and political conditions surrounding their objects of study (King 2005). In a contextualized reading, one strives to understand how a discursive network produces a cultural phenomenon, and, in turn, how that cultural phenomenon may shift and transform the network.

Contextualized reading goes hand in hand with discourse analysis. According to feminist scholar Nicola Gavey (1989), the primary goal of discourse analysis is to discern patterns of meaning through careful reading of texts. This task involves questioning elements of social existence such as language and social practices, which are typically taken for granted as true, natural, and inevitable. Therefore, discourse analysis is not about describing what is true in reality, but is about understanding the conditions of possibility that allow certain things to count as truth (Adams 1997). My study of mainstream news media representations of SlutWalk is not about assessing SlutWalk as a social movement or the media's accuracy in portraying it. Rather, I am committed to assessing the climate that enables only some portrayals of feminist political action to achieve such mainstream notoriety. It is with this intent that I limited my primary sources to Canadian coverage of North American SlutWalks across a range of media including newspapers, nightly news clips, radio clips, and photos. My final sample included 90 written texts, with publication dates ranging from 21 March to 30 December 2011.

I also compiled 378 visual texts (94 published photos, 284 screen shots). The majority of texts were published in April, May, and June 2011, which coincided with SlutWalks in Toronto (3 April), Ottawa (10 April), Boston (7 May), Vancouver (15 May), Saskatoon (28 May), Montreal (29 May), Edmonton (4 June), Hamilton (5 June), and Calgary (11 June).

Following Kaitlynn Mendes's work (2011), I read through or viewed each text once, noting 'emerging themes, quotations, [and] angles or positions that seemed salient or ideologically rich' and paying attention to word choices, other rhetorical devices, and 'the presence or absence of particular voices' (p. 486). I paid attention to the racial, gender, and age diversity of the SlutWalk participants and interviewees; the intelligibility of placards and chants; participants' attire (scantily clad, costume, regular); the media and police presence; and the composition and focal point of the image or video.

Analysis: media representations of SlutWalk

Overall, my research suggests that mainstream media representations of SlutWalk reproduce a watered-down version of feminism and a decontextualized understanding of sexual violence that resonates most with white, heteronormative, educated women. Essentially, the media oversimplifies the 'slut' and the 'walk' in SlutWalk by portraying i) slut-shaming as a male-perpetrated oppression that affects women everywhere and ii) SlutWalk as an inclusive and diverse movement that welcomes 'all walks of life.' Such media representations rely on and reinforce problematic norms of whiteness and postfeminism. In addition to this oversimplification, the spectacle of SlutWalk elevates the 'slut' controversy to public consciousness and makes ensuing feminist discussions more widely available for the general public. I challenge readers to question whether or not the spectacle overshadows the movement's political substance about victim solidarity and violence prevention.

Oversimplifying the problem and the protest: the facts

The mainstream news media I examined provide readers with an accessible understanding of the problem of slut-shaming and the nature of feminist resistance in SlutWalk by establishing three 'facts.' The first is to position Constable Sanguinetti as the poster-boy for slut-shaming. The second is to portray women as victims of slut-shaming worthy of sympathy. The third is to depict SlutWalk as an inclusive movement that invites diverse peoples to unite in resistance against slut-sham-ing. At first glance, the media portray feminist resistance positively and make feminist ideas accessible to wider audiences. Upon closer inspection, the media rely on problematic norms of whiteness and postfeminism. Namely, the mainstream media depoliticize the prob-lem of slut-shaming by discursively positioning men as perpetrators of isolated attacks. In turn, the media (perhaps inadvertently) absolve women of any responsibility for perpetuating the 'slut' stereotype. Simultaneously, the media exclusively feature young white women, thus reproducing white privilege in popular portrayals of feminism and sexual violence.

Sanguinetti: poster-boy for slut-shaming

Within my sample of media texts, little space is devoted to unpacking what made Sanguinetti's use of the word 'slut' so controversial and enraging, presumably because 'slut' is taken for granted as a widespread gender-based slur. Most journalists use Sanguinetti as the 'hook' for their stories, and then delve further into the notion of slut-shaming. In her 12 May *Globe and Mail* column, Judith Timson (2011) offers an example of this journalistic efficiency:

> SlutWalk started, of course, with poor Michael Sanguinetti, the Toronto cop who now goes down in the annals of feminist history ('Daddy, tell me again how you ended up in the Ms. Magazine Hall of Shame?') because he suggested that women could avoid being raped if they stopped 'dressing like sluts.' (Timson 2011)

To be 'in' on Timson's implicit feminist critique, readers must rely on existing knowledge of the word 'slut.' In most texts, the facts are presented in a way that requires readers to assume the political incorrectness of Sanguinetti's remark. For example, a CBC report (2011a) began as follows:

> A group of Toronto marchers took to the streets Sunday afternoon in what they're calling a 'slut walk' in response to controversial comments made by a police constable earlier this year. In January, Toronto Police Const. Michael Sanguinetti told a personal security class at York University that 'women should avoid dressing like sluts in order not to be victimized.' Sanguinetti apologized for his com-ments, but his apology failed to satisfy walk organizer Sonya Barnett. (CBC 2011a)

Some reporters flourish their descriptions of Sanguinetti to make his error more explicit to readers. For example, *Globe and Mail* reporter Greg McArthur characterizes Sanguinetti's advice as 'ill-advised,' and an example of when 'public officials ... say things that offend' (2011), the *Associated Press* calls it a 'flippant comment' (Associated Press 2011), and *Ottawa Citizen* columnist Joanne Laucius calls it a 'grave mistake' (Laucius 2011). The tendency to skip over an explanation of the slut stereotype is a tactic used by reporters who are relatively supportive (for example, Timson) and those who are openly critical (for example, Furey 2011) of SlutWalk. In his column in the *Ottawa Citizen*, Anthony Furey (2011) calls the Sanguinetti comment 'a classic case of blaming the victim,' explaining that apologies were issued, and moving immediately into his critique of SlutWalk. If there is further elaboration about the problem, it is often about victim-blaming in sexual assault cases rather than 'slut-shaming.' For the most part, journalists do not spend time explaining why or how slut is a derogatory term beyond the context of campus safety.

Under similar time and space restrictions, I might have expedited my explanation of slut-shaming much the same way that Laucius and Furey do. Still, I worry about the cultural implications of journalism that requires readers to 'read between the lines' to identify misogyny and sexism. On a superficial level, the press might be said to have demonstrated gender studies savvy. Sanguinetti's slut comment was an offensive, politically incorrect, gender-based slur, thus slut-shaming was so simple that it hardly required explanation. I counter that such a reading is too generous and shortsighted in light of the abundant evidence of the mainstream news media's complacency and active contribution to slut-shaming and victim-blaming, treatment of 'gender' or 'women's issues' as soft news (Mendes 2011), avoidance of structural causes of male violence against women (Worthington 2008), and continued failure on gender parity in hiring.

Paradoxically, the news media rely on readers' tacit understanding of 'slut,' only to then write about slut-shaming in ways that deter readers from acknowledging their potential participation in the problem. Sanguinetti is made to be the poster-boy and scapegoat. His very publicized wrongdoing enables SlutWalkers, journalists, readers, and even the police themselves to feel better about having pinpointed the problem. Sanguinetti is central to mainstream media explanations of slut-shaming, and thus serves as the focal point of the outrage culminating in SlutWalk. According to *Vancouver Province* reporter Ian Austin, 'Sanguinetti's words galvanized women who saw the officer's speech as typical of male bias, often blaming the victims of sexual assaults' (2011). I believe that this oversimplification inadvertently encourages an interpretation of slut-shaming as a male-perpetrated oppression which deters an exploration of slut-shaming as part of the general cultural phenomenon known as rape culture. The news media rarely cite examples of woman-to-woman slut-shaming, and fail to acknowledge the ubiquitous presence of the term 'slut' in mainstream pop culture, music, and political debates. The omnipresence of Sanguinetti as the lone exemplar might partly explain (or enable) the lack of commentary about women's participation in sexism throughout the media coverage of SlutWalk. In this context, women are most easily understood as victims. I explore the construction of women-as-victims in the following section.

Women: the shamed, not the shamers

The second part of the oversimplified media portrayal of slut-shaming is a focus on women as the victims of slut-shaming. Journalists cement slut as a gender-based slur used to injure women, particularly by relying on the explanations of SlutWalk participants and organizers. For example, *Hamilton Spectator* reporter Danielle Wong describes slut as a pejorative term for women by quoting Hamilton SlutWalk co-organizer Nikki Wilson:

> 'The word slut is used to make women feel uncomfortable about how they're presented to the world and to shame (them), and make them feel they need to police their bodies and police their sexualities in the way they express themselves,' said Wilson, 22. (Wong 2011a)

Similarly, Timson quotes a speaker at Boston SlutWalk:

> A slut is someone, usually a woman, who's stepped outside of the very narrow lane that good girls are supposed to stay within. Sluts are loud. We're messy. We don't behave. In fact, the original definition of 'slut' meant 'untidy woman.' But since we live in a world that relies on women to be tidy in all ways, to be quiet and obedient and agreeable and available (but never aggressive), those of us who color outside the lines get called sluts. And that word is meant to keep us in line. (Timson 2011)

Many media texts I examined establish slut-shaming as a relatable experience for women that serves as a basis for solidarity. In on-camera interviews with CBC and CTV, Vancouver SlutWalk co-organizer Katie

Raso explains the galvanizing function of slut-shaming, particularly for women, declaring, 'I don't know a woman who hasn't been called slut. And you know, it's something that affects all of us' (CBC News 2011b) and 'Everyone I know has been called a slut and yet we're all very different women and we all dress very differently' (Daflos 2011). Similarly, *Ottawa Citizen* reporter Zev Singer paraphrases Ottawa SlutWalk participant Katryna Schafer's feelings about SlutWalk as a form of solidarity, saying 'If a police officer, or anyone else, wants to call a woman a slut in a way that blames a victim, then they'll have to call all of the marchers sluts, too' (2011).

On the one hand, these candid descriptions of the effects of slut-shaming make feminist ideas more accessible to readers, and are thus positive features of the SlutWalk media coverage. Readers are afforded a sense of how 'slut' is used to monitor the rigid boundaries of feminine norms. The second passage from the Boston speaker is particularly nuanced, for it historicizes the term and pushes past common-sense understandings revolving around promiscuity. Unfortunately, such detailed accounts of slut-shaming are relatively uncommon and thus not characteristic of the sample. Nonetheless, the media acknowledge slut-shaming as a widespread issue by offering space for SlutWalk supporters to explain a common oppression based on female gender and sexualities, which include multiple mentions of 'us' and 'we' in reference to women. The media reproduce SlutWalk as a movement for uniting people in outrage and solidarity. As a result, the media represent slut-shaming as happening everywhere and affecting all women. The extent to which 'all women' could be said to participate in the culture of slut-shaming is unacknowledged. That is, slut-shaming is described as not something women do, but as something that is done to them.

So, SlutWalk participants and supporters are rendered invisible as potential or actual 'slut-shamers' in the mediascape. Woman-to-woman slut-shaming, a prime example of female sexist thinking, is mostly obscured from view in discourses about SlutWalk. In the context of SlutWalk, many supporters frame their descriptions of slut-shaming in passive voice (for example, 'slut is used to make women feel'). Dominant discourses of sexism and violence against women frequently adopt this passive framing of the problem, wherein men are the implicit operators of violence and women are the objects of violence (Marcus 1992). For the most part, the only identifiable operator of slut-shaming is Sanguinetti. More importantly, women and SlutWalk supporters are seemingly absolved of any personal or collective responsibility for the popular currency of the 'slut' stereotype.

The mainstream depiction of slut-shaming hinges on what hooks (2000a) describes as the 'shared sympathy for [women's] common suffering' (p. 15). In this popular incarnation of feminist resistance in SlutWalk, there are limited representations of struggle against patriarchal injustice in all of its forms, including when women 'judge each other without compassion and punish one another harshly' (hooks 2000a, p. 14). Therefore, to the typical mainstream media consumer, slut-shaming would be most readily understood as a male-perpetrated phenomenon that affects and outrages women everywhere, and, presumably, equally. In my experience, feminist politics are a lot messier than what might be captured by an 'us' versus 'them'/'him' dichotomy, especially one that assumes an inherent opposition between men and women.

A dichotomous and oppositional understanding of slut-shaming is problematic because it fails to accurately reflect how sexism takes hold in dominant culture, including through woman-to-woman slut-shaming. hooks (2000a) reminds us that a critique of women's internalized sexism was the foundation of political solidarity in the feminist movement in the 1970s and 1980s, and remains crucial in contemporary versions. I admit, in high school and my early university days, I personally referred to other women as slutty behind their backs and laughed at jokes about sluts. I reaped the social rewards of my collusion with the 'slut' stereotype amongst friends. Even as an unabashed feminist, I don't have the greatest track record, and I wonder, what are the odds that anyone does? It is all the more curious to me, then, that the majority of media coverage of SlutWalk gives the impression that most people do have a good track record.

Joanne Laucius's (2011) *Ottawa Citizen* column from 9 April is a notable exception, in that it breaks from the media pattern of treating slut-shaming as an attack on women, for which few people (mostly men) are accountable. Laucius calls young women's usage of slut as 'a double-edge word [sic],' as it could be complimentary of a friend's 'chutzpah' or intended to undermine an enemy. Laucius cites a pop culture example of female sexism, reminding readers of the popular currency of slut-shaming:

> 'In girl world, Halloween is the one night a year when girls can dress like a total slut and no other girls can say anything about it,' notes Lindsay Lohan in Mean Girls, which takes an anthropological – and humorous – look at the backstabbing world of high school girls. (Laucius 2011)

Laucius does here what few other journalists did – she acknowledges that slut has a history and a social location, and, in turn, recognizes the lived messiness of the problem. It's a simple and significant moment, for it demonstrates that the mainstream media can address social issues through a feminist lens *and* garner readership. On a wider scale, the mainstream media might acknowledge that women and girls can also shame each other through the use of the label 'slut,' and thus demonstrate that patriarchal consciousness spreads far beyond the Sanguinettis of the world. In turn, this might encourage some critical introspection (a crucial part of feminist consciousness-raising) amongst readers. As it stands, the media emphasis on calling out only Sanguinetti for slut-shaming precludes an exploration of slut-shaming as a general cultural phenomenon that SlutWalk participants and media consumers themselves might have been sustaining at one point or another.

'All walks of life': a whitewashed banner of diversity and inclusion

In this section, I argue that the media discourses about diversity and inclusiveness point to a sense of universal solidarity within SlutWalk, which might encourage wider participation. Unfortunately, the written accounts of diversity stand in contradiction to visual representations of Slutwalk agitators as overwhelmingly young, white, and female students. In media coverage of SlutWalk, the contradiction between a diversity-inclusiveness discourse and a white visual economy reinforces the broader reproduction of white privilege in the media representations of feminism, social movements, and 'gender issues.'

Many news reports I examined describe SlutWalk as an inclusive movement representing a diverse cross-section of people. Participants are repeatedly described as coming from 'all walks of life' (McArthur 2011; Nguyen 2011; Walters 2011), and from 'all age groups and genders' (Daflos 2011), making the crowd constitutive of 'almost every representation of people ... People of different races, people of different abilities, people of different orientations' (Paikin 2011) and 'represent[ing] a cross-section of the city' (Onstad 2011). In addition to emphasizing diversity in relation to race, ability, age, sexual orientation, and gender, some news reports also refer to the differing political slants and lifestyles of participants. For instance, according to *Globe and Mail* reporter Greg McArthur, the Toronto SlutWalk featured 'all walks of life, including activists, Goths, native protesters, artists, and a good smattering of men' (2011). The sense of diversity and inclusiveness is also established, though to a lesser extent, through the acknowledgment of the attendance of families and parents (Associated Press 2011; CBC News 2011c) and multiple generations of women (Ho 2011; Walters 2011), and the range of attire worn by the crowd (Mallick 2011; Thomas 2011; Wong 2011b).

Some media outlets point to the inclusiveness and diversity as evidence of SlutWalk's potential to help victims of slut-shaming. In her 30 March 2011 column, *Toronto Star* columnist Heather Mallick writes the following about the then upcoming Toronto SlutWalk:

> [SlutWalk] will feature people in all sorts of garments and gear, dressed for the office, clubbing, yoga, walking the dog, whatever it is that people wear as they go about their lives not asking to be raped. It is a message of love and strength to all women (and men), especially those who have been assaulted at the core of their being. (Mallick 2011)

Ottawa Citizen columnist Joanne Laucius explicitly affiliates SlutWalk with third-wave feminism and praises its inclusive approach, saying that:

> Perhaps the best thing about Third Wave feminism is that these young women recognize that feminism in the new millennium is not about exclusion. There might be a trace of anger behind SlutWalk, but also a sense of camaraderie in fishnets and stilettos. Everyone is welcome at SlutWalk. (Laucius 2011)

The media also recognize diverging opinions about the appropriation of slut, though these were typically positioned as secondary to the goal of marching in solidarity with victims. For instance, *Ottawa Citizen* reporter Zev Singer highlights the tension between the two goals of SlutWalk with reference to Ottawa SlutWalk participant Katryna Schafer. Singer describes Shafer as not being in favor of 'the idea of identifying as a slut on a personal level' but in favor of 'calling the event the SlutWalk, as a form of solidarity' (Singer 2011). *Vancouver Province* reporter Ian Austin captures a similar sentiment from protester Rory Marck, who says, 'There's such a variety of opinions – some people like the idea, but don't like the term, "SlutWalk." It's kind of like feminism'

(Austin 2011). *Vancouver Sun* reporter Daphne Bramham explains that her discomfort with the word slut matters less than showing solidarity with the movement. Bramham states, 'what's more important is that the SlutWalk symbolizes how a new generation of women has been energized to take on an old fight' (Bramham 2011). In other words, the diversity of opinions about the provocative title do not dismantle the notion of unity and inclusiveness. SlutWalk participants apparently share 'a common message' (Daflos 2011) and are 'united by a surge of well-placed fury' (Onstad 2011).

These overlapping narratives of diversity and inclusiveness are contradicted by the visual and audio-visual representations of SlutWalk events, which feature young white women (many of whom had performed the word slut based on their signage and attire). With a handful of exceptions, photos and interviews do not feature a diverse cross-section of people; they do not include, for instance, men, women of color, people with disabilities, or older individuals. The most high-profile photographs and news footage of the SlutWalk events feature posed photos of young, white, scantily clad women, many of whom are identified as university students. Across 18 video clips, there is only one black woman interviewed on camera, albeit briefly as she marched during the relatively less publicized Winnipeg SlutWalk (CTV News 2011b). While there is an abundance of images showing individuals and groups of young white women at SlutWalk, there are only a handful of such images of women of color in a slideshow from Edmonton SlutWalk.

Not only are white women the most conspicuous participants and organizers of SlutWalk in the press, they are also overrepresented as invited experts and critical commentators on shows like TVO's *The Agenda* with Steve Paikin, CBC's *Q* with Jian Ghomeshi, and CBC's *Connect* with Mark Kelley. The banner of diversity and inclusiveness is held up by white women, the voices of outrage and solidarity are those of young white female university students, and the chief supporters and dissidents of the latest feminist demonstration are white female professors and journalists. The people participating in, benefiting from, and discussing SlutWalk in the mainstream news media occupy positions of racial, cultural, and economic privilege. By frequently quoting or soliciting feedback from white female organizers and academics, the press establish a gendered framing of the problem and the protest and reproduce the whiteness and elitism of the media coverage of SlutWalk.

The media juxtapose discourses of inclusive diversity with representations of whiteness. This juxtaposition shapes whether or not media consumers identify with the movement and, in turn, informs their expectations about whether they will be welcomed in the movement. Do all media consumers 'see' themselves as recognized participants of the movement? Activist and *rabble.ca* contributor Harsha Walia speaks to the relationship between media representation and expectations. Recalling the Vancouver SlutWalk, she explains, 'I expected to see only a handful of women of color, mothers and children, older women. I was surprised at the actual diversity on the streets, not captured by photographers seeking sensationalist images of bras and fish nets' (2011). Walia points to several issues in that quote, and throughout her analysis of SlutWalk in *rabble.ca* notes that the extent to which SlutWalk can be read by media consumers as inclusive and diverse stands in tension with its overwhelmingly unmarked white vision of female sexual empowerment. In turn, this tension is damaging for the development of a mass-based feminist movement and for sexual violence prevention, because it tends to subsume difference in an apolitical and whitewashed 'we' that relatively few people can identify with. Overall, the news media proffer a narrative of SlutWalk as welcoming of and working for everyone while also reproducing white supremacy in the movement and marginalizing non-white voices and opinions.

Debating 'SlutWalk': (white) feminists at the table

Throughout the first half of this chapter, I developed an argument about supposedly factual and straightforward media coverage. In the second half, I carry forward the threads of that argument about media reproduction of whiteness, but I do so with a broader scope of evidence and interpretations. Namely, I shift the focus of my analysis to moments of debate and contention in the media coverage of SlutWalk, drawing on media excerpts that reflect a more dynamic, dialogic, and layered style of journalism. I focus on moments where reporters and TV hosts took a stance themselves and/or captured the divergent opinions of invited commentators.

In the following section, I demonstrate how the media are preoccupied with debating the merits of the branding and marketing tactics of organizers, rather than the political substance of the movement. I show how a mutually beneficial interplay between savvy SlutWalk-ers and journalists seeking catchy copy propels the SlutWalk from a local event to a worldwide mediated spectacle. The problem is that SlutWalk's spectacular mainstream existence is circumscribed by postfeminist ideals and is premised on whiteness, which distracts from conversations about sexual violence prevention and undermines the intersectional feminist politics that prevention requires.

The spectacle of SlutWalk: rising above the noise, silencing others

> But whatever you may think of SlutWalk (and part of the genius of its organizers has been figuring out that 'slut' is a search-engine optimizer), one strongly positive thing has emerged from it: a new, energetic cohort of feisty feminists are on the move. They've used social media to mobilize in a hell of a hurry (the longest part was probably wondering what to wear). And they've figured out a way to be front and center in the public conversation. (Timson 2011)

> Ultimately, protesters face a difficult challenge. News coverage is important to achieving protest goals, yet such coverage may not be forthcoming unless protesters engage in dramatic and even violent action. However, those very actions that attract media attention are often central features of stories that delegitimize the protesters. (Boyle et al. 2012)

Since the story broke, media outlets explained the widespread attention to SlutWalk as being obviously connected to its controversial name. For instance, the day before the Toronto demonstration, a *Globe and Mail* editorial explains that SlutWalk was 'picking up public steam, thanks to its provocative calling card' (2011). Several media outlets characterize the protest name as provocative, scandalous, or controversial in their headlines, bylines, body, and captions. It was only on rare occasions that the descriptor for the movement was 'feminist' or 'quasi-feminist.' According to the press, the most marketable aspect of SlutWalk is its brand, not necessarily its message. If we delve deeper into these media texts, we learn more about the relationship between feminist activists and mainstream news media.

In her 10 May article, *Globe and Mail* journalist Elizabeth Church (2011) explores the worldwide spread of the SlutWalk movement in the context of feminist debates about its provocative title. Church calls SlutWalk 'an in-your-face response to violence against women' and frames SlutWalk positively as the latest example of social media activism. Church provides space for organizers and supporters to explain their strategies and goals. In an interview, co-founder Sonya Barnett explains that the slut brand is a way of 'grabbing attention' and '[rising] above the noise' while also intending to 'teach people about the harmful use of language' (Church 2011). Barnett is 'skeptical that a protest by any other name would [make] headlines in the British press and on

Fox News or [elicit] messages from would-be march organizers halfway around the world.' Karen Pickering, an organizer of the Melbourne SlutWalk, echoes Barnett, explaining that her efforts as a long-time organizer of women's events failed to get mainstream attention until SlutWalk. In the same article, Church paraphrases York professor Kate McPherson as describing the slut brand as a clever and effective strategy 'that has allowed organizers to put the issue of women's sexuality on the table and then focus on a more pressing topic – why society has failed to address sexual violence.' My concern is that the media fixation on the former prevented an exploration of the latter.

In open forums (such as radio programs and TV shows), more in-depth debates emerge about whether SlutWalk's mainstream incarnation as a highly visual media spectacle might undermine the legitimacy of SlutWalk as a feminist movement and signal its cooptation by corporate media. *Globe and Mail* columnist Margaret Wente is most succinct in this regard:

> The walks are drawing major media coverage, because news directors think their audiences will be stirred by images of valiant feminists reclaiming their power and their agency. Either that, or by images of nubile young women in thigh-high cutoffs and tube tops. You really have to wonder who's using whom. (Wente 2011)

Sarcastic tone aside, Wente rightly points to the irreconcilable tension that all activists experience in securing a place in mainstream dialogue and subsequently paying the price of being represented in ways that coalesce with market-driven news values and the white visual economy (Martin & Mohanty 1986). That is, just as activists capitalized on their controversial name to secure a platform for their political message, the media capitalized on the controversial name and sexy costumes of protesters to sell newspapers.

During TVO's *The Agenda*, Heather Jarvis shows frustration about SlutWalk's mainstream representation, telling host Steve Paikin that:

> [S]ome people have become so focused on this word that they are losing sight of the rest of the work that we are doing. We are calling into question male sexuality, we are trying different forms of education and pushing different angles to bring this piece together ... SlutWalk is doing a lot more than just talking about reclaiming slut, and why aren't we talking about those things? (2011)

Jarvis's frustration speaks to what Kellie Bean (2007) calls the 'double bind of any liberal political movement' (p. 10). This double bind stems from the fact that '[t]he mainstream media, as an emphatically patriarchal, seriously conservative, willfully biased capital institution can be nothing but pernicious to liberal political thinking, [yet it] ... also represents the best access to the largest audience' (p. 10). To gain access to the mainstream club of news producers, the activists paid the cover fee with 'slut,' only to realize that subsequent conversations were fixated on their provocative nametag rather than their march. Both SlutWalk's successful marketing and its struggle to be taken seriously derive from the same thing: its controversial name. I will explore the paradox of 'slut' through a close reading of two interactions between media figures and SlutWalk activists on the debate segment of CBC's *Q with Jian Ghomeshi* – a left-leaning radio program – and *Connect with Mark Kelley* – a news talk show. I will provide pertinent quotes from each show separately, but will interpret them together.

Ghomeshi centers the 10 May *Q* debate around the question, 'Is [the word slut] empowering to women or an affront to the feminist progress?,' and monitors the subsequent discussion between Gail Dines, notable as both an anti-porn scholar and outspoken critic of SlutWalk, and Heather Jarvis, SlutWalk co-founder. Ghomeshi asks Jarvis:

> Do you feel conflicted at all, as you see slut emblazoned across headlines in papers all over the world? ... Do you think the media coverage is getting your re-definition, or at times, taking advantage of it for a catchy copy? (2011)

Jarvis agrees, saying, 'I definitely think people are taking advantage of it, as they always have of feminism, and women, sometimes. It's never going to not happen. We've seen that, it's the reality.'

On his 9 June broadcast, Mark Kelley speaks on-camera with his invited guest, Shira Tarrant (social critic and author, featured speaker at Los Angeles SlutWalk), primarily about the controversial name and reclamation of slut. The conversation takes place against the studio backdrop of photos of scantily clad white female protesters from various SlutWalks. Kelley opens by asking, 'Why try to reclaim the word itself?' Tarrant explains:

> SlutWalks are about saying it doesn't matter what she's wearing, it doesn't matter who she sleeps with, it doesn't matter what she does for a living. The question is never 'What was she wearing?' but rather 'Why was he raping?' (2011)

Kelley responds:

> I understand the point behind [SlutWalk] but I guess it's what's out front of it. It's like the advertising on a packaging on something. And that makes people uncomfortable, and so I wonder if that only serves to distance the good message that you're trying to get across? (2011)

Tarrant responds in disagreement, 'Well I don't think so. I think it's actually bringing so much attention. I mean the fact is that I'm on your show tonight because it's called SlutWalk.'

Both the Q debate and the *Connect* segment involve 'meta' discussion about mainstream depictions of SlutWalk, that is, the media talking about the media talking about SlutWalk. Ghomeshi and Kelley both acknowledge feminist efforts to navigate the muddy waters of the mainstream news circuit, while also distancing themselves from their power in ideological production and issue-framing. Although Ghomeshi suggests that the media catered the SlutWalk message for profit, he does not take accountability for his own complacency in the same distortion. Ghomeshi frames and monitors his Q debate segment around 'the politics of the word "slut,"' rather than, say, the politics of sexual violence prevention. The Q debate reinforces the notion that the most discussion-worthy element of SlutWalk is its spectacular name, a move which more readily reflects and reinforces market-driven news values (that is, newspaper sales) than feminist politics to end violence.

Kelley also focuses his conversation around the controversy of reclaiming slut, positioning himself as sympathetic to the underlying message of SlutWalk, though never really engaging with it. Kelley's line of questioning signals a preoccupation with unpacking the controversy and widespread attention of the movement, rather than the issue of sexual violence. Perhaps inadvertently, Kelley's emphasis on the controversial branding of the movement serves as a barrier to a conversation about 'the good message that [SlutWalk is] trying to get across.' Like Ghomeshi, Kelley amplifies the 'slut' in SlutWalk, and then calls on Tarrant, as a SlutWalk affiliate, to explain the media fixation on the branding and its impact on the cause.

SlutWalk supporters Jarvis and Tarrant demonstrate a similar awareness of how the controversial name secured their spots on the panel while also imposing rigid boundaries on the content of their dialogue. Jarvis's comment sheds light on the historically complex relationship between feminism and the media, but it also suggests that the media distortion of feminism is inevitable. In other words, Jarvis suggests that feminist politics simply do not and will not ever fit in the media landscape, without the media engaging in at least some profitable distortion of feminism. Similarly, Tarrant seems confident about the 'fact' that her invitation to provide feedback on *Connect* was contingent on the SlutWalk brand stirring controversy; she thus echoes the aforementioned sentiments of Toronto SlutWalk co-founder Barnett, Melbourne SlutWalk organizer Pickering, and feminist scholar MacPherson in Church's *Globe and Mail* article (Church 2011).

In the context of extended debate and dialogue, it is unfortunate that both the media producers and SlutWalk supporters[1] employ totalizing language and stances to describe the fraught relationship between feminist activism and the mainstream news media. In particular, Jarvis's statement denotes a slippage from publicly acknowledging structural power differences between feminist agitators and media producers (post-structuralist) and characterizing those differences as inevitable and unchanging (essentialist). These widely available debates, panel discussions, and interviews between prominent media figures and lesser known feminist activists and scholars provide an important opportunity for the general public to 'listen in' and even participate in discussions pertaining to feminist activism and violence prevention. Unfortunately, upon listening to the discussion between Ghomeshi and Jarvis, for instance, media consumers might come to oversimplify the relationship between feminism and the mainstream media, and, by extension, mainstream culture, as inevitably at odds. This might serve to further disenchant the public from engaging with feminist politics, including those concerned with violence prevention. I do not have space within this chapter to critically explore the responsibility of feminists and activists to carefully navigate mainstream spaces, nor the research on the congruency (or lack thereof) of feminist values and journalistic standards in mainstream news production. Briefly, I should acknowledge that such projects are necessary and ongoing in the work of organizations such as Women, Action, and the Media! (WAM!) and in mass communication and framing studies (for example, Worthington 2008).

More central to my project is an exploration of the conditions of possibility that enabled a discursive preoccupation with the *Slut*Walk rather than the Slut*Walk* within media coverage. The media made SlutWalk visible in the mainstream partly by camouflaging its feminist rhetoric in a provocative, attention-getting package. Against the best efforts of SlutWalk organizers and supporters, debates about the SlutWalk branding tactics dominate the mediascape, thus overshadowing dialogue about ending sexual violence and victim-blaming. Although some journalists, such as the *Globe and Mail's* Elizabeth Church, do manage to redirect attention to those feminist issues (and speak to the difficulty of such a task), the subsequent discussions tend to privilege the viewpoints of white educated women at the exclusion of others. In both the major mediated forums for discussion (CBC's *Q* and *Connect*, and TVO's *The Agenda*) and the brief televised interviews (for example, CTV News 2011a) invited panelists and commentators are exclusively white women in various positions of privilege and authority, including university students, professors, and journalists. Organizers and supporters may have jockeyed for a position at the table with their shock marketing, but such maneuvering seemed contingent on only some white educated women participating in a narrow line of questioning.

Conclusion

Throughout this chapter, I aimed to help my readers understand how newspaper columnists and news programs filter and reproduce specific messages about slut-shaming for wider audiences in ways that promote some feminist values at the expense of others. In the first section, I argued that the media, despite its gestures of good faith toward victims and feminists, rely on and reproduce depoliticized understandings of solidarity and resistance that ignore the complexities of sexual violence and undermine intersectional feminist politics. In the final section, I argued that the media circumvent crucial discussions about violence prevention in favor of sensationalized stories about the controversial 'slut' branding tactics. In so doing, the media promote the views of relatively privileged white feminist activists and scholars. Overall, I argued that media representations of the problem, protesters, and strategies of SlutWalk can be described as 'generous' only through superficial readings. Upon further inspection, we see how the media reproduce oversimplified understandings of slut-shaming as a male-perpetrated attack on women, without sufficient attention to its wider cultural roots. Moreover, the media represent the issue of slut-shaming and participation in SlutWalk from an unmarked white positionality, which renders invisible the experiences of people of color in relation to SlutWalk.

Note

1. I have represented media producers and Slutwalk supporters as separate and distinct for argument's sake. These are, at times, fluid and overlapping categories. For instance, Jarvis and SlutWalkers are also media producers in the

burgeoning spheres of new media in the internet age (social networking), but, unlike Ghomeshi and others, are not necessarily paid for it.

References

Adams, M.L. (1997) *The Trouble with Normal: Postwar Youth and the Making of Heterosexuality* (University of Toronto Press).

Associated Press (2011) 'Toronto "Slut Walk" Spreads to US,' *CBC News*, 6 May, online.

Austin, I. (2011) 'SlutWalk is "Kind of Like Feminism": Women Condemn Dress, Sex-Assault Link,' *Vancouver Province*, 16 May, online.

Bean, K. (2007) *Post-backlash Feminism: Women and the Media since Reagan–Bush* (Jefferson, NC: McFarland).

Berns, N. (2001) 'Degendering the Problem and Gendering the Blame: Political Discourse on Women and Violence,' *Gender & Society*, 15(2), 262–81.

Boyle, M., McLeod, D.M. and Armstrong, C.L. (2012) 'Adherence to the Protest Paradigm: The Influence of Protest Goals and Tactics on News Coverage in U.S. and International Newspapers,' *The International Journal of Press/Politics*, Online First, 2 February.

Bramham, D. (2011) 'SlutWalk Movement Sends Message Rapists, not Victims, Are at Fault,' *Vancouver Sun*, 12 May, online.

CBC News (2011a) 'Toronto "Slut Walk" Takes to City Streets,' *CBC News Toronto*, 3 April, online.

CBC News (2011b) (Radio broadcast) 'Slutwalk,' *On the Coast*, 13 May, online.

CBC News (2011c) 'Calgarians Strut for "SlutWalk",' *CBC News Calgary*, 21 August, online.

Church, E. (2011) 'SlutWalk Sparks Worldwide Movement,' *Globe and Mail*, 11 May, online.

CTV News (2011a) 'SlutWalk Movement Comes to Montreal,' *CTV News Montreal*, 29 May, online [video].

CTV News (2011b) (Video) 'Hundreds March in Winnipeg's SlutWalk,' *CTV News Winnipeg*, 15 October, online.

Daflos, P. (2011) (Video) 'Slutwalk Marching into Vancouver,' *CTV News British Columbia*, 14 May, online.

Furey, A. (2011) 'The Problem with SlutWalk,' *Ottawa Sun*, 10 April, online.

Gavey, N. (1989) 'Feminist Poststructuralism and Discourse Analysis,' *Psychology of Women Quarterly*, 13, 459–75.

Ghomeshi, J. (2011) (Radio broadcast) 'Can the Word Slut be Empowering?,' *Q with Jian Ghomeshi*, 10 May, online.

Globe and Mail (2011) 'Editorial: The Overcoming of Stigma,' *Globe and Mail*, 12 May, online.

Ho, C. (2011) 'Slutwalk Sheds Assault Blame,' *Edmonton Journal*, 21 August, online.

hooks, b. (1990) *Yearning: Race, Gender and Cultural Politics* (Boston: South End Press).

hooks, b. (2000a) *Feminism is for Everybody: Passionate Politics* (London: Pluto Press).

hooks, b. (2000b) *Feminist Theory: From Margin to Center* (Cambridge, MA: South End Press).

Johnson, R., Chambers, D., Raghuram, P. and Tincknell, E. (2004) *The Practice of Cultural Studies* (London: Sage).

Kelley, M. (2011) (Video) 'A Goalie's Tough Job, Slutwalk, and One Embarrassing Dad,' *Connect with Mark Kelley*, 9 June, online.

King, S.J. (2005) 'Methodological Contingencies in Sports Studies,' in D. Andrews, D. Mason, and M. Silk (eds) *Qualitative Methods in Sport Studies* (Oxford: Berg), 21–38.

Laucius, J. (2011) 'Sensible Shoes and a Grey Cardigan at SlutWalk,' *Ottawa Citizen*, 9 April, online.

Mallick, H. (2011) 'What to Wear for SlutWalk,' *Toronto Star*, 30 March, online.

Marcus, S. (1992) 'Fighting Bodies, Fighting Words: A Theory and Politics of Rape,' in J. Butler and J.W. Scott (eds) *Feminists Theorize the Political* (London: Routledge), 385–403.

Martin, B. and Mohanty, C. (1986) 'Feminist Politics: What's Home Got to Do with It?,' in T. de Lauretis (ed.) *Feminist Studies, Critical Studies* (Bloomington: Indiana University Press), 191–212.

McArthur, G. (2011) 'Women Walk the Talk after Officer's Offending "Slut" Remarks,' *Globe and Mail*, 4 April, online.

McRobbie, A. (2009) *The Aftermath of Feminism* (Thousand Oaks, CA: Sage).

Mendes, K. (2011) 'Reporting the Women's Movement: News Coverage of Second-Wave Feminism in UK and US Newspapers, 1968–1982,' *Feminist Media Studies*, 11(4), 483–98.

Nguyen, L. (2011) 'March to Protest Remarks Made about Assault Victims,' *Edmonton Journal*, 2 April, online.

Onstad, K. (2011) 'Feminism and Fashion: The (Other) Two Solitudes,' *Globe and Mail*, 16 April, online.

Paikin, S. (2011) (Video) 'SlutWalks and Modern Feminism,' *The Agenda with Steve Paikin*, 9 May, online.

Singer, Z. (2011) 'Don't Blame Victims: Marchers,' *Ottawa Citizen*, 11 April, online.

Thomas, N. (2011) 'Women Rally against "Slut" Stereotypes,' *Toronto Star*, 4 April, online.

Timson, J. (2011) 'Why SlutWalk Raises Hackles – and Hopes,' *Globe and Mail*, 13 May, online.

Walia, H. (2011) 'Slutwalk: To March or Not to March,' *Rabble*, 18 May, online.

Walters, K. (2011) 'Slutwalk Marching into Vancouver,' *CTV News British Columbia*, 14 May, online.

Wente, M. (2011) 'Embrace Your Inner Slut? Um, Maybe Not,' *Globe and Mail*, 12 May, online.

Wong, D. (2011a) 'SlutWalk: The Victim is Not to Blame,' *Hamilton Spectator*, 24 May, online.

Wong, D. (2011b) 'Slutwalk Hits the Streets of Hamilton,' *Hamilton Spectator*, 6 June, online.

Worthington, N. (2008) 'Progress and Persistent Problems: Local TV News Framing of Acquaintance Rape on Campus,' *Feminist Media Studies*, 8(1), 1–16.

Index